CW01020925

365 Yummy Fruit Pie Recipes

(365 Yummy Fruit Pie Recipes - Volume 1)

Sarah Williams

Copyright: Published in the United States by Sarah Williams/ © SARAH WILLIAMS

Published on December, 02 2020

All rights reserved. No part of this publication may be reproduced, stored in retrieval system, copied in any form or by any means, electronic, mechanical, photocopying, recording or otherwise transmitted without written permission from the publisher. Please do not participate in or encourage piracy of this material in any way. You must not circulate this book in any format. SARAH WILLIAMS does not control or direct users' actions and is not responsible for the information or content shared, harm and/or actions of the book readers.

In accordance with the U.S. Copyright Act of 1976, the scanning, uploading and electronic sharing of any part of this book without the permission of the publisher constitute unlawful piracy and theft of the author's intellectual property. If you would like to use material from the book (other than just simply for reviewing the book), prior permission must be obtained by contacting the author at publishing@crumblerecipes.com

Thank you for your support of the author's rights.

Content

CHAPTER 9: RHUBARB PIE RECIPES .144

CHAPTER 10: STRAWBERRY PIE RECIPES 169

CHAPTER 11: AWESOME FRUIT PIE RECIPES.................................... 204

Chapter 1: Blackberry Pie Recipes

***

1. Apple Blackberry Pie

Serving: 6 | Prep: 20mins | Cook: 50mins | Ready in:

Ingredients

- 1/4 cup butter
- 1 tablespoon all-purpose flour
- 1/4 cup water
- 1/2 cup white sugar
- 1/2 cup brown sugar
- 1 teaspoon lemon juice
- 1 (6 ounce) container blackberries, halved - divided
- 1 recipe pastry for a 9-inch double-crust pie
- 4 large Granny Smith apple - peeled, cored, and sliced

Direction

- Turn on the oven at 425°F (220°C) to preheat.
- On medium-low heat, put on a saucepan and melt butter. Add in flour; stir well until it turns into a smooth paste. Add in lemon juice, brown sugar, white sugar and water; whisk well. Let it simmer for about 3 minutes until it thickens with constant whisks. Add to the sauce 6 blackberry halves; lower the heat to low and keep cooking with occasional stirs while preparing other steps.
- Use a crust to line a 9-inch pie dish. Arrange apples and the rest of blackberries onto the crust. Cut the remaining crust into about 1-inch wide slices; use pie crust strips to make a lattice crust on top; seal the strips and crust edges. Pour the hot blackberry sauce onto the top of the pie and let it completely absorb through the openings in the top crust. Transfer to baking sheet to catch drippings.
- Put into the oven for 15 minutes to bake. Lower the heat to 350°F (175°C); keep baking for 35-45 more minutes until the sauce bubbles and the crust turns into golden brown color.

Nutrition Information

- Calories: 433 calories;
- Total Carbohydrate: 69.7
- Cholesterol: 20
- Protein: 2.9
- Total Fat: 17.8
- Sodium: 217

2. Apple Berry Pie

Serving: 8 | Prep: 20mins | Cook: 50mins | Ready in:

Ingredients

- 1 pastry for a 9 inch double crust pie
- 1 cup white sugar
- 4 teaspoons tapioca
- 1/2 teaspoon ground cinnamon
- 2 cups fresh blackberries
- 2 cups apples - peeled, cored and sliced
- 2 tablespoons butter, cut into small pieces

Direction

- Set oven at 190°C (375°F) and start preheating. Take one crust to a light-floured surface, roll it out and put in a 9-inch pie dish. Roll the top crust out and put aside.
- Combine cinnamon, tapioca and sugar in a big bowl. Mix in sliced apples and blackberries. Gently toss to coat without the berries getting mashed. Let rest for 20 minutes.

- Add the filling into the pastry-lined pan. Dot butter over. Brush the edge of the pastry to with water moisten. Put the top crust over, cut and fold the edges. Slit the top crust few times for the steam to escape while baking. Use foil to cover edges to avoid overbrowning.
- Put the pie in the preheated oven and start baking for 25 minutes. Take out the foil, keep baking until the crust turns golden brown, or for 20 to 25 minutes. Take the pie to a wire rack and let cool.

Nutrition Information

- Calories: 385 calories;
- Total Fat: 18
- Sodium: 255
- Total Carbohydrate: 54.1
- Cholesterol: 8
- Protein: 3.4

---

3. Berry Custard Pie

Serving: 8 | Prep: | Cook: | Ready in:

Ingredients

- 1 cup baking mix
- 1 1/2 tablespoons white sugar
- 1/3 cup milk
- 1/2 teaspoon lemon zest
- 1 1/2 cups raspberries
- 1 cup fresh blackberries
- 1/2 cup fat free sour cream
- 2 egg whites
- 1/2 cup white sugar
- 3 tablespoons all-purpose flour
- 1/2 teaspoon ground cinnamon
- 1/4 teaspoon ground nutmeg
- 1/2 teaspoon vanilla extract

Direction

- Mix lemon rind, milk, 1 1/2 tablespoons sugar, and baking mix. Then use your floured fingers to press at the bottom and up sides of the pie dish that has been coated with nonstick cooking spray. Dust berries onto crust. Whisk vanilla extract, spices, flour, 1/2 cup white sugar, egg whites, and sour cream. Place on fruit. Use foil to cover the edges of the crust.
- Bake for 10 minutes at 450°F (230°C). Lower heat to 350°F (175°C), then bake for 30 minutes, or until the middle is set.

Nutrition Information

- Calories: 164 calories;
- Total Carbohydrate: 35.7
- Cholesterol: 3
- Protein: 4.4
- Total Fat: 0.7
- Sodium: 320

---

4. Berry Rhubarb Pie

Serving: 8 | Prep: | Cook: | Ready in:

Ingredients

- 1 cup fresh blackberries
- 1 cup raspberries
- 2 cups rhubarb, cut into 1/2 inch pieces
- 3/4 cup white sugar
- 1/4 cup all-purpose flour
- 2 cups all-purpose flour
- 1 teaspoon salt
- 2/3 cup shortening
- 2 tablespoons butter
- 4 tablespoons ice water
- 1 tablespoon butter, melted
- 1 teaspoon lemon juice
- 1 1/2 tablespoons half-and-half cream
- 2 tablespoons white sugar

Direction

- For the filling: Mix rhubarb, raspberries, and blackberries together in a medium-sized bowl. Combine 1/4 cup flour and 3/4 cup sugar in another bowl. Sprinkle over the fruit mixture and lightly mix. Put a cover on and chill overnight.
- For the crust: Combine salt and 2 cups flour in a big bowl. Cut in 2 tablespoons butter and shortening until the texture resembles coarse cornmeal. Transfer 1/3 of the mixture to another bowl. Pour water into the smaller portion and whisk until forming a paste. Add this mixture to the other portion of the flour mixture and whisk until the dough just turns into a ball. Let sit for a minimum of 20 minutes, and then roll out. Split the dough into 2 portions. Roll the bottom crust out and put in a 9-in. pie pan.
- Turn the oven to 400°F (200°C) to preheat.
- Stir lemon juice and 1 tablespoon melted butter into the fruit filling, and then add to the pie pan lined with the pastry. Roll the top crust out and put onto the filling. Crimp the edges and slice slits to vent steam in the top. Lightly brush half and half over and lightly sprinkle sugar over.
- Bake for 10 minutes in the preheated oven. Lower the oven heat to 350°F (175°C) and bake until the crust turns golden brown, about another 40-50 minutes.

Nutrition Information

- Calories: 427 calories;
- Protein: 4.4
- Total Fat: 22.3
- Sodium: 325
- Total Carbohydrate: 53.8
- Cholesterol: 12

5. Blackberry Butter Tarts

Serving: 12 | Prep: 15mins | Cook: 25mins | Ready in:

Ingredients

- 12 (3 inch) unbaked tart shells
- 1 cup fresh blackberries, rinsed and patted dry
- 1 lemon, zested
- 3/4 cup brown sugar
- 1/3 cup honey
- 1 egg
- 2 tablespoons melted butter
- 1 tablespoon vanilla extract
- 1 pinch salt

Direction

- Pre heat the oven to 200 degrees C (400 degrees F). Put the tart shells onto the baking sheet.
- Smash together the lemon zest and blackberries slightly in the small-sized bowl. Split the blackberry mixture equally in bottom of the tart shells.
- Stir together the salt, vanilla extract, butter, egg, honey and brown sugar in the bowl; scoop the mixture equally on the blackberries in the shells.
- Bake in preheated oven for 22-27 minutes or till the shells turns golden and the filling becomes bubbling.

Nutrition Information

- Calories: 232 calories;
- Total Carbohydrate: 36.8
- Cholesterol: 21
- Protein: 2.2
- Total Fat: 8.8
- Sodium: 126

6. Blackberry Peach Pie

Serving: 8 | Prep: 15mins | Cook: 50mins | Ready in:

Ingredients

- 3 cups fresh blackberries

- 3 fresh peaches - peeled, pitted, and sliced
- 3 tablespoons cornstarch
- 3/4 cup white sugar
- 1 double crust ready-to-use pie crust
- 2 tablespoons butter, melted
- 1 tablespoon ground cinnamon
- 1/2 teaspoon ground nutmeg

Direction

- Pre heat the oven to 230 degrees C (450 degrees F).
- Combine sugar, cornstarch, peaches and blackberries in the big bowl.
- Press one pie crust in bottom of the 9-in. pie pan. Add blackberry mixture to pie crust. Use the rest of pie crust to cover. Crimp edges of 2 crusts together to seal it up. Slice the slits in pie's top to vent. Use the melted butter to brush top. Drizzle nutmeg and cinnamon on top.
- Bake in the preheated oven for 15 minutes. Lower oven temperature to 175 degrees C (350 degrees F) and keep cooking for 35-40 minutes or till the top crust turns golden-brown.

Nutrition Information

- Calories: 363 calories;
- Total Fat: 18.2
- Sodium: 255
- Total Carbohydrate: 48
- Cholesterol: 8
- Protein: 3.6

7. Blackberry Pie I

Serving: 8 | Prep: 40mins | Cook: 40mins | Ready in:

Ingredients

- 4 cups fresh blackberries
- 1/2 cup white sugar
- 1/2 cup all-purpose flour

- 1 recipe pastry for a 9 inch double crust pie
- 2 tablespoons milk
- 1/4 cup white sugar

Direction

- Set oven to 425 0 F (220 0 C) and preheat.
- Mix together 3 1/2 cups berries with the flour and sugar. Pour the mixture into an unbaked pie shell. Spread the leftover half cup berries on top of the sweetened berries and put on the top crust to cover. Seal and crimp the edges; let steam escape by cutting vents in the top crust.
- Brush milk over the top crust and dust with 1/4 cup sugar.
- Put in the prepared oven and bake for 15 minutes. Lower the temperature of the oven to 375 0 F (190 0 C) and bake for 20 to 25 minutes more, or until the filling is bubbly and the crust turns golden brown. Cool on wire rack.

Nutrition Information

- Calories: 248 calories;
- Protein: 3.3
- Total Fat: 8
- Sodium: 119
- Total Carbohydrate: 42.1
- Cholesterol: < 1

8. Blackberry Pie II

Serving: 8 | Prep: | Cook: | Ready in:

Ingredients

- 4 1/2 cups fresh blackberries, rinsed and drained
- 1 1/2 cups white sugar
- 1/4 cup tapioca flour
- 1 recipe pastry for a 9 inch double crust pie
- 1 egg white, beaten
- 1 tablespoon white sugar

Direction

- Combine sugar and tapioca flour, and stir the mixture into the berries.
- Use pastry to line a pie dish. Pour the filling into pie shell, and put the top crust on top to cover. Pinch or flute the edge to seal. Brush egg white over the top and dust with a little sugar. Slit the top to let steam escape.
- Put into oven and bake at 350 0 F (175 0 C) until pie is golden brown and bubbly, about 30 to 40 minutes.

Nutrition Information

- Calories: 430 calories;
- Protein: 4.4
- Total Fat: 15.3
- Sodium: 242
- Total Carbohydrate: 71
- Cholesterol: 0

9. Blackberry Pie III

Serving: 8 | Prep: | Cook: | Ready in:

Ingredients

- 1 recipe pastry for a 9 inch double crust pie
- 4 cups fresh blackberries
- 3 tablespoons all-purpose flour
- 1 cup white sugar
- 1 tablespoon lemon juice
- 1 tablespoon butter

Direction

- Turn the oven to 450°F (230°C) to preheat.
- Line 1/2 the pastry into a 9-inch pie pan. Reserve the leftover pastry to use for the top crust. Refrigerate both while you prepare the blackberries.
- Mix together lemon juice, sugar, flour, and berries. Scoop to the pie shell, dot margarine

or butter over. Put on the top crust to cover and cut in a few spots.
- Bake for 15 minutes. Lower the temperature to 350°F (175°C). Keep baking until brown, about 35-40 minutes.

Nutrition Information

- Calories: 379 calories;
- Total Carbohydrate: 54.8
- Cholesterol: 4
- Protein: 4.1
- Total Fat: 16.8
- Sodium: 245

10. Blackberry Puff Pastry Tarts

Serving: 12 | Prep: 15mins | Cook: 15mins | Ready in:

Ingredients

- 1 (10 ounce) package frozen puff pastry shells, thawed
- 1 (8 ounce) package cream cheese, at room temperature
- 1/2 cup white sugar
- 1/2 teaspoon ground cinnamon
- 1/4 cup milk
- 1/4 cup turbinado sugar
- 1 1/2 cups fresh or frozen blackberries

Direction

- Turn the oven to 375°F (190°C) to preheat. Lightly oil a cookie sheet.
- In a bowl, combine cinnamon, sugar, and cream cheese until well mixed. Put aside.
- On the prepared cookies sheet, put puff pastry shells. Brush milk over each shell and sprinkle turbinado sugar over.
- Bake for 10-15 minutes in the preheated oven until the shells turn golden brown and expand. Watch carefully to ensure that the shells bake thoroughly without overbaking.

Take the shells out of the oven and remove the cap from each shell with a fork. Put the caps aside.

- Scoop each shell with 2 tablespoons of the cream cheese mixture. Put 6-8 blackberries on top. Top berries in each shell with a puff pastry cap.
- Put the filled pastry shells back to the oven, and bake for another 5 minutes until the filling is warm and the pastry tops turn golden brown.

Nutrition Information

- Calories: 219 calories;
- Sodium: 175
- Total Carbohydrate: 22.9
- Cholesterol: 21
- Protein: 3.8
- Total Fat: 13.2

11. Blackberry And Blueberry Pie

Serving: 8 | Prep: 30mins | Cook: 45mins | Ready in:

Ingredients

- Pie Crust:
- 2/3 cup shortening, chilled
- 2 cups all-purpose flour
- 1 teaspoon salt
- 5 tablespoons cold water
- Filling:
- 3/4 cup white sugar
- 1/3 cup all-purpose flour
- 1/2 teaspoon ground cinnamon
- 4 cups fresh blueberries
- 1 1/2 cups fresh blackberries
- 1 tablespoon lemon juice
- 2 tablespoons butter

Direction

- Mash shortening into salt and 2 cups flour until the shortening has the size of small peas. Sprinkle in water, 1 tablespoon each time, until the flour moisten. Form into a ball, use plastic to wrap, and chill for a minimum of 30 minutes. Split the dough into 2 portions and roll 1 portion out on a board lightly scattered with flour. Line the pastry into a 9-inch pie dish. Roll the top crust out and put aside.
- Turn the oven to 425°F (220°C) to preheat.
- Combine cinnamon, 1/3 cup flour, and sugar. Mix in berries to coat. Add the filling to the pan lined with the pastry. Use lemon juice to sprinkle over and dot butter on top. Put on the top crust to cover, make slits in the top for vent. Seal the crust and flute the edges.
- To avoid over-browning, use foil to cover the crust edges. Put in the preheated oven and bake for 45 minutes until the juices are bubbly and the crust turns golden brown. Take off the foil during the final 12 minutes of baking.

Nutrition Information

- Calories: 436 calories;
- Total Fat: 20.7
- Sodium: 313
- Total Carbohydrate: 59.9
- Cholesterol: 8
- Protein: 4.7

12. Blackberry Chocolate Chip Pie

Serving: 8 | Prep: 20mins | Cook: 35mins | Ready in:

Ingredients

- 1 (15 ounce) package pastry for a 9 inch double crust pie
- 3/4 cup white sugar
- 1/3 cup all-purpose flour
- 3/4 teaspoon ground cinnamon
- 4 cups blackberries
- 3/4 cup semisweet chocolate chips

- 1/2 tablespoon lemon juice

Direction

- Turn the oven to 425°F (220°C) to preheat. In the bottom of a 9-inch pie plate, put 1 of the pie crusts.
- Combine cinnamon, flour, and sugar in a bowl. Lightly mix in chocolate chips and blackberries. Sprinkle lemon juice over. Remove to the pie plate with the pie crust. Top with the leftover pie crust, and use your fingers to flute or press using a fork onto the bottom crust to seal.
- Bake in the preheated oven for 35 minutes until the top turns golden brown. Let cool briefly before cutting.

Nutrition Information

- Calories: 445 calories;
- Total Carbohydrate: 62
- Cholesterol: 0
- Protein: 5.2
- Total Fat: 21.3
- Sodium: 256

13. Blackberry Lemon Pie

Serving: 8 | Prep: 20mins | Cook: 1hours | Ready in:

Ingredients

- 1 recipe pastry for a 9 inch double crust pie
- 3/4 cup brown sugar
- 1 tablespoon lemon zest
- 4 cups fresh blackberries, rinsed and drained
- 1 cup white sugar
- 1/2 cup all-purpose flour
- 1 tablespoon lemon zest
- 1 tablespoon butter

Direction

- Turn the oven to 350°F (175°C) to preheat.

- In a 9-inch pie pan, put bottom crust. Crumble the leftover pie crust in a medium bowl with a tablespoon lemon zest and brown sugar. Use your hands to combine until the dough turns into crumbs with size of pea. Put aside.
- Mix 1 tablespoon lemon zest, flour, white sugar, and blackberries together in a big bowl. Add the blackberry mixture to the bottom pie crust until full. Sprinkle the mixture with the crumb topping and dot butter over.
- Put in the preheated oven and bake until the berries are bubbly and the crust is brown, about 45-60 minutes. Let sit until then serve.

Nutrition Information

- Calories: 449 calories;
- Total Fat: 16.8
- Sodium: 249
- Total Carbohydrate: 72
- Cholesterol: 4
- Protein: 4.6

14. Blackberry Mango Tart

Serving: 8 | Prep: 10mins | Cook: 35mins | Ready in:

Ingredients

- cooking spray
- 1 (9 inch) refrigerated pie crust
- 1 cup white sugar
- 3 eggs
- 1 cup mango puree
- 1/4 cup butter, melted
- 2 tablespoons lemon juice
- 1 (6 ounce) container fresh blackberries

Direction

- Preheat oven at 425 0 F (220 0 C). Grease a pie pan using cooking spray. Put pie crust in pan, trimming the edges to fit.

- Pour water into a saucepan halfway and bring to a simmer. Mix together sugar and eggs in a heatproof bowl and place on top of the simmering water. Mix in lemon juice, melted butter and mango puree. Cook while stirring constantly for about 15 minutes until filling is dissolved and thickened.
- Take the filling away from heat and pour into prepared pie crust. Let stand for 5 minutes. Distribute blackberries equally on top of mango mixture.
- Put in the prepared oven and bake for 15 to 20 minutes until partially firm and beginning to brown on top. Refrigerate completely before serving.

Nutrition Information

- Calories: 314 calories;
- Total Fat: 15.1
- Sodium: 182
- Total Carbohydrate: 42.5
- Cholesterol: 77
- Protein: 4

15. Bramblewood Blackberry Pie

Serving: 8 | Prep: | Cook: | Ready in:

Ingredients

- 2 1/4 cups all-purpose flour
- 1 teaspoon salt
- 1/2 cup vegetable oil
- 3 tablespoons cold water
- 2/3 cup white sugar
- 1/2 teaspoon ground cinnamon
- 3 cups fresh blackberries

Direction

- Set the oven to 425°F (220°C) and start preheating.

- In a medium mixing bowl, mix salt and 2 cups flour. Create a well in the center; pour in water and oil; stir together.
- Divide dough into 2 balls, the first ball uses 3/4 the dough and the second uses the remaining 1/4. Put a sheet of wax paper over the bigger dough ball; roll it out; it might be crumbly, and the wax paper will prevent it from separating to pieces. Line an 8 inch pie pan with dough. Do the same with the second ball of dough; put aside.
- Mix cinnamon, 1/4 cup flour and sugar in a small bowl. Place berries in a large bowl; top the berries with sugar mixture. Stir gently to coat. Spread the filling into the pie pan lined with dough. Place top crust on top to cover; pinch crusts together. Create holes in the top to release steam when baking. Use tint foil to line the edges of the crust so as not to let it burn.
- Bake until crust turns light brown and filling becomes hot and bubbly or for 30-45 minutes.

Nutrition Information

- Calories: 338 calories;
- Total Carbohydrate: 48.8
- Cholesterol: 0
- Protein: 4.4
- Total Fat: 14.4
- Sodium: 292

16. Brigid's Blackberry Pie

Serving: 8 | Prep: 15mins | Cook: 1hours | Ready in:

Ingredients

- 1 (15 ounce) package pastry for a 9 inch double crust pie
- 4 cups fresh blackberries
- 1 1/2 cups white sugar
- 1/2 cup all-purpose flour
- 1/4 teaspoon salt

- 1 tablespoon butter

Direction

- Turn the oven to 325°F (165°C) to preheat. Line 1 of the crusts into a 9-inch deep-dish pie pan.
- In a big bowl, put blackberries. Combine salt, flour, and sugar. Sprinkle over the berries and mix to coat. Add to the pie crust. Dot butter over. Top with the second pie crust and flute with the bottom crust using your fingers or press with a fork to seal. Use a sharp knife to slice a design in the top crust to release steam.
- Put in the preheated oven and bake until the top crust turns brown, about 60 minutes. Let cool to nearly room temperature until the filling sets then serve.

Nutrition Information

- Calories: 463 calories;
- Total Carbohydrate: 72.6
- Cholesterol: 4
- Protein: 4.8
- Total Fat: 18
- Sodium: 337

17. Bumbleberry Pie I

Serving: 8 | Prep: | Cook: | Ready in:

Ingredients

- 2 (9 inch) unbaked pie crusts
- 1 1/3 cups white sugar
- 1/3 cup all-purpose flour
- 2 cups thinly sliced apples
- 1 cup raspberries
- 1 cup fresh blackberries
- 1 cup fresh rhubarb, cut into 1 inch pieces

Direction

- Set the oven to 350°F (175°C), and start preheating.
- In a large bowl, combine flour and sugar. Add rhubarb, blackberries, raspberries and apples. Toss together, then pour into pie shell. Cover up with pastry top. Trim and seal edges. Slice vents on top.
- Bake in the oven for about 45 minutes at 175 degrees C (350 degrees F), until the apple is cooked and crust turns brown.

Nutrition Information

- Calories: 404 calories;
- Total Fat: 14.5
- Sodium: 281
- Total Carbohydrate: 67.2
- Cholesterol: 0
- Protein: 3

18. Deluxe Blackberry Pie

Serving: 8 | Prep: 30mins | Cook: 40mins | Ready in:

Ingredients

- 4 cups fresh blackberries
- 1 1/4 cups white sugar
- 4 tablespoons cornstarch
- 2 tablespoons blackberry brandy
- 1 teaspoon ground nutmeg
- 1 tablespoon ground cinnamon
- 1 recipe pastry for a 9 inch double crust pie
- 1 tablespoon white sugar

Direction

- In a blender, puree 2 cups of the blackberries until it turns into liquid. Filter the seeds out and add to a saucepan. Stir in 1 1/4 cups sugar. Cook over medium heat until it comes to a boil, whisking continually and scraping the bottom. Continue to boil for 5 minutes, and then take away from heat.

- In a cup, combine brandy and cornstarch. Once thoroughly blended, stir into the pan; whisk until the mixture boils again. Take away from heat. Mix in cinnamon and nutmeg. Test the mixture's consistency; it should have the consistency of a thin pudding. If needed, put in the water-cornstarch mixture at a 2:1 ratio to thicken.
- Pour the leftover 2 cups of blackberries into the pie shell filling it. Pour fresh berries with the blackberry puree, evenly covering. Cover with dough strips in a criss-cross pattern, or use a slit-cut solid dough sheet. Dust over the top with sugar.
- Bake for 35 minutes in a preheated 400°F (205°C) oven until the crust is brown.

Nutrition Information

- Calories: 421 calories;
- Total Fat: 15.5
- Sodium: 235
- Total Carbohydrate: 66.8
- Cholesterol: 0
- Protein: 3.8

19. Double Berry Custard Pie

Serving: 8 | Prep: 15mins | Cook: |Ready in:

Ingredients

- 1 (3.4 ounce) package instant vanilla pudding mix
- 1 1/4 cups heavy cream
- 1 (9 inch) prepared graham cracker pie crust
- 1/2 cup seedless raspberry jam
- 6 ounces fresh blackberries
- 6 ounces fresh raspberries

Direction

- In a bowl, whip cream and pudding mix for 2 minutes until extremely thick. Evenly spoon

the mixture into the pie crust and even out. Put a cover and refrigerate for 30 minutes.
- In a small saucepan, heat jam over low heat for 2-3 minutes, whisking from time to time.
- Combine raspberries and blackberries. Mound over the pudding mixture with berries and drizzle top with warm jam. Cover loosely and refrigerate for a minimum of 30 minutes and a maximum of 1 day.

Nutrition Information

- Calories: 392 calories;
- Total Fat: 21.5
- Sodium: 356
- Total Carbohydrate: 49.8
- Cholesterol: 51
- Protein: 2.5

20. Fresh No Bake Fruit Pie

Serving: 8 | Prep: 15mins | Cook: 5mins |Ready in:

Ingredients

- 1 (16 ounce) package fresh strawberries, hulled and large berries cut in half
- 1 pint fresh blueberries
- 1 (6 ounce) container fresh raspberries
- 1 (6 ounce) container fresh blackberries
- 1 cup water
- 1/2 cup white sugar
- 3 tablespoons cornstarch
- 1/4 cup water
- 1 (9 inch) prepared shortbread pie crust (such as Keebler®)

Direction

- In a bowl, mix blackberries, raspberries, blueberries, and strawberries thoroughly. Spoon out 3/4 cup of mixed berries and put into a saucepan with sugar and a cup water;

put remaining berries aside. Boil the mixture and turn heat down to medium-low.

- In a bowl, whip 1/4 cup water and cornstarch until smooth and mix the cornstarch mixture into the hot fruit syrup; mix about 2 minutes until the mixture thickens. Let cool completely, mixing sometimes for about 20 minutes.
- Put the thick berry mixture into fresh berries until well-combined; put sauce and berries into shortbread pie shell. Put into refrigerator at least 1 hour until chilled.

Nutrition Information

- Calories: 232 calories;
- Sodium: 104
- Total Carbohydrate: 44.2
- Cholesterol: 0
- Protein: 2.2
- Total Fat: 5.6

21. Fruit Of The Forest Pie

Serving: 12 | Prep: 10mins | Cook: 30mins | Ready in:

Ingredients

- 1 apple - peeled, cored, and sliced
- 1 cup strawberries
- 1 cup blackberries
- 1 cup fresh raspberries
- 1/2 cup sliced rhubarb
- 2 tablespoons lemon juice
- 2 tablespoons white sugar, or more to taste
- 1 (15 ounce) package pastry for a 9-inch double crust pie

Direction

- Turn the oven to 350°F (175°C) to preheat.
- In a bowl, combine rhubarb, raspberries, blackberries, strawberries, and apple. Add lemon juice and sprinkle the fruit mixture with sugar and mix to coat.

- Line prepared pie pastry into a 9-inch pie pan. Transfer apple mixture in pie pan. Put on the leftover pie pastry to cover and press and crimp the edges enclose the crusts. Slice a few slits in the pastry top.
- Put in the preheated oven and bake for 30-40 minutes until the fruit is bubbly and soft and the crust turns golden.

Nutrition Information

- Calories: 194 calories;
- Total Carbohydrate: 22.3
- Cholesterol: 0
- Protein: 2.4
- Total Fat: 11
- Sodium: 169

22. Gramama's Great Black Berry Pie

Serving: 8 | Prep: 15mins | Cook: 50mins | Ready in:

Ingredients

- 1 recipe pastry for double-crust pie
- 1 cup white sugar
- 1 teaspoon vanilla extract
- 1/2 cup maple syrup
- 1/2 teaspoon ground cardamom
- 1/2 teaspoon ground cinnamon
- 4 cups blackberries

Direction

- Set the oven to 350°F (175°C) to preheat. Push 1 crust up the sides and into the bottom of a 9 inch pie pan.
- Combine the cinnamon, cardamom, maple syrup, vanilla and sugar in a big bowl. Carefully mix in blackberries until evenly covered. Add to the pie crust. Cover with the top crust and enclose the edges. Score top with a few holes to vent steam.

- Bake in the prepared oven for 45 to 50 minutes, until crust turn golden brown.

Nutrition Information

- Calories: 295 calories;
- Total Fat: 7.9
- Sodium: 119
- Total Carbohydrate: 55.7
- Cholesterol: 0
- Protein: 2.4

23. Grandma's Blackberry Pie

Serving: 10 | Prep: 40mins | Cook: 40mins | Ready in:

Ingredients

- 1 egg
- 1 teaspoon distilled white vinegar
- 2 1/2 cups all-purpose flour
- 2 tablespoons white sugar
- 1 teaspoon salt
- 3/4 cup cold unsalted butter, cut into small cubes
- 7 tablespoons ice water, plus more as needed
- 6 cups fresh blackberries
- 1 apple, peeled and cut into 1/2-inch thick slices
- 1/2 cup white sugar
- 1 tablespoon white sugar

Direction

- In a small bowl, beat the vinegar and egg, and put aside. In a mixing bowl, whisk salt, 2 tablespoons sugar and flour together. Slice in the cold butter with a pastry blender or a knife till the mixture looks like coarse crumbs. (Another way is using a food processor: pulse the shortening or cold butter till getting the small pea size. Put in a bowl and proceed). Mix in the vinegar mixture and egg. Add a tablespoon of ice water at a time, toss it using a fork till the mixture turns moist. Make sure not to add too much water than necessary: check by squeezing a handful of the moistened pastry mixture, it should shape into a ball. Separate the dough in two equal parts and form into balls. Wrap in plastic and let it stay in the fridge for at least half an hour or up to three days.
- Set the oven to 375°F (190°C) and start preheating.
- Roll out one ball to fit a 9 inch pie plate. Put the bottom crust in pie plate and refrigerate for no less than 20 minutes prior to baking. Roll out the top crust and put aside. Place the apple slices on the bottom of the pie crust, then sprinkle the blackberries on top. Sprinkle in 1/2 cup of sugar. Put the second pie crust on the top of fruit mixture, then pinch together the top of the crusts with their bottom. Slightly drizzle water on the top crust, then sprinkle 1 tablespoon sugar. Use a fork to pierce a few holes in the top of crust to let the steam escape while baking.
- Put into the preheated oven and bake for 40-45 minutes until turn golden brown.

Nutrition Information

- Calories: 340 calories;
- Total Fat: 15
- Sodium: 339
- Total Carbohydrate: 47.8
- Cholesterol: 53
- Protein: 5.2

24. Logan's Fruity Fresh Pie

Serving: 8 | Prep: 10mins | Cook: | Ready in:

Ingredients

- 1 cup milk
- 1 (3.4 ounce) package instant vanilla pudding mix

- 1 large banana, sliced
- 1 pound fresh strawberries, sliced
- 1 teaspoon lemon juice
- 1 pint fresh blackberries
- 1 pint fresh blueberries
- 1 (6 ounce) container berries and cream yogurt
- 1 (9 inch) prepared graham cracker crust
- 1 cup miniature marshmallows

Direction

- In a bowl, mix the milk with vanilla pudding together for 2 minutes. Let sit for 5 minutes to start to set. In another bowl, toss the banana and strawberries with the lemon juice. Fold in the pudding, yogurt, blueberries and blackberries gently. Add to the prepared graham cracker crust and scatter marshmallows on to serve.

Nutrition Information

- Calories: 324 calories;
- Sodium: 379
- Total Carbohydrate: 59.2
- Cholesterol: 4
- Protein: 4.4
- Total Fat: 8.8

25. Poppin' Jalapeno Blackberry Pie

Serving: 8 | Prep: 30mins | Cook: 1hours5mins | Ready in:

Ingredients

- 4 cups blackberries
- 1/4 cup honey
- 2 jalapeno peppers, sliced
- 1 tablespoon lemon juice
- 1 1/2 cups brown sugar, divided
- 3 tablespoons cornstarch
- 2 1/2 cups all-purpose flour, or as needed
- 1 cup butter, cubed

- 1/4 cup ice water, or as needed
- 1 cup quick-cooking oats

Direction

- Set oven to 425°F (220°C) to preheat. Put a baking tray on the bottom rack of the oven.
- In a big bowl, mix lemon juice, jalapeno peppers, honey and blackberries. In a bowl, stir cornstarch and 1/2 cup brown sugar; mix into blackberry mixture until sugar dissolves.
- In another big bowl, mix flour with half cup brown sugar; stir butter into flour mixture with a food processor or pastry blender until mixture forms balls with the same size as peas. Put in ice water and stir with your hands until dough is well incorporated, putting in a little water if the mixture is too dry and flour if the mixture is too sticky.
- Split dough in half and form each half into a 9-inch circle on a floured surface. Push a circle into a 9-inch pie dish.
- Discard jalapeno peppers from blackberry mixture. Add blackberry mixture slowly into pie shell, letting about 1/4-inch space between top edge of pie crust and top of filling.
- In a bowl, stir oats with 1/2 cup brown sugar; scatter on top of blackberry filling. Cover pie with another pie crust. Trim excess edges from top shell and fold bottom crust edges over top crust edges; pinch to seal. Score 2 slits on top of crust for ventilation.
- Put pie on the middle rack of the oven, over a baking tray on the bottom rack to catch drips. Bake for about 25 minutes until crust begins to turn golden. Turn down temperature to 350°F (175°C) and bake for about 40 minutes more until crust is golden brown entirely.

Nutrition Information

- Calories: 563 calories;
- Total Fat: 24.4
- Sodium: 174
- Total Carbohydrate: 82.1
- Cholesterol: 61
- Protein: 6.7

26. She's My Blackberry Pie

Serving: 8 | Prep: 15mins | Cook: 40mins |Ready in:

Ingredients

- 1 double crust ready-to-use pie crust
- 4 cups fresh blackberries, or more to taste
- 1/2 cup white sugar
- 3 tablespoons all-purpose flour
- 1 tablespoon lemon juice
- 2 tablespoons water, or as needed
- 1 egg, beaten

Direction

- Set oven to 425 0 F (220 0 C) and preheat. Press a pie pastry into bottom of a 9-inch pie pan.
- In a large bowl, combine lemon juice, flour, sugar and blackberries together. Put into the prepared crust.
- Cut the second pie crust into 1-inch strips; place the strips over the top of the pie in a lattice pattern. Seal the lattice ends to the bottom pastry using a dab of water; crimp the edges together. Brush beaten egg over lattice top.
- Put the pie in prepared oven and bake for 15 minutes. Lower the heat to 375 0 F (190 0 C) and bake for additional 15 minutes. Use aluminum foil to loosely cover pie to avoid burning; bake until pie is bubbling for 10 - 15 minutes longer.

Nutrition Information

- Calories: 327 calories;
- Sodium: 243
- Total Carbohydrate: 42.4
- Cholesterol: 23
- Protein: 4.9
- Total Fat: 15.9

27. Todd And Jenny's Favorite Summertime Fluff Pie

Serving: 12 | Prep: 10mins | Cook: |Ready in:

Ingredients

- 2 (6 ounce) containers lemon yogurt
- 1 (8 ounce) container extra-creamy whipped dessert topping
- 1 cup blueberries
- 1 cup raspberries
- 1 cup blackberries (optional)
- 1 (9 inch) prepared deep dish graham cracker pie crust

Direction

- In a large bowl, combine lemon yogurt and whipped dessert topping together. Mix blackberries, raspberries and blueberries into the yogurt mixture; pour the mixture into prepared pie crust.
- Put in refrigerator for about 4 hours until the mixture sets.

Nutrition Information

- Calories: 181 calories;
- Total Fat: 7.7
- Sodium: 120
- Total Carbohydrate: 24.6
- Cholesterol: < 1
- Protein: 2.5

28. Wheat And Dairy Free Blackberry Pie

Serving: 8 | Prep: 20mins | Cook: 40mins |Ready in:

Ingredients

- 1/2 cup margarine, softened

- 1 1/2 cups potato flour
- 1/4 cup ice water
- 1 pinch salt
- 4 cups blackberries
- 1 cup white sugar
- 1/3 cup potato flour
- 2 tablespoons lime juice
- 1/4 cup margarine, melted and divided

Direction

- Whip together salt, ice water, 1.5 cups of the potato flour, and half cup of the margarine in the bowl with the electric mixer till the mixture looks like the big crumbs. Shape into the ball of dough; keep chilled in the fridge for 60 minutes.
- Whisk together lime juice, 1/3 cup of the potato flour, sugar and blackberries in the bowl.
- Pre heat the oven to 175 degrees C (350 degrees F).
- Split the dough into two even halves. Roll each half using the rolling pin to 12-in. in diameter. Press one of the crusts into the 9-in. pie pan. Spoon the blackberry filling to prepped pan. Sprinkle 3 tbsp. of the margarine on the blackberry filling.
- Gently press other pie crust over the top of blackberry filling and seal edges to edges of the bottom layer. Use the rest 1 tbsp. of the melted margarine to brush the top crust. Slide 2-3 slits in top crust to let the steam escape when baking.
- Bake the pie in preheated oven for roughly 40 minutes or till the blackberries become bubbly and the crust turns golden-brown.

Nutrition Information

- Calories: 410 calories;
- Total Fat: 17.3
- Sodium: 218
- Total Carbohydrate: 62.9
- Cholesterol: 0
- Protein: 3.7

29. Wild Blackberry Pie

Serving: 8 | Prep: 30mins | Cook: 35mins | Ready in:

Ingredients

- 1 1/2 cups all-purpose flour
- 1 teaspoon baking powder
- 1/2 teaspoon salt
- 1/2 cup butter
- 3 tablespoons boiling water
- 3/4 cup white sugar
- 3 tablespoons all-purpose flour
- 1 teaspoon ground cinnamon
- 1/8 teaspoon salt
- 4 cups fresh blackberries, rinsed and drained
- 1 tablespoon lemon juice
- 2 tablespoons butter

Direction

- For the pastry dough, sift 1/2 teaspoon salt, baking powder, and 1 1/2 cups flour. Cut in 1/2 cup margarine or butter. Pour boiling water into the flour mixture. Whisk until the mixture holds together into a ball. Split the dough into 2 portions, and roll out 2 crusts.
- Mix together 1/8 teaspoon salt, cinnamon, 3 tablespoons flour, and sugar. Stir with berries. In an unbaked pie crust, put the berry filling. Sprinkle lemon juice over and dot margarine or butter over.
- Fit and seal the upper crust.
- Put on the lower rack of the oven and bake for 30-40 minutes at 425°F (220°C).

Nutrition Information

- Calories: 328 calories;
- Sodium: 346
- Total Carbohydrate: 46.4
- Cholesterol: 38
- Protein: 3.9
- Total Fat: 15

Chapter 2: Blueberry Pie Recipes

***

30. Amazing Blueberry Rhubarb Pie

Serving: 8 | Prep: 15mins | Cook: 45mins | Ready in:

Ingredients

- 1/4 cup white sugar
- 1/4 cup light brown sugar
- 1/4 cup quick-cooking tapioca
- 1/4 teaspoon salt
- 3 cups diced rhubarb
- 3 cups fresh blueberries
- 1 pastry for a 9-inch double crust pie

Direction

- Pre heat the oven to 200 degrees C (400 degrees F).
- Whisk together salt, tapioca, brown sugar and white sugar in a big bowl. Put in the blueberries and rhubarb; coat by tossing.
- Halve the pie dough and roll each half into one 9 in. round. Position one round of the dough in pie plate's bottom. Pile the blueberry-rhubarb mixture over the dough and add the rest of the dough round on top. Trim off the excess dough from top crust to leave a half-an-in. border below top rim of pie plate. Tuck top edges of crust under bottom crust and crimp the border together. Position the pie plate onto a rimmed baking sheet.
- Bake in preheated oven for 20 minutes. Lower the oven temperature to 175 degrees C (350 degrees F) and keep baking for 25-30 minutes longer till filling becomes bubbly and crust

turns golden-brown. Let it cool down for 2 hours.

Nutrition Information

- Calories: 324 calories;
- Total Carbohydrate: 44.8
- Cholesterol: 0
- Protein: 3.6
- Total Fat: 15.2
- Sodium: 310

31. Bluebarb Pie

Serving: 8 | Prep: 25mins | Cook: 1hours5mins | Ready in:

Ingredients

- 3 cups diced rhubarb
- 1 1/2 cups fresh blueberries
- 1 pinch salt
- 1/8 teaspoon ground nutmeg
- 1/2 teaspoon lemon juice
- 1 1/3 cups white sugar
- 1/3 cup all-purpose flour
- 1 double crust ready-to-use pie crust
- 2 tablespoons butter, cut up
- 1 tablespoon white sugar

Direction

- Start preheating the oven at 425°F (220°C). Line aluminum foil on a baking sheet and position on the lower oven rack.
- Combine blueberries and rhubarb in a bowl with flour, 1 1/3 cups of sugar, lemon juice, nutmeg, and salt, until well-mixed. Pour into the pie shell and use butter to dot.
- Place the top crust over the filled crust and flute the edges. In the top crust, slice some decorative steam vents. Sprinkle 1 tablespoon of sugar over the crust; to prevent over-

browning, cover the fluted edges with aluminum foil.

- Bake in the prepared oven on the baking sheet for 15 minutes; lower the heat at 350°F (175°C) and bake for an additional 35 minutes. Take out the foil and keep baking until the crust turns to golden and juice bubbles through the slits, about an additional 15 minutes. Let cool completely before enjoying.

Nutrition Information

- Calories: 432 calories;
- Sodium: 276
- Total Carbohydrate: 65.4
- Cholesterol: 8
- Protein: 3.9
- Total Fat: 18.1

32. Blueberry Cream Pie

Serving: 16 | Prep: 20mins | Cook: 30mins | Ready in:

Ingredients

- 1 recipe pastry for a (10 inch) single crust pie
- 1 cup white sugar
- 2 egg yolks
- 1 tablespoon quick-cooking tapioca
- 1 pinch salt
- 1 tablespoon lemon juice
- 1/4 cup milk
- 1 quart fresh blueberries
- 2 egg whites
- 1 tablespoon all-purpose flour
- 1 tablespoon white sugar

Direction

- Start preheating the oven to 425°F (220°C). In a 10-in. deep-dish pie pan, put pie pastry that you've prepared.
- Using an electric mixer; beat egg yolks on high speed in a big bowl until pale. Slowly add 1

cup of sugar while whisking. Whisk until the yolks are pale and thick, and the sugar has fully dissolved. You will need 15 minutes to complete this. Stir in lemon juice, salt, and tapioca. Mix in milk, and then gently fold in blueberries. Whip egg whites in a big metal or glass bowl until forming stiff peaks. Fold into the blueberry mixture with egg whites.

- Mix together flour and the leftover 1 tablespoon of sugar, and sprinkle over the bottom of the unbaked pie crust. This will prevent the pie from leaking and absorb excess juice. Pour into the prepared crust with the filling.
- Bake in the preheated oven for 10 minutes, and then lower the temperature to 350°F (175°C). Bake until the pie is set, or about another 40-60 minutes.

Nutrition Information

- Calories: 160 calories;
- Total Fat: 5.4
- Sodium: 82
- Total Carbohydrate: 27
- Cholesterol: 26
- Protein: 2.1

33. Blueberry Crumb Pie

Serving: 8 | Prep: 30mins | Cook: 40mins | Ready in:

Ingredients

- 1 (9 inch) unbaked pie crust
- 3/4 cup white sugar
- 1/3 cup all-purpose flour
- 2 teaspoons grated lemon zest
- 1 tablespoon lemon juice
- 5 cups fresh or frozen blueberries
- 2/3 cup packed brown sugar
- 3/4 cup rolled oats
- 1/2 cup all-purpose flour
- 1/2 teaspoon ground cinnamon

- 6 tablespoons butter

Direction

- Heat the oven to 375°F (190°C).
- In a pie plate of 9 inches, press the pie crust into the bottom and onto the sides. Mix flour and sugar together in a large bowl. Stir in lemon juice and lemon zest. Carefully mix in blueberries. Add into pie crust.
- Combine cinnamon, flour, oats and brown sugar together in a medium bowl. Stir in butter with a fork until crumbly. Spread the crumb evenly over the pie filling.
- Bake for 40 minutes, or until it is browned on top. Let cool on a wire rack.

Nutrition Information

- Calories: 461 calories;
- Protein: 4.5
- Total Fat: 17
- Sodium: 185
- Total Carbohydrate: 75.6
- Cholesterol: 23

34. Blueberry Custard Pie

Serving: 8 | Prep: 20mins | Cook: 50mins | Ready in:

Ingredients

- 3 cups fresh blueberries
- 1 (9 inch) prepared graham cracker crust
- 1 cup all-purpose flour, divided
- 1/2 cup white sugar
- 1/8 teaspoon salt
- 2/3 cup sour cream
- 2 eggs
- 1/2 cup brown sugar
- 1/2 cup cold butter, cut into cubes

Direction

- Set the oven to 175 °C (350 °F) to preheat.

- On the bottom of the graham cracker crust, spread blueberries.
- In a bowl, mix salt, white sugar, and half cup flour together.
- In a separate bowl, whisk eggs and sour cream together. Fold in flour mixture. Pour over the blueberries with batter.
- In a bowl, combine brown sugar and half cup of leftover flour. Use 2 knives or a pastry cutter to cut in butter until mixture forms coarse crumbs. Sprinkle crumb topping over the pie.
- Bake in the prepared oven for 50 to 55 minutes, until topping and custard are golden brown. Bring to a rack and cool entirely before serving.

Nutrition Information

- Calories: 497 calories;
- Total Fat: 24.5
- Sodium: 321
- Total Carbohydrate: 66.2
- Cholesterol: 85
- Protein: 5.6

35. Blueberry Meringue Pie

Serving: 8 | Prep: 15mins | Cook: 40mins | Ready in:

Ingredients

- 1 (9 inch) pie shell, partially baked
- 4 cups blueberries
- 1 cup white sugar
- 1 teaspoon ground cinnamon
- 3 tablespoons cornstarch
- 2 tablespoons lemon juice
- 2 egg whites
- 1/4 cup white sugar

Direction

- Set the oven to 400°F (200°C).

- Mix the cornstarch, cinnamon and sugar in a big bowl. Put in blueberries and lemon juice, then gently mix to coat berries. Add to the pie shell.
- Bake in the prepared oven for 30 minutes. In a big glass or metal bowl, beat the egg whites until soft peak when the pie is done. Scatter sugar gradually while whipping into a stiff meringue. Spread on top of the hot filling to seal the meringue to the crust all around.
- Bake for 10 minutes longer, or until nicely browned on top. Let cool to room temperature before chilling or serving.

Nutrition Information

- Calories: 298 calories;
- Total Fat: 8
- Sodium: 137
- Total Carbohydrate: 55.8
- Cholesterol: 0
- Protein: 2.9

36. Blueberry Mulberry Custard Tart

Serving: 8 | Prep: 10mins | Cook: 23mins | Ready in:

Ingredients

- Custard:
- 1 (14 ounce) can fat-free sweetened condensed milk
- 1/2 cup low-fat sour cream
- 1/2 lemon, juiced, divided
- 2 teaspoons vanilla extract
- 1 (9 inch) prepared graham cracker crust
- Fruit Topping:
- 1/2 cup blueberry preserves
- 2 tablespoons dry white wine
- 1 cup fresh blueberries
- 1 cup fresh mulberries

Direction

- Set oven to preheat at 425°F (220°C).
- Mix together the vanilla extract, sour cream, half of the lemon juice, and condensed milk in a saucepan on medium heat. Simmer and stir on medium heat till the custard slightly thickens, for about 5 minutes. Take off from heat and let it cool down, for about 5 minutes. Transfer into the graham cracker crust.
- Mix together the remaining lemon juice, wine, and blueberry preserves in a different saucepan on medium heat; simmer and stir on medium heat till the preserves liquefy, for about 3 to 5 minutes. Stir blueberries and mulberries into the mix till coated with the preserves and warmed completely, for about 5 minutes. Take off from heat and let it cool down, for about 5 minutes. Pour on top of the custard.
- In preheated oven, bake until the crust's edges are golden, for about 10 minutes. Let it cool down on a wire rack, about 15 minutes.
- Chill in the refrigerator until custard sets before serving, no less than 1 hour.

Nutrition Information

- Calories: 376 calories;
- Protein: 6
- Total Fat: 13.6
- Sodium: 244
- Total Carbohydrate: 58.2
- Cholesterol: 23

37. Blueberry Pie

Serving: 8 | Prep: 15mins | Cook: 50mins | Ready in:

Ingredients

- 3/4 cup white sugar
- 3 tablespoons cornstarch
- 1/4 teaspoon salt
- 1/2 teaspoon ground cinnamon
- 4 cups fresh blueberries

- 1 recipe pastry for a 9 inch double crust pie
- 1 tablespoon butter

Direction

- Preheat an oven to 190°C/375°F.
- Mix cinnamon, salt, cornstarch and sugar; sprinkle on blueberries.
- Line 1 pie crust on pie dish. Put berry mixture into crust; dot with butter. Cut leftover pastry to 1/2 - 3/4-in. wide strips; create lattice top. Crimp, then flute edges.
- Bake pie on lower oven shelf till crust is golden brown, about 50 minutes.

Nutrition Information

- Calories: 366 calories;
- Total Fat: 16.6
- Sodium: 318
- Total Carbohydrate: 52.6
- Cholesterol: 4
- Protein: 3.3

38. Blueberry Pie Pops

Serving: 16 | Prep: 40mins | Cook: 20mins | Ready in:

Ingredients

- 2 (9 inch) unbaked pie crusts
- 1/2 cup white sugar, or to taste
- 1 teaspoon ground cinnamon
- 1/4 teaspoon ground nutmeg
- 2 teaspoons lemon zest
- 1 tablespoon cornstarch
- 1 1/4 cups blueberries
- 1 egg
- 1 tablespoon white sugar, for sprinkling
- 16 sturdy cookie pop or lollipop sticks

Direction

- Prepare the oven by preheating to 375°F (190°C). Use a parchment paper to line a baking sheet.
- Roll out to 1/8 inch thickness one of the pie crusts then from the rolled out crust, cut 16 3-inch circles. Line with crust circles each of the 16 mini muffin cups of a 24-cup mini muffin pan. Place inside the refrigerator for about 15 minutes to chill. In the meantime, roll out the other crust to 1/8 inch thickness and cut out 16 2 1/2-inch circles; onto the prepared baking sheet, put the 16 circles and place inside the refrigerator.
- In a bowl, mix together the corn starch, lemon zest, nutmeg, cinnamon and sugar. Mix in the blueberries and lightly toss to coat with sugar mixture. In a small separate bowl, beat the eggs. Scoop about 1 tablespoon of blueberry mixture into each crust-lined muffin cup without over-filling. Put a cookie pop stick horizontally into the filled pop leaving the end sticks out by few inches. Dab a bit of beaten eggs evenly around the edges of the filled crust using a pastry brush; put a 2 1/2 inch crust circle on top of the filled crust then seal the edges by pinching to secure the filling and close the crust around the stick. Use a toothpick to poke three or four steam holes into the top crust. Brush each top of pie pop with beaten egg and dust with sugar.
- Place inside the preheated oven and bake for about 20 minutes until the tops are golden brown in color. Let it cool for five minutes before slowly separating it from muffin tin cups. Use a small knife to run around the edges and under the stick to help release the pops.

Nutrition Information

- Calories: 154 calories;
- Total Fat: 7.8
- Sodium: 121
- Total Carbohydrate: 19.6
- Cholesterol: 12
- Protein: 1.9

39. Blueberry Pie In A Jar

Serving: 42 | Prep: 20mins | Cook: 20mins | Ready in:

Ingredients

- 7 quarts fresh blueberries
- 4 1/2 cups white sugar
- 3 tablespoons lemon juice
- 1 tablespoon salt
- 10 cups water, divided
- 1 cup cornstarch

Direction

- In a big, non-reactive pot, put 8 cups of water, salt, lemon juice, sugar and blueberries, then boil on high heat. In the leftover 2 cups of water, dissolve the cornstarch and mix it into the boiling blueberries until it becomes thick. Let it cook and stir for another 2 minutes.
- Ladle the mixture to seven sterilized quart jars with rings and lids. Process for 5 minutes in a pressure canner at 5 lbs. of pressure. Take out the jars from the canner and put it on the wood or cloth-covered surface and place it a couple of inches apart, until it cools down. When it cools, use your finger to press the top of every lid and make sure that it's tightly sealed (the lid doesn't move down or up at all). You can keep the sealed jars for a maximum of 1 year.

Nutrition Information

- Calories: 160 calories;
- Cholesterol: 0
- Protein: 0.9
- Total Fat: 0.4
- Sodium: 169
- Total Carbohydrate: 41

40. Blueberry Pie With Flax And Almonds

Serving: 8 | Prep: 30mins | Cook: 30mins | Ready in:

Ingredients

- FOR THE CRUST
- 1 cup graham cracker crumbs
- 3/4 cup flax seed meal
- 3/4 cup finely ground almonds (almond meal)
- 1/4 cup melted butter
- FOR THE FILLING
- 1/2 cup sour cream
- 1/2 cup plain non-fat yogurt
- 1/4 cup rolled oats, ground into flour
- 1/4 cup white sugar
- 1/4 cup honey
- 1 teaspoon vanilla extract
- 1/4 teaspoon salt
- 1 egg
- 4 cups fresh blueberries
- 2 tablespoons honey

Direction

- Preheat the oven to 190 °C or 375 °F.
- In a bowl, mix ground almonds, flax seed meal and graham cracker crumbs; mix in liquified butter. Put several drops of water, if needed, to make crumb mixture to combine. Force 1/2 of crumb mixture into the base and up the sides of a pie pan, 9-inch in size; crust should just be approximately 1/8-inch thick. Reserve another half of crumb mixture.
- In a blender, mix salt, vanilla, honey, sugar, ground oats, yogurt and sour cream. Process till mixed. To pie pan, put blueberries and add in the filling.
- To prepare the topping, into reserved mixture of crumb, mix 2 tablespoons of honey to taste. It should create an extremely thick paste. Drop topping by teaspoonfuls over the top of pie.
- In the center rack of prepped oven, let the pie bake for 30 to 45 minutes, or till middle is firm and a knife pricked close to the middle of pie

gets out clean. Switch the oven off and allow pie to sit in warm oven for 10 minutes.
- Take pie out of oven and cool on a wire rack. Refrigerate to chill till pie is firm and cool.

Nutrition Information

- Calories: 418 calories;
- Protein: 9.1
- Total Fat: 23.6
- Sodium: 209
- Total Carbohydrate: 47.6
- Cholesterol: 46

41. Blueberry Pigs

Serving: 6 | Prep: 35mins | Cook: 1hours | Ready in:

Ingredients

- 3 cups all-purpose flour
- 1 teaspoon salt
- 3/4 cup shortening
- 6 tablespoons cold water
- 4 cups blueberries
- 1 pinch ground cinnamon
- 1/4 cup white sugar
- 1/4 cup butter, chilled and diced

Direction

- Heat an oven to 175°C or 350°F.
- Mix salt and flour in a big bowl. Mash shortening in till mixture looks much like coarse crumbs. Mix water in to form mixture into ball. Split dough in 1/2 and form to balls. Roll from middle to edges on floured counter, to 12-inch round. Do not roll too thin.
- Smear about 2 cups of blueberries over every rolled pastry, or sufficient to create a one blueberries layer, keeping a 2-inch form edge bare. Scatter with sugar, slices of butter and cinnamon.

- Roll the pastry, jelly-roll style, folding ends while rolling, and put onto cookie sheet.
- Bake for an hour in prepped oven till golden brown.

Nutrition Information

- Calories: 610 calories;
- Total Fat: 34.2
- Sodium: 445
- Total Carbohydrate: 70.2
- Cholesterol: 20
- Protein: 7.3

42. Blueberry Raspberry Pie

Serving: 8 | Prep: 30mins | Cook: 45mins | Ready in:

Ingredients

- Pie Crust:
- 2 cups all-purpose flour
- 3/4 teaspoon salt
- 2/3 cup shortening
- 6 tablespoons cold water, or more as needed
- 1 egg white
- 1 tablespoon water
- Filling:
- 3/4 cup white sugar
- 1/4 cup cornstarch
- 2 tablespoons grated lemon peel
- 1 teaspoon vanilla extract
- 1/4 teaspoon ground cinnamon
- 3 cups fresh blueberries
- 1 cup fresh raspberries
- 1 tablespoon water
- 1 tablespoon white sugar

Direction

- Preheat the oven to 200 degrees C/400 degrees F.
- In a bowl, mix salt and flour. With a pastry cutter/fork, mash shortening into flour

mixture until mixture becomes crumbly. As needed, add cold water gradually, using a fork to toss until dough shapes to a ball. Use plastic wrap to wrap the dough. Keep in the fridge for 30 minutes.

- On a flat work surface that's been dusted with flour, turn out dough. Halve dough. Shape each dough half to a ball. From center to edges, roll dough ball to a circle that's 2-in. bigger than the pie plate and about 1/8-in. thick. Wrap the dough around the rolling pin, beginning at one circle's side. Unroll it above a pie plate. Trim dough. Roll leftover dough ball to a crust so it fits the pie's top. Put aside.
- Beat 1 tbsp. water and egg white. Brush on bottom of crust. Put aside.
- In a bowl, mix cinnamon, vanilla extract, lemon peel, cornstarch and 3/4 cup sugar. Stir raspberries and blueberries gently into the mixture to coat. Put into crust. Put reserved pie crust on top. Brush 1 tbsp. water on top of the pie crust. Sprinkle 1 tbsp. sugar on moistened top. Use a sharp knife to cut several slits into the top crust.
- Bake in the preheated oven for about 45 minutes until filling is bubbly and crust is golden brown. Put pie on a wire rack; completely cool. Refrigerate.

Nutrition Information

- Calories: 402 calories;
- Total Fat: 17.7
- Sodium: 227
- Total Carbohydrate: 57.9
- Cholesterol: 0
- Protein: 4.3

43. Bumbleberry Pie II

Serving: 16 | Prep: 45mins | Cook: 1hours | Ready in:

Ingredients

- 5 1/2 cups all-purpose flour
- 1/4 teaspoon salt
- 2 cups shortening
- 3/4 cup cold water
- 1 egg
- 1 tablespoon vinegar
- 4 cups apples - peeled, cored and chopped
- 2 cups chopped fresh rhubarb
- 2 cups sliced fresh strawberries
- 2 cups fresh blueberries
- 2 cups fresh raspberries
- 2 tablespoons lemon juice
- 2 cups white sugar
- 2/3 cup all-purpose flour
- 2 tablespoons tapioca
- 1 egg yolk, beaten
- 2 tablespoons water

Direction

- Set oven to preheat at 350°F (175°C).
- In a large bowl, combine salt and flour. Cut in shortening until mixture looks like coarse crumbs. Whisk together vinegar, egg, and 3/4 cup water. Mix into flour until mixture creates a ball. Split the dough into 4 balls. Use plastic to wrap and chill in refrigerator for 4 hours or overnight. Roll out the dough pieces to fit a 9 inch pie pan. To 2 of pie pans, place the bottom crusts. Put the top crusts aside.
- In a large bowl, combine lemon juice, raspberries, blueberries, strawberries, rhubarb, and apples. Mix together tapioca, 2/3 cup flour, and 2 cups sugar; toss gently with the fruit mixture. Split the mixture into 2 pastry lined pie pans. Cover using top crusts; trim the edges and crimp. Brush the tops using egg wash (2 tablespoons water beaten with 1 egg yolk). Slice several slits in the top to vent the steam.
- In preheated oven, bake for 50 to 60 minutes, or until top becomes golden brown and filling is bubbly in center.

Nutrition Information

- Calories: 554 calories;
- Total Fat: 27
- Sodium: 44
- Total Carbohydrate: 73.7
- Cholesterol: 24
- Protein: 6.2

44. Cherry Berry Peach Pie

Serving: 8 | Prep: 30mins | Cook: 55mins | Ready in:

Ingredients

- 1 (15 ounce) package pastry for a double crust 9-inch pie
- 3 cups peeled, sliced peaches
- 1 cup Bing cherries, pitted and halved
- 1 cup blueberries
- 1 tablespoon lemon juice
- 1/2 cup white sugar
- 1/4 cup brown sugar
- 3 tablespoons all-purpose flour
- 1/4 teaspoon ground cinnamon
- 1/8 teaspoon salt
- 1 tablespoon milk, or as needed
- 1 teaspoon white sugar, or as needed

Direction

- Preheat the oven to 230°C (450°F). Pat 1 pie crust pastry into a 9 inch pie plate. Slice the leftover pie crust pastry into 3/4-inch strips to be used for the lattice top.
- In a large bowl, stir lemon juice together with blueberries, cherries and peaches. Put in salt, cinnamon, flour, brown sugar and 1/2 cup of white sugar; mix to coat. In the prepared pie crust, spread the fruit blend. With the pie crust strips, weave a lattice top atop the fruit filling. Brush the top crust with milk; dust with about 1 teaspoon of white sugar.
- Bake for 10 minutes in the preheated oven. Lower heat to 175°C (350°F); bake for 45 to 50 minutes until the lattice top is lightly browned and fruit filling is bubbling.

Nutrition Information

- Calories: 370 calories;
- Total Fat: 16.5
- Sodium: 294
- Total Carbohydrate: 53.1
- Cholesterol: < 1
- Protein: 3.7

45. Cherry Blueberry Pie

Serving: 8 | Prep: 15mins | Cook: 45mins | Ready in:

Ingredients

- 1 (15 ounce) package refrigerated pie crusts
- 1/2 cup white sugar
- 2 tablespoons cornstarch
- 1/4 teaspoon ground cinnamon
- 1 (21 ounce) can cherry pie filling
- 1 1/2 cups frozen blueberries
- 1 egg white
- 1 teaspoon water
- 2 teaspoons sugar

Direction

- Preheat an oven to 220 ° C or 425 ° F.
- Force one of pie crusts into one pie plate, 9-inch in size. Mix cinnamon, cornstarch and half cup sugar together in a big bowl. Mix in blueberries and cherry pie filling. Scoop into pie crust. Put another crust on top, and pinch edges to enclose. Crimp edges, or force using fork tines. Whip water and egg white together in cup using fork. Brush on pie surface, then scatter 2 teaspoons sugar over.
- In the prepped oven, bake till crust turn golden brown for 45 to 55 minutes. Cover crust edges in aluminum foil in case they seem to be getting very dark. To let filling set, cool for a minimum of 2 hours prior to serving.

Nutrition Information

- Calories: 409 calories;
- Sodium: 274
- Total Carbohydrate: 62
- Cholesterol: 0
- Protein: 3.9
- Total Fat: 16.4

46. Company Special

Serving: 18 | Prep: | Cook: | Ready in:

Ingredients

- 3 1/2 cups graham cracker crumbs
- 3/4 cup butter, melted
- 1 (8 ounce) package cream cheese, softened
- 4 cups frozen whipped topping, thawed
- 1 (3 ounce) package cook and serve vanilla pudding
- 1 cup milk
- 1 (16 ounce) can blueberry pie filling

Direction

- To preheat: Set oven to 150°C (300°F).
- Combine melted butter with graham cracker crumbs in a large bowl. Spread the mixture into bottom of a 9x13 inch pan.
- Put into the preheated oven and bake at 150°C (300°F) for 10 minutes or till golden brown color forms. Let cool down.
- Combine milk and pudding in a saucepan and cook as instructed on package label. It will become very stiff.
- Combine cream cheese and pudding in a large bowl, mix until the mixture gets smooth. Fold in whipped topping. Use the mixture to spread on cooled graham cracker crust.
- Put fruit filling on top. Keep in the fridge until ready to serve.

Nutrition Information

- Calories: 303 calories;
- Total Carbohydrate: 32.8
- Cholesterol: 35
- Protein: 2.9
- Total Fat: 18.2
- Sodium: 238

47. Creamy Apple Blueberry Pie

Serving: 8 | Prep: 20mins | Cook: 1hours | Ready in:

Ingredients

- 3 cups sliced apples
- 1 cup blueberries
- 1 (9 inch) unbaked deep dish pie crust
- 1/4 cup all-purpose flour
- 1/2 cup white sugar
- 1/4 teaspoon salt
- 1/4 teaspoon ground nutmeg
- 1/4 teaspoon ground cinnamon, or more to taste
- 1 cup plain yogurt
- 1 egg
- 1 teaspoon vanilla extract
- 1/2 cup all-purpose flour
- 1/2 cup chopped pecans
- 1/2 cup rolled oats
- 1/4 cup brown sugar
- 1/2 cup butter

Direction

- Set oven to preheat at 400°F (200°C). Toss blueberries and apples in the unbaked pie crust.
- Mix cinnamon, nutmeg, salt, white sugar, and 1/4 cup flour in a bowl. Mix in vanilla extract, egg, and yogurt; pour batter over apples and blueberries.
- Mix together brown sugar, oats, pecans, and 1/2 cup flour in a mixing bowl. Use a knife or pastry blender to cut in butter until the mixture looks like coarse crumbs; put aside.

- In preheated oven, bake for 15 minutes; lower the heat to 350°F (175°C) and continue to bake pie crust until light brown, for about 30 minutes. Sprinkle the mixture of crumb on top of the pie and bake for about 15 more minutes until golden brown. Let it cool down before serving.

Nutrition Information

- Calories: 464 calories;
- Sodium: 335
- Total Carbohydrate: 54.5
- Cholesterol: 56
- Protein: 6.3
- Total Fat: 25.6

48. Creamy Blueberry Pie

Serving: 8 | Prep: 25mins | Cook: 55mins | Ready in:

Ingredients

- 3 cups fresh blueberries
- 1 (9 inch) deep dish pie crust
- For the Custard:
- 1 cup white sugar
- 1/3 cup all-purpose flour
- 1/8 teaspoon salt
- 2 eggs, beaten
- 1/2 cup sour cream
- For the Streusel:
- 1/2 cup white sugar
- 1/2 cup all-purpose flour
- 1/4 cup butter

Direction

- Heat the oven to 350°F (175°C). In the pastry shell, add blueberries and put aside.
- Mix salt, 1/3 cup of flour and 1 cup sugar together. Put in sour cream and eggs, stirring until combined. Add over the blueberries.

- In a separate bowl, mix 1/2 cup flour and 1/2 cup sugar together. Use pastry blender to cut in the butter until the mixture looks like coarse meal. Sprinkle over the sour cream mixture in the crust.
- Bake in the oven until it is lightly browned, about 50 - 55 minutes. Let cool on wire rack.

Nutrition Information

- Calories: 440 calories;
- Cholesterol: 68
- Protein: 4.8
- Total Fat: 17.8
- Sodium: 250
- Total Carbohydrate: 67.3

49. Easy Summer Pie

Serving: 8 | Prep: 25mins | Cook: 15mins | Ready in:

Ingredients

- 1 (9 inch) frozen pie crust, thawed
- 1 (8 ounce) package cream cheese, softened
- 1/3 cup white sugar
- 1 (11 ounce) can mandarin oranges, drained
- 1 cup fresh strawberries, halved
- 4 kiwi, peeled and sliced
- 1 cup fresh raspberries
- 1 cup fresh blueberries

Direction

- Preheat the oven to 200 ° C or 400 ° F.
- Roll the pastry making an 11-inches round. Spread flat on pizza pan or baking sheet. Puncture a few times using fork. In prepped oven, bake till pale brown, for 12 to 15 minutes. Take off and cool fully.
- Whip sugar and cream cheese together in small mixing bowl till mixture is smooth and creamy. Scatter equally onto the cooled pastry.

Decoratively place fruit on layer of cream cheese. Refrigerate till set to serve.

Nutrition Information

- Calories: 282 calories;
- Sodium: 189
- Total Carbohydrate: 34.6
- Cholesterol: 31
- Protein: 3.8
- Total Fat: 15.4

---

50. Finnish Blueberry Pie

Serving: 12 | Prep: 35mins | Cook: 25mins | Ready in:

Ingredients

- 3/4 cup white sugar
- 3/4 cup butter, softened
- 1 egg
- 1 teaspoon baking powder
- 2 1/4 cups all-purpose flour
- 1/2 cup milk
- 2 pints fresh blueberries
- 1/2 cup white sugar, or more to taste

Direction

- Start preheating the oven to 400°F (200°C), line parchment paper on a 9-by-13-in. baking pan.
- Beat butter with 3/4 cup of sugar until creamy and smooth. Beat in egg. Put in baking powder, stir in flour, half cup at once, alternating with a few tablespoons of milk, until all milk and flour are incorporated. Dough will become sticky as the sugar cookie dough. Spread prepared baking dish with dough, making a raised edge around dish.
- In a bowl, put blueberries with half cup sugar, using a potato masher to mash berries. Spread the crust top with blueberry mixture, in an even layer.

- Bake in prepared oven for 15 to 25 mins or until filling is bubbling and thickened, crust has slightly browned.

Nutrition Information

- Calories: 310 calories;
- Cholesterol: 47
- Protein: 3.8
- Total Fat: 12.5
- Sodium: 133
- Total Carbohydrate: 47.3

---

51. Fresh Blueberry Pie I

Serving: 8 | Prep: 30mins | Cook: 40mins | Ready in:

Ingredients

- 1 recipe pastry for a 9 inch double crust pie
- 4 cups fresh blueberries
- 2/3 cup white sugar
- 2 tablespoons all-purpose flour
- 1 tablespoon quick-cooking tapioca
- 1/4 teaspoon ground nutmeg
- 1/4 teaspoon salt
- 1 tablespoon grated lemon zest
- 1 1/2 tablespoons lemon juice
- 1/2 tablespoon butter

Direction

- Preheat an oven to 230°C/450°F.
- Prepare pastry to make 2 crust pies; pick over, then wash blueberries.
- Mix salt, spices, tapioca, flour and sugar; mix into blueberries. Add lemon rind and juice; stand for 10-15 minutes, then stir well. Put into 9-in. pastry-lined pie plate; use small pieces of margarine/butter to dot over. Use top crust to cover.
- In preheated oven, position pie on lowest rack; bake for 10 minutes. Lower oven temperature

to 175°C/350°F; bake for 30 minutes more.
Serve cold or warm.

Nutrition Information

- Calories: 238 calories;
- Cholesterol: 2
- Protein: 2.2
- Total Fat: 8.5
- Sodium: 196
- Total Carbohydrate: 40.2

52. Fresh Blueberry Pie II

Serving: 8 | Prep: | Cook: |Ready in:

Ingredients

- 1 prepared 8 inch pastry shell, baked and cooled
- 2 pints fresh blueberries
- 1 tablespoon all-purpose flour
- 1 tablespoon butter
- 1 tablespoon lemon juice
- 1/2 cup white sugar

Direction

- Add a pint of the blueberries into the baked pie shell.
- Put sugar, lemon juice, butter, flour together. Mix well. Put in the remaining pint of blueberries and bring just to a boil on medium heat. Berries should begin cracking open.
- Transfer cooked berries on fresh berries. Chill the pie then serve with whipped cream.

Nutrition Information

- Calories: 177 calories;
- Sodium: 93
- Total Carbohydrate: 31.6
- Cholesterol: 4
- Protein: 1.3

- Total Fat: 5.9

53. Fresh Blueberry Pie IV

Serving: 8 | Prep: 30mins | Cook: 15mins |Ready in:

Ingredients

- 1 (9 inch) pie crust, baked
- 3/4 cup white sugar
- 2 1/2 tablespoons cornstarch
- 1/4 teaspoon salt
- 2/3 cup water
- 1 cup fresh blueberries
- 2 tablespoons butter
- 1 1/2 tablespoons lemon juice
- 1 1/2 tablespoons orange liqueur
- 2 cups fresh blueberries
- 2 cups whipped cream for garnish (optional)

Direction

- Mix water, salt, cornstarch and sugar in a big saucepan. Stir well, then put in a cup of blueberry. Heat up over low heat, mixing frequently, until mixture comes to a boil. Boil and mix about for 15 minutes until very thick. Take off from heat.
- Mix liqueur, lemon juice, and butter or margarine into mixture. Let cool. Mix in leftover 2 cups blueberries. Refrigerate for an hour. Scoop into pastry crust and chill for at least 2 more hours before serving. Top with whipped cream (optional).

Nutrition Information

- Calories: 333 calories;
- Total Carbohydrate: 39
- Cholesterol: 49
- Protein: 1.8
- Total Fat: 19.3
- Sodium: 207

54. Fresh Fruit Flan

Serving: 12 | Prep: 30mins | Cook: 12mins | Ready in:

Ingredients

- Crust:
- 2 1/8 cups all-purpose flour
- 1/2 teaspoon cream of tartar
- 1/2 teaspoon baking soda
- 1/2 cup white sugar
- 1/2 cup confectioners' sugar
- 1/2 cup butter
- 1/2 cup vegetable oil
- 1 egg
- 1/2 teaspoon vanilla extract
- Filling:
- 1 (8 ounce) package cream cheese, softened
- 1/3 cup white sugar
- 1/2 teaspoon vanilla extract
- Fruit:
- 3 cups fresh strawberries, hulled and halved
- 1 cup fresh blueberries, rinsed and dried
- 3 kiwifruit, peeled and thinly sliced
- Glaze:
- 1 tablespoon cornstarch
- 1/4 cup white sugar
- 1/2 cup water
- 1/2 cup orange juice
- 2 tablespoons lemon juice

Direction

- Preheat oven to 350° F (175°C). Grease a 10-by-15 inch jelly roll pan.
- To make the crust, sift together cream of tartar, flour, and baking soda into a mixing bowl. Cream egg, vanilla, white sugar, confectioner's sugar, vegetable oil and butter together in another bowl. Combine the dry ingredients. Mix well. Place the dough on the bottom of the greased pan and spread evenly. Bake for 10 to 12 minutes until golden brown. Cool completely.
- For the filling, combine the vanilla, cream cheese and sugar and cream together. Place the mixture over the cooled crust and spread evenly. Top the cream cheese filling with fruits and refrigerate.
- For the glaze, combine sugar and cornstarch in a small pan. Mix in the lemon juice, orange juice, and water. Let the mixture boil on medium heat and boil gently for 1 minute. Take off from heat and let cool completely.
- Brush or drizzle the glaze evenly over the fruit. Keep refrigerated until ready to serve.

Nutrition Information

- Calories: 430 calories;
- Protein: 4.9
- Total Fat: 24.2
- Sodium: 170
- Total Carbohydrate: 50.1
- Cholesterol: 56

55. Gluten Free Berry Rhubarb Pie

Serving: 8 | Prep: 35mins | Cook: 1hours10mins | Ready in:

Ingredients

- Gluten-Free Pie Crust:
- 3 cups gluten-free all-purpose baking flour (such as Cup4Cup™)
- 1 tablespoon white sugar
- 1 teaspoon fine salt
- 1 cup cold unsalted butter, cut into cubes
- 3/4 cup ice cold water
- Filling:
- 4 cups hulled and halved strawberries
- 4 cups fresh blueberries
- 4 cups thinly sliced rhubarb
- 1 lemon, zested
- 1 teaspoon vanilla extract
- 1 cup white sugar
- 1/4 cup gluten-free cornstarch

- 1/4 teaspoon salt
- 1 egg
- 1/4 cup water
- 1 tablespoon raw sugar, or to taste

Direction

- Whisk together the flour, sugar, and salt in a bowl. Toss butter into the mixture of flour till coated. Turn the mixture into a food processor and, in short bursts, pulse till butter has crumbs the size of hazelnuts. Drizzle ice water into the mix through the feed tube, in quick 4-second bursts, pulse till the dough forms a ball.
- Split the dough into 2 equal balls. Flatten them out into disks and use parchment paper and plastic wrap to wrap each disk. Place them in refrigerator till firm, for about 1 hour.
- Set oven to preheat at 425°F (220°C).
- Roll 1 disk out into a circle 11-inch wide. Place it into a 9-inch pie plate. Trim the excess dough, leave 1 inch overhang.
- In the preheated oven, bake till golden, for about 15 to 20 minutes. Let the crust cool down while making the filling. Keep the oven on.
- Toss the vanilla extract, blueberries, rhubarb, lemon zest, and strawberries in a large bowl. Mix sugar, cornstarch, and salt in a different bowl. Toss the fruit mixture into the mixture of sugar right before pouring on top of the crust.
- Beat together the egg and water in a small bowl to create an egg wash. Use the egg wash to brush the bottom crust's rim.
- Roll the second disk out into an 11-inch circle. Place it on top the filled pie carefully. Cut off the edges and tuck the top crust over the bottom crust's rim to tightly seal. Decoratively crimp the edge. Slice an X-shape into the top crust. Use egg wash to brush the top and sprinkle it with raw sugar.
- Put the pie onto a baking sheet and bake for 20 minutes, turn the pie halfway through baking. Lower the temperature to 350°F (175°C). Keep on baking till crust is golden and juices thicken and begin to bubble out through the X on the top, for about 35 to 40 minutes.
- Put the pie onto a rack to cool completely, for no less than 1 hour.

Nutrition Information

- Calories: 585 calories;
- Total Fat: 25.9
- Sodium: 380
- Total Carbohydrate: 88.4
- Cholesterol: 81
- Protein: 7.6

56. Grandma's Blueberry Pie

Serving: 8 | Prep: 40mins | Cook: 40mins | Ready in:

Ingredients

- 1 1/4 cups white sugar
- 3 tablespoons quick-cooking tapioca
- 1/2 teaspoon ground cinnamon
- 3 cups blueberries
- 1 tablespoon lemon juice
- 1 tablespoon butter
- 1 pastry for a 9 inch double crust pie

Direction

- Start preheating the oven to 400°F (200°C). Roll out 1/2 pastry then line a 9-in. pie pan; trim crust to the pan rim. Cover loosely in plastic wrap. Place in the refrigerator.
- Combine cinnamon, tapioca and sugar. In a mixing bowl, toss blueberries with sugar mixture and pour lemon juice over the top. Allow to stand for 15 mins. In the meantime, roll to form top crust into a 10-in. circle. Slice into 1/2-inch strips. Add blueberry mixture to the chilled pie shell then dot with butter. Put in pastry strips, 1 at a time, weaving a lattice. Flute the edges.

- Arrange the pie on baking sheet to catch drips. Bake for 40-50 mins in prepared oven, until the crust turns light brown and the filling is bubbly. Let it cool completely before enjoying.

Nutrition Information

- Calories: 290 calories;
- Cholesterol: 4
- Protein: 1.8
- Total Fat: 9.1
- Sodium: 128
- Total Carbohydrate: 52.2

57. Green Blueberry Pie

Serving: 14 | Prep: 10mins | Cook: | Ready in:

Ingredients

- 1 cup boiling water
- 1 (3 ounce) package lime-flavored Jell-O® mix
- 1 pint vanilla ice cream, softened
- 1 pint fresh blueberries
- 1 (9 inch) prepared graham cracker pie crust, frozen

Direction

- In a bowl, add boiling water on top of lime-flavored gelatin mix; mix to dissolve gelatin. Stir softened vanilla ice cream into the hot gelatin mixture and mix quickly to melt ice cream into the mixture. Put blueberries into the bowl; mix to coat. Add to frozen pie shell. Chill at least 3 hours prior to serving.

Nutrition Information

- Calories: 157 calories;
- Total Fat: 6.4
- Sodium: 141
- Total Carbohydrate: 24.2
- Cholesterol: 8

- Protein: 2.1

58. Lemon Blueberry Custard Pie

Serving: 8 | Prep: 20mins | Cook: 50mins | Ready in:

Ingredients

- 1 (9 inch) unbaked pie crust
- 1 tablespoon butter
- 2/3 cup white sugar
- 2 tablespoons all-purpose flour
- 3 tablespoons lemon juice
- 1 tablespoon grated lemon zest
- 2 egg yolks
- 1 cup milk
- 2 egg whites
- 1 3/4 cups fresh blueberries

Direction

- Set oven to 350°F (175°C) to preheat.
- Whip butter in a big bowl. Stir in lemon zest, lemon juice, flour and sugar. Whip in egg yolks then the milk.
- Whip egg whites in a big glass or metal mixing bowl until stiff peaks create. Fold into the lemon mixture gently. Pour filling into pie crust. Sprinkle blueberries over the top evenly.
- Bake for approximately 50 minutes in the prepared oven, or until filling is firm. Cover the pie with foil after about half an hour to prevent browning. Let cool slightly before serving.

Nutrition Information

- Calories: 250 calories;
- Protein: 4.4
- Total Fat: 10.7
- Sodium: 156
- Total Carbohydrate: 35.3
- Cholesterol: 57

59. Lemon Blueberry Pie

Serving: 16 | Prep: | Cook: | Ready in:

Ingredients

- 1 (14 ounce) can sweetened condensed milk
- 1/4 cup lemon juice
- 1 1/2 cups fresh blueberries
- 2 egg yolks
- 2 (9 inch) pie shells, baked
- 8 egg whites
- 1/4 cup white sugar
- 1/4 teaspoon cream of tartar

Direction

- Blend together egg yolks and sweetened condensed milk; add lemon juice slowly, mixing till it is well blended and thickened. Fold in blueberries gently; put filling into the baked pie shells.
- Beat cream of tartar and room temperature egg whites till foamy in another bowl. Add sugar slowly, beating till egg whites are stiff; spread meringue on filling carefully, sealing edges.
- Bake at 200°C/400°F for about 6 minutes till meringue browns; cool. Refrigerate leftovers.

Nutrition Information

- Calories: 233 calories;
- Total Fat: 10.5
- Sodium: 182
- Total Carbohydrate: 29.7
- Cholesterol: 34
- Protein: 5.6

60. Mango Cheese Tart With Blueberries

Serving: 8 | Prep: 30mins | Cook: 20mins | Ready in:

Ingredients

- 1 1/2 cups all-purpose flour
- 1/2 cup confectioners' sugar
- 1/2 tablespoon butter
- 2 egg yolks
- 2 tablespoons water
- 1 (8 ounce) package cream cheese, softened
- 1/2 cup white sugar
- 2 mangos, peeled, seeded and chopped
- 2 tablespoons lemon juice
- 2 cups blueberries
- 1/3 cup confectioners' sugar for dusting

Direction

- Preheat an oven to 175°C/350°F.
- Sift 1/2 cup confectioners' sugar and flour into a big bowl; cut in butter till it looks like coarse crumbs. Stir in enough water and egg yolks to make a ball; gently knead till smooth on a lightly floured surface. Roll out to line 8-in. tart shell/flan ring. In preheated oven, bake till pastry is golden, about 20 minutes; cool.
- Mix together lemon juice, mangoes, 1/2 cup sugar and cheese; beat till fairly smooth, with chunks of mangoes; spread into the baked pastry shell. Put blueberries over; lightly dust confectioners' sugar. Serve.

Nutrition Information

- Calories: 357 calories;
- Sodium: 92
- Total Carbohydrate: 58.7
- Cholesterol: 84
- Protein: 5.7
- Total Fat: 12.1

61. Marry Me Blueberry Pie

Serving: 8 | Prep: 15mins | Cook: 50mins | Ready in:

Ingredients

- Crust:
- 2 cups self-rising flour
- 2/3 cup vegetable oil
- 1/3 cup water
- Filling:
- 2 cups blueberries, or more to taste
- 1 cup white sugar
- 1/4 cup all-purpose flour
- 1 tablespoon lemon juice
- 1 pinch salt
- 2 tablespoons butter, cut into small cubes

Direction

- Set oven to 400°F (200°C) to preheat.
- In a bowl, combine water, oil, and two cups self-rising flour until pie dough is well-combined; split into 2 balls. Shape each ball between two pieces of waxed paper until flattened to about 9 inches in diameter. Flip 1 piece of dough on top of pie pan and remove top piece of waxed paper. Cut off excess crust if necessary. Put leftover dough aside.
- In a bowl, mix salt, lemon juice, a quarter cup all-purpose flour, sugar and blueberries together until evenly combined; add to the pie shell. Cover blueberry filling with leftover dough, crimp to close the edges together. Put butter cubes evenly over top crust.
- Bake for about 50 minutes in the prepared oven until crust is golden brown and filling is thick.

Nutrition Information

- Calories: 429 calories;
- Protein: 3.8
- Total Fat: 21.5
- Sodium: 437
- Total Carbohydrate: 56.6
- Cholesterol: 8

62. Meyer Lemon And Blueberry Cheese Tart

Serving: 16 | Prep: 20mins | Cook: 20mins | Ready in:

Ingredients

- 4 1/2 ounces thin lemon tea cookies (such as Trader Joe's® Meyer Lemon Cookies), crushed
- 3 tablespoons butter, melted
- 1 pound fresh blueberries
- 2/3 cup white sugar
- 1 tablespoon cornstarch
- 1 (8 ounce) container mascarpone cheese
- 3 tablespoons lemon curd
- 1/2 (8 ounce) container frozen whipped topping, thawed

Direction

- In a bowl, thoroughly mix butter and crushed lemon cookies.
- Press cookie mixture on bottom of 8-in. springform pan.
- Bring sugar and blueberries to a saucepan on medium low heat; simmer for 10 minutes till a thin sauce forms and sugar dissolves.
- Mix cornstarch into blueberry sauce and simmer for about 10 minutes till sauce is thick; take off heat. Cool for 10 minutes.
- Mix whipped topping, lemon curd and mascarpone till smooth and well blended in a bowl.
- Spread mascarpone mixture on crust in springform pan; use waxed paper to cover. Freeze for about 10 minutes till semi-firm.
- Spread blueberry sauce on mascarpone layer; use waxed paper to cover. Refrigerate for a minimum of 1 hour till set.

Nutrition Information

- Calories: 198 calories;

- Total Fat: 11.8
- Sodium: 59
- Total Carbohydrate: 22.8
- Cholesterol: 26
- Protein: 1.9

- Cholesterol: 46
- Protein: 4
- Total Fat: 9.7
- Sodium: 254

63. My Grandmother's Best Berry Pie

Serving: 8 | Prep: | Cook: | Ready in:

Ingredients

- 1 3/4 cups all-purpose flour
- 3/8 cup butter
- 3 teaspoons baking powder
- 1 teaspoon vanilla extract
- 3/8 cup white sugar
- 1 egg
- 2 1/2 cups fresh blueberries

Direction

- To prepare crust: Beat the butter or margarine and the flour thoroughly. Mix in egg, sugar, vanilla and baking powder; mix thoroughly. Allow the dough to sit for about 25 minutes.
- Cover the pie dish in the center of the pan with enough dough and spread the dough equally over the sides and bottom of the pan. Reserve the leftover dough for the top of the pie. Make holes here and there along the bottom of the pie dough using a fork. Allow the pie dough to rest again for 25 minutes longer.
- Place the berries inside the pie dish, then spread the rest of the crumb dough over it.
- Put in the oven and bake at 400 0F (205 0 C) for 25-30 minutes.

Nutrition Information

- Calories: 249 calories;
- Total Carbohydrate: 37.4

64. Mystery Ingredient Wild Blueberry Pie

Serving: 8 | Prep: 15mins | Cook: 45mins | Ready in:

Ingredients

- 1 recipe pastry for a double-crust 9-inch pie, divided
- 5 cups fresh blueberries (preferably wild)
- 1/2 cup white sugar
- 1/4 cup all-purpose flour
- 1/2 teaspoon ground cinnamon, or more to taste
- 1/4 teaspoon almond extract
- 1/4 cup butter, cut into small pieces
- 1 tablespoon milk (optional)

Direction

- Set oven to 375°F (190°C) to preheat. Push a pie crust pastry into the sides and the bottom of a 9-inch pie plate.
- In a big bowl, mix cinnamon, flour, sugar, and blueberries. Put in almond extract; mix to coat. Add blueberry mixture into the prepped pie shell. Dot butter pieces on the blueberry mixture. Top with another pie crust, crimping the 2 crusts together. Brush top crust using milk. Create several incisions with a knife into the top crust to let steam escape during baking. Encase the edges of the pie with aluminum foil to prevent burning.
- Bake for 25 minutes in the prepared oven. Take the foil and keep baking for 20 to 25 minutes more until crust turn brown and blueberry filling is bubbling. Let cool before serving.

- Calories: 394 calories;
- Cholesterol: 15
- Protein: 4
- Total Fat: 21.1
- Sodium: 276
- Total Carbohydrate: 49.3

65. Old Fashioned Blueberry Custard Pie

Serving: 8 | Prep: 25mins | Cook: 50mins |Ready in:

Ingredients

- 2 (9 inch) prepared pie crusts
- 3 eggs, slightly beaten
- 1 3/4 cups white sugar
- 4 tablespoons all-purpose flour
- 3 tablespoons cornstarch
- 2 tablespoons milk
- 1/2 teaspoon ground nutmeg
- 1/2 teaspoon ground cinnamon
- 1/4 teaspoon salt
- 3 cups fresh blueberries

Direction

- Set the oven to 410°F (210°C) to preheat. Line a pie pan with a pie crust.
- In a big bowl, whip eggs slightly. Combine in salt, cinnamon, nutmeg, milk, cornstarch, flour and sugar. Put in blueberries; mix to combine. Add blueberry mixture over the bottom shell.
- Shape the top crust into a 10-inch circle. Slice into 1/2-inch strips using a pastry wheel or sharp paring knife. With a small amount of water, moisten the rim of the pie. Lay the first 2 in an X in the center of the pie, starting with the longest strips. Alternate vertical and horizontal strips, weaving them in an under-and-over pattern. For the edges of the lattice, use the shortest strips. Fold the ends of the lattice strips under the edge of the bottom shell and flute the shell.
- Bake for about 50 minutes in the prepared oven until center is firm.

Nutrition Information

- Calories: 483 calories;
- Cholesterol: 70
- Protein: 6.1
- Total Fat: 17.2
- Sodium: 335
- Total Carbohydrate: 78.4

66. Orange Blueberry Pie

Serving: 8 | Prep: | Cook: |Ready in:

Ingredients

- 3 eggs
- 3 tablespoons orange juice
- 1 cup water
- 1/2 cup white sugar
- 1 pinch salt
- 1 cup water
- 1 (3 ounce) package orange flavored Jell-O® mix
- 1 (9 inch) pie crust, baked
- 1 1/2 teaspoons orange zest
- 1 pint fresh blueberries
- 1 cup heavy cream

Direction

- Beat egg yolks slightly. In a saucepan, combine 1/4 cup sugar, 1 cup water, and egg yolks. Cook and stir over low heat until mixture slightly thickens up. Take away from heat. Put gelatin in, and stir until incorporated. Add orange juice, orange rind, and 1/2 cup water. Refrigerate until slightly thickened.
- Beat together salt and egg whites until foamy. Beat 1/4 cup sugar in gradually, and keep on

beating until stiff peaks form. Fold thickened gelatin in. Mix well. Fold 1 1/2 cups blueberries in. Spoon filling into pie crust. Refrigerate until firm.

- Beat whipping cream until soft peaks are formed. Top each serving with reserved blueberries and whipped cream.

Nutrition Information

- Calories: 323 calories;
- Total Fat: 18.2
- Sodium: 178
- Total Carbohydrate: 37
- Cholesterol: 111
- Protein: 5

67. Peach Blueberry Pie

Serving: 8 | Prep: 15mins | Cook: 45mins |Ready in:

Ingredients

- 1 pastry for a double-crust 9-inch pie
- 3 cups sliced peaches
- 1 cup blueberries
- 2 tablespoons fresh lemon juice
- 1 cup white sugar
- 2 tablespoons quick-cooking tapioca
- 1/2 teaspoon salt
- 2 tablespoons margarine, cut into pieces

Direction

- Start preheating the oven at 425°F (220°C). Arrange 1 pie crust onto a pie plate.
- Combine lemon juice, blueberries, and peaches in a bowl. Combine salt, tapioca, and sugar in a small bowl and transfer to peach mixture; toss to blend. Let fruit rest for 15 minutes, and then place into prepared pie plate. Spread margarine pieces over the fruit and brush water on the edge of the pie. Cover pie with

the crust left; press and enclose the top and bottom of crusts.

- Bake in the prepared oven until the crust turns golden brown and fruit is bubbly, 45 to 50 minutes.

Nutrition Information

- Calories: 378 calories;
- Total Fat: 17.7
- Sodium: 412
- Total Carbohydrate: 53.1
- Cholesterol: 0
- Protein: 3

68. Red, White, And Blueberry Cheesecake Pie

Serving: 8 | Prep: 40mins | Cook: 50mins |Ready in:

Ingredients

- 8 sheets phyllo dough
- 1/4 cup butter, melted
- 2 (8 ounce) packages cream cheese
- 1/2 cup white sugar
- 1 teaspoon vanilla extract
- 2 eggs
- 2 cups fresh blueberries
- 1/2 cup strawberry jelly
- 1 cup heavy cream, whipped (optional)

Direction

- Heat the oven to 220°C or 425°F.
- Put a phyllo dough sheet on an even counter. Brush liquified butter on it, and top with one more phyllo piece to cover. Redo till all eight sheets are used. Cut piled phyllo with kitchen scissors, to a circle, 12- to 13-inch in size. Cautiously force circle to an oiled pie plate, 9-inch in size; softly fan the edges. Bake for 6 to 8 minutes in prepped oven till edges are barely

golden; partially cool on wire rack. Lower oven heat to 175°C or 350°F.

- Use electric mixer to whip sugar, vanilla and cream cheese in medium bowl till fluffy and light. Whip eggs in till thoroughly incorporated. Fold a cup blueberries in. Put the filling to prepped crust.
- Bake for 40 to 50 minutes at 175°C or 350°F till set. On the final 25 minutes of baking time, slowly cover pie using foil to avoid crust from excessive-browning. Cool fully on wire rack.
- Whip jelly in small bowl till smooth; scatter on cheese filling. Place one cup of blueberries over in a star design.

Nutrition Information

- Calories: 496 calories;
- Total Carbohydrate: 43.6
- Cholesterol: 144
- Protein: 7.8
- Total Fat: 33.3
- Sodium: 322

69. Summer Fruit Galettes

Serving: 10 | Prep: 15mins | Cook: 14mins | Ready in:

Ingredients

- 2 (9 inch) refrigerated pie crusts
- 3 fresh peaches - peeled, pitted, and sliced
- 1 pint fresh strawberries, sliced
- 1/2 pint fresh blueberries
- 4 tablespoons white sugar, divided
- 4 tablespoons all-purpose flour, divided
- 6 tablespoons turbinado sugar, divided

Direction

- Set oven to 450°F (230°C) to preheat.
- On a baking tray lined with parchment or on a baking stone, roll out 1 pie crust, leaving room for another pie crust next to it.

- In a bowl, combine 2 tablespoons of the sugar with 2 tablespoons of the flour, half the blueberries and sliced peaches. Add on top of one pie crust, leaving a 1-inch border. Fold up the uncovered border on top of the edge of the fruit and crimp into pleats. Dust the crust and fruit filling using 3 tablespoons of turbinado (or raw) sugar.
- On the baking tray, roll out the second pie crust. In the bowl, combine 2 tablespoons of sugar, 2 tablespoons of flour, the rest of the blueberries and the sliced strawberries. Add on top of the second pie crust and create the galette the same as the first. Sprinkle with 3 tablespoons of turbinado sugar.
- Bake for 12 to 14 minutes in the prepared oven until crust is lightly browned. Scatter with more sugar (optional). Serve at room temperature or warm.

Nutrition Information

- Calories: 269 calories;
- Sodium: 192
- Total Carbohydrate: 37.9
- Cholesterol: 0
- Protein: 2.9
- Total Fat: 12.1

70. Summer Fruit Tart From Almond Breeze®

Serving: 8 | Prep: 10mins | Cook: 10mins | Ready in:

Ingredients

- 1 egg
- 1 tablespoon cornstarch
- 1 tablespoon maple syrup
- 1 cup Unsweetened Vanilla Almond Breeze Almondmilk
- 1 prepared tart shell
- 1/2 cup sliced fresh strawberries
- 1/2 cup fresh raspberries

- 1/2 cup fresh blueberries
- 1/2 cup fresh blackberries

Direction

- In a pan, beat maple syrup, corn starch and egg together to make custard. Gently whip in almond milk over medium heat. Heat up to a boil, beating constantly, take off the heat and cool 5 minutes.
- Transfer custard into tart crust and garnish with fruit.
- Chill 30 minutes prior to serving.

Nutrition Information

- Calories: 96 calories;
- Protein: 1.7
- Total Fat: 3.5
- Sodium: 92
- Total Carbohydrate: 15
- Cholesterol: 23

71. Summer Is Here Triple Berry Peach Pie

Serving: 8 | Prep: 30mins | Cook: 45mins | Ready in:

Ingredients

- For the Pie:
- 1 pastry for a 9 inch double crust pie
- 1 egg white, lightly beaten
- 3 fresh peaches - peeled, pitted, and sliced
- 1 pint fresh strawberries, hulled and large berries cut in half
- 1 pint fresh blueberries
- 2 (6 ounce) containers fresh raspberries
- 1/3 cup all-purpose flour
- 3 tablespoons cornstarch
- 1/2 cup brown sugar
- 1/2 cup white sugar
- 2 teaspoons ground cinnamon
- 1/4 teaspoon ground nutmeg

- 2 tablespoons butter, cut into small pieces
- For the Topping:
- 1 teaspoon ground cinnamon
- 1 tablespoon white sugar

Direction

- Set an oven to 350°F (175°C) to preheat. Line a 9 inch pie pan using half of the dough and brush with 1/2 of the beaten egg white.
- In a big bowl, mix raspberries, blueberries, strawberries and the sliced peaches; put aside. Combine the nutmeg, 2 teaspoons cinnamon, 1/2 cup white sugar, brown sugar, cornstarch and flour together. Fold the flour mixture into the fruit gently, be sure not to crush the berries. Add the fruit mixture to the pastry-lined pie pan. The filling will be mounded high but will reduce as it cooks. Dot with butter.
- Top the pie with a full top crust or a lattice crust (score decorative slits in the shell to let steam escape). Brush the top crust or lattice using the leftover egg white. Mix 1 tablespoon sugar and 1 teaspoon cinnamon and scatter the mixture on the shell. Put the pie on a baking tray to catch drips.
- Bake the pie for 45 to 60 minutes, until the shell is golden brown and the filling is bubbly. Turn off the oven and allow pie to set for half an hour; turn onto a cooling rack. The filling will be loose if served while warm, but will hardens when the pie is cooled completely.

Nutrition Information

- Calories: 463 calories;
- Total Carbohydrate: 72.1
- Cholesterol: 8
- Protein: 4.9
- Total Fat: 18.4
- Sodium: 268

72. Sweet Blueberry Cream Cheese Pie

Serving: 8 | Prep: 15mins | Cook: 40mins | Ready in:

Ingredients

- 1 cup all-purpose flour
- 3/4 cup chopped pecans
- 1/2 cup margarine, melted
- 4 cups blueberries
- 1 cup white sugar
- 2 tablespoons cornstarch
- 1 teaspoon lemon juice
- 1 (8 ounce) package cream cheese, softened
- 1 (14 ounce) can sweetened condensed milk
- 1/3 cup lemon juice

Direction

- Preheat the oven to 150 degrees C (300 degrees F).
- Combine the margarine, pecans and flour in the bowl. Press the dough into the 9x13-in. baking plate to shape a crust.
- Bake in the preheated oven for roughly half an hour or till it turns golden-brown. Let the crust cool down totally.
- At the same time, heat 1 tsp. of the lemon juice, cornstarch, sugar and blueberries on medium heat in a saucepan for roughly 10 minutes or till the berries burst and the juice becomes thick. Let the blueberry sauce cool down totally.
- Whip the cream cheese till fluffy. Put in the sweetened condensed milk and blend well. Whisk in one-third cup of the lemon juice. Add the cream cheese filling to the cooled crust and spread the blueberry sauce on the cream cheese. Keep chilled in the fridge for no less than 2 hours prior to serving.

Nutrition Information

- Calories: 631 calories;
- Total Fat: 33
- Sodium: 278
- Total Carbohydrate: 79.1
- Cholesterol: 47
- Protein: 9.2

73. Three Berry Pie

Serving: 8 | Prep: 45mins | Cook: 45mins | Ready in:

Ingredients

- Pastry for a Double-Crust Pie:
- 2 cups all-purpose flour
- 1/2 teaspoon salt
- 2/3 cup shortening, chilled
- 6 tablespoons cold water
- Three-Berry Filling:
- 1 cup fresh strawberries, halved
- 2 cups fresh raspberries
- 1 1/2 cups fresh blueberries
- 1/2 cup white sugar
- 3 tablespoons cornstarch

Direction

- Mix the salt and flour. Mash in the shortening with a pastry blender until small pea-sized pieces form. Scatter a tablespoon of the water on part of the mixture, then toss with a fork gently. Press moistened part to the side of the bowl. Repeat with a tablespoon of water at a time, until all is moist. Spit the dough in half. Roll each half into a ball and flatten slightly. Encase in plastic and chill for no less than 30 minutes.
- Put one piece of dough onto a lightly floured surface. Stretch the dough from the center to the edges to form a 12-inch circle. Roll the crust around the rolling pin. Roll out on a 9-inch pie pan. Ease the shell into the pie pan, be sure not to stretch it. Cut off the bottom crust evenly with the rim of the pie pan, and put the pastry-lined-pie-pan back to the fridge.
- Mix the sugar with cornstarch in a big mixing bowl. Put in the blueberries, raspberries, and strawberries; toss gently until berries are

covered. Let fruit mixture sit for about 15 minutes.

- Set the oven to 375°F (190°C) to preheat. Put a baking tray in the oven to preheat.
- Unroll the leftover pastry for the top crust. Mix the berry mixture and add the filling to the pastry-lined pie pan. Put the top crust on top of the pie and cut off the edges, leaving a 1/2-inch overhang. Fold the top shell under the bottom shell, lightly pinch to seal. Crimp the edges of the shell and score vents in the top to let steam escape. To avoid over-browning, cover the edge of the pie using foil.
- Bake for 25 minutes in the prepared oven on the baking sheet. Take off the foil.
- Bake for 20 to 30 minutes more, or until the crust is golden and the filling is bubbling. Let cool on a wire rack.

Nutrition Information

- Calories: 361 calories;
- Total Fat: 17.7
- Sodium: 147
- Total Carbohydrate: 48
- Cholesterol: 0
- Protein: 3.8

74. Topless Blueberry Pie

Serving: 8 | Prep: 30mins | Cook: 30mins | Ready in:

Ingredients

- 3/4 cup white sugar
- 3 tablespoons cornstarch
- 1 pinch salt
- 1 cup water
- 4 cups fresh blueberries
- 1 tablespoon butter
- 1 (9 inch) pie crust, baked

Direction

- Mix salt, cornstarch and sugar in saucepan; mix in 1 cup blueberries and water. Mix and cook on medium heat for about 8-10 minutes till thick.
- Add butter; cool for about 5 minutes. Mix in leftover blueberries.
- Put into baked pie shell; cool for 2-4 hours in the fridge.

Nutrition Information

- Calories: 219 calories;
- Sodium: 113
- Total Carbohydrate: 39.8
- Cholesterol: 4
- Protein: 1.3
- Total Fat: 6.8

75. True Blue Custard Crunch Pie

Serving: 8 | Prep: 15mins | Cook: 40mins | Ready in:

Ingredients

- 8 ounces sour cream
- 3/4 cup sugar
- 1 egg
- 2 tablespoons flour
- 2 teaspoons vanilla extract
- 1/4 teaspoon salt
- 2 1/2 cups fresh blueberries
- 1 (9 inch) unbaked pie crust
- Topping:
- 3 tablespoons all-purpose flour
- 2 tablespoons white sugar
- 3 tablespoons chilled butter, cut into small pieces
- 4 tablespoons chopped pecans

Direction

- Set oven to 400°F (200°C) to preheat.
- In a mixing bowl, whip together salt, vanilla extract, 2 tablespoons flour, egg, 3/4 cup sugar

and sour cream until smooth. Fold the blueberries gently into the sour cream mixture. Scoop the filling into the unbaked pie crust.

- Bake for 25 minutes in the prepared oven.
- Make the streusel crunch topping while the filling is baking: Mix 3 tablespoons flour with 2 tablespoons sugar in a medium bowl. Mash the cold butter into the flour mixture until crumbly. Fold the chopped pecan in. Scatter the streusel crunch topping on top of the pie after the filling has baked 25 minutes.
- Bake about 15 minutes more until the topping is golden brown.

Nutrition Information

- Calories: 378 calories;
- Sodium: 245
- Total Carbohydrate: 44.3
- Cholesterol: 47
- Protein: 4.3
- Total Fat: 21.2

76. Yogurt Blueberry Oreo® Pie

Serving: 8 | Prep: 20mins | Cook: 5mins | Ready in:

Ingredients

- 1/2 cup white sugar
- 2 cups frozen blueberries, thawed
- 1 (.25 ounce) envelope unflavored gelatin
- 2 cups vanilla yogurt
- 1 (6 ounce) prepared chocolate cookie pie crust (such as Oreo®)

Direction

- In a bowl add sugar over blueberries to make juice, mash the berries into little pieces. Pour pieces off and keep the juice.
- In a medium saucepan put blueberry juice and gelatin together and mix on low heat. Cook for

about 2 minutes till gelatin is dissolved. Put the mixture into a bowl.

- Add yogurt into the bowl containing gelatin mixture. Put in the remaining blueberries. Transfer the mixture into crust.
- Keep the pie in the fridge for about 2 hours until it is set.

Nutrition Information

- Calories: 231 calories;
- Protein: 5
- Total Fat: 7.6
- Sodium: 186
- Total Carbohydrate: 37.3
- Cholesterol: 3

Chapter 3: Cherry Pie Recipes

***

77. A Piece Of The Tropics Pie

Serving: 8 | Prep: 15mins | Cook: 1hours | Ready in:

Ingredients

- 1 (8 ounce) can crushed pineapple, with juice
- 1 cup sugar
- 1 cup light corn syrup
- 2 1/2 tablespoons all-purpose flour
- 1/2 cup flaked coconut
- 1/2 cup chopped macadamia nuts
- 1/2 cup chopped maraschino cherries
- 3 eggs, beaten
- 1 teaspoon vanilla extract
- 1 (9 inch) unbaked deep dish pie crust
- 1/4 cup butter, melted

Direction

- Preheat an oven to 175°C/350°F.
- Mix flour, corn syrup, sugar and pineapple with juice in a bowl. Mix in vanilla, eggs, cherries, macadamia nuts and coconut, one by one. Scoop filling mixture into crust; drizzle melted butter on pie.
- In preheated oven, bake for 30 minutes, loosely covered with foil; to avoid spillage, you can sit the pie on cooking sheet or something similar. Remove foil; bake for 30 minutes. Cool; chill before serving for 2-3 hours in the fridge.

Nutrition Information

- Calories: 534 calories;
- Sodium: 254
- Total Carbohydrate: 82.4
- Cholesterol: 85
- Protein: 4.6
- Total Fat: 22.8

78. Baked Fresh Cherry Pie

Serving: 8 | Prep: 30mins | Cook: 50mins | Ready in:

Ingredients

- 1 recipe pastry for a 9 inch double crust pie
- 4 tablespoons quick-cooking tapioca
- 1/8 teaspoon salt
- 1 cup white sugar
- 4 cups pitted cherries
- 1/4 teaspoon almond extract
- 1/2 teaspoon vanilla extract
- 1 1/2 tablespoons butter

Direction

- Set the oven to 400°F (205°C) for preheating. Press the bottom crust into the pie pan, and reserve the top crust covered.

- Mix tapioca, extracts, sugar, salt, and cherries in a large mixing bowl. Let it stand for 15 minutes. Pour the mixture on top of the bottom crust and dot with butter. Use the reserved top crust to cover the mixture. Flute its edges and cut vents on its top. Place the pie on a cookie sheet lined with foil in case of any drips.
- Let it bake inside the preheated oven for 50 minutes until golden brown. Make sure to cool for couple of hours before slicing.

Nutrition Information

- Calories: 410 calories;
- Total Carbohydrate: 60.9
- Cholesterol: 6
- Protein: 3.7
- Total Fat: 17.8
- Sodium: 286

79. Cannoli Pie

Serving: 8 | Prep: 15mins | Cook: | Ready in:

Ingredients

- 1 cup confectioners' sugar
- 1 (15 ounce) container ricotta cheese
- 1/4 cup blanched slivered almonds
- 1/4 cup chopped maraschino cherries
- 1/4 cup miniature semisweet chocolate chips
- 1 (9 inch) graham cracker crust

Direction

- With a spoon, whisk together ricotta cheese and confectioners' sugar in a medium-sized bowl until thoroughly combined. Fold in chocolate chips, cherries, and almonds. Add to graham cracker crust by a spoon. Freeze until set, about 3 hours. Take out of the freezer before cutting, about 10-15 minutes. Freeze any leftovers again.

Nutrition Information

- Calories: 343 calories;
- Total Fat: 15.6
- Sodium: 239
- Total Carbohydrate: 44.4
- Cholesterol: 17
- Protein: 8.6

80. Cherry Cheese Pie I

Serving: 8 | Prep: 15mins | Cook: | Ready in:

Ingredients

- 1 (9 inch) prepared graham cracker crust
- 1 (8 ounce) package cream cheese, softened
- 1/2 cup white sugar
- 2 cups frozen whipped topping, thawed
- 1 (21 ounce) can cherry pie filling

Direction

- Beat sugar and softened cream cheese together in a medium mixing bowl until fluffy and light. Fold whipped topping in and blend until smooth. Layer into graham cracker crust and scoop pie filling over the top. Use plastic wrap to cover and refrigerate for 2 hours before serving.

Nutrition Information

- Calories: 421 calories;
- Sodium: 251
- Total Carbohydrate: 55.5
- Cholesterol: 31
- Protein: 3.7
- Total Fat: 21.1

81. Cherry Cheese Pie II

Serving: 8 | Prep: 15mins | Cook: | Ready in:

Ingredients

- 1 (8 ounce) package cream cheese
- 1 (14 ounce) can sweetened condensed milk
- 1/3 cup lemon juice
- 1 teaspoon vanilla extract
- 1 (9 inch) prepared graham cracker crust
- 1 (21 ounce) can cherry pie filling

Direction

- Whip cream cheese in a large bowl until fluffy. Whisk in milk until smooth. Mix in vanilla and lemon juice, put entire mixture into graham cracker crust.
- Cover and chill for 3 hours, or until firm. Garnish with pie filling in a desired amount before serving. Chill leftovers.

Nutrition Information

- Calories: 492 calories;
- Sodium: 329
- Total Carbohydrate: 68.7
- Cholesterol: 47
- Protein: 7.6
- Total Fat: 21.5

82. Cherry Folditup

Serving: 6 | Prep: 15mins | Cook: 35mins | Ready in:

Ingredients

- 6 ounces white whole wheat flour
- 1 teaspoon white sugar
- 1/2 teaspoon salt
- 6 tablespoons chilled unsalted butter, cut into 1/2-inch chunks
- 1/4 cup ice cold water
- 1 tablespoon ice cold orange vodka (optional)

- 1 cup cherry pie filling
- 2 teaspoons milk
- 2 tablespoons white sugar

Direction

- In a bowl, mix together salt, sugar and flour. Use a pastry blender to cut cold butter into the mixture until coarse and crumbly. In the middle of the dry mixture, make a well; put in vodka (optional) and water. Use a fork to toss until moist; form dough into a ball by hands. Flatten dough into a disc; use plastic wrap to wrap; chill in the refrigerator for no less than two hours.
- Set oven to 190°C (375°F) and start preheating. Use silicone baking mat or parchment paper to line a baking sheet.
- Roll dough into a big disk with a 1/8-in. thickness and 13-in. width. Place dough on the baking sheet.
- Spread cherry filling into the center of the dough to within 3 inches around the rim. Fold the dough's outer edge over the filling, creating occasional pleats.
- Brush the dough with milk; liberally scatter sugar over top. Bake for 35 minutes in 190°C (375°F) until the tart crust turns golden and the filling bubbles.

Nutrition Information

- Calories: 275 calories;
- Total Fat: 12.1
- Sodium: 206
- Total Carbohydrate: 38.1
- Cholesterol: 31
- Protein: 4.2

83. Cherry Lattice Pie

Serving: 10 | Prep: 30mins | Cook: 1hours | Ready in:

Ingredients

- Pie Crust:
- 2 1/2 cups all-purpose flour
- 1/2 teaspoon sea salt, divided
- 1 cup unsalted butter, well chilled and cut into cubes
- 1/2 cup ice water
- Filling:
- 1 3/4 pounds fresh cherries, stemmed and pitted (or frozen cherries, partially thawed)
- 1/2 cup Stevia In The Raw®
- 1/4 cup cornstarch
- 2 tablespoons fresh lemon juice
- 2 tablespoons 2% milk
- 1 tablespoon Stevia In The Raw® (optional)

Direction

- Pulse flour with salt in a food processor to blend. Put in butter and blend until pea-sized. Put in 6 tablespoons water and blend 15 times. (Pour in more water if dough is still dry, a tablespoon at a time, until dough holds together.)
- Split dough in half, roll into discs, cover in plastic wrap, and chill for at least an hour.
- Set oven to 425°F to preheat.
- Mix lemon juice, cornstarch, stevia and cherries in a big bowl.
- On a lightly floured surface, shape half the dough into a 12-inch circle.
- Add to a 9-inch pie pan, pushing into the corners gently. Cut off edges to let the dough hang 1/4 inch over the sides. Chill.
- Shape the rest of the dough as above and slice into 3/4-inch wide strips.
- Put 1/2 of the dough strips 1/2-inch apart on a lightly floured cookie tray, then weave the leftover strips through them in a perpendicular, alternating under, over pattern.
- Take crust out of the fridge and add filling into it.
- Slide lattice off the cookie tray directly over the pie.
- Cut off lattice strips, leaving a 1/4-inch overhang.
- Under the edge of the bottom shell, tuck ends of the strips; crimp the edge.

- Brush the pie's top using milk, then scatter Sugar in The Raw (optional) over.
- Bake for 30 mins, then turn down heat to 350°F and bake for about 25 to 30 minutes until the juices thickens and bubbles.
- Let cool on a rack.

Nutrition Information

- Calories: 348 calories;
- Protein: 4.5
- Total Fat: 19.5
- Sodium: 5
- Total Carbohydrate: 41.6
- Cholesterol: 49

84. Cherry Pie Filling

Serving: 6 | Prep: 25mins | Cook: 15mins | Ready in:

Ingredients

- 4 cups pitted tart red cherries
- 1 cup white sugar
- 1/4 cup cornstarch

Direction

- Put the cherries in a saucepan over medium heat then cover the pan; heat the cherries until they release their juice and come to a simmer, 10 to 15 minutes.
- Stir the cornstarch with sugar in a bowl until smooth; pour into the hot cherries and juice, then thoroughly mix. Bring back to low heat, bring to a simmer and cook for about 2 minutes, until the filling has thickened; take away from the heat, allow to cool, then use as a pie filling.

Nutrition Information

- Calories: 219 calories;
- Total Fat: 0.9

- Sodium: < 1
- Total Carbohydrate: 54.2
- Cholesterol: 0
- Protein: 1.2

85. Cherry Pie I

Serving: 8 | Prep: | Cook: | Ready in:

Ingredients

- 1 (9 inch) prepared vanilla wafer crust
- 1 (.25 ounce) package unflavored gelatin
- 2 tablespoons cold water
- 4 cups pitted cherries
- 1 cup white sugar
- 2 tablespoons cornstarch
- 4 teaspoons lemon juice
- 3 drops red food coloring

Direction

- Soften gelatin in cold water in a small bowl. Put aside.
- Mash the sugar with half of the cherries in a medium saucepan. Mix in food coloring, lemon juice and cornstarch. Cook over medium heat, mixing until transparent and thick. Take away from the heat. Put in gelatin and briskly mix.
- Cut the leftover cherries into the crust then pour the gelatin blend over the cherries. Chill for minimum of 4 hours prior to serving.

Nutrition Information

- Calories: 277 calories;
- Total Fat: 8.7
- Sodium: 115
- Total Carbohydrate: 50.1
- Cholesterol: 9
- Protein: 2.4

86. Cherry Pie II

Serving: 8 | Prep: 45mins | Cook: 40mins | Ready in:

Ingredients

- 1 pastry for a 9 inch double crust pie
- 2 1/2 cups pitted sour cherries
- 3/4 cup white sugar
- 3 tablespoons all-purpose flour
- 1 tablespoon butter
- 1 pinch salt

Direction

- Turn oven to 400°F (200°C) to preheat. Line pastry over a 9-inch pie plate.
- Combine salt, flour and sugar. Toss cherries with sugar mixture until well mixed; pour into pie shell with the cherry filling. Top with dots of butter.
- Make a lattice top pastry by weaving strips pf pastry. Position the pie on a baking sheet.
- Bake for approximately 40 minutes in the preheated oven until crust turns golden brown and filling is bubbly. Allow pie to cool on a wire rack.

Nutrition Information

- Calories: 348 calories;
- Total Fat: 16.6
- Sodium: 246
- Total Carbohydrate: 47.4
- Cholesterol: 4
- Protein: 3.6

87. Cherry Pie III

Serving: 8 | Prep: 30mins | Cook: 45mins | Ready in:

Ingredients

- 2 cups all-purpose flour
- 1 cup shortening, chilled
- 1/2 cup cold water
- 1 pinch salt
- 2 cups pitted sour cherries
- 1 1/4 cups white sugar
- 10 teaspoons cornstarch
- 1 tablespoon butter
- 1/4 teaspoon almond extract

Direction

- Slice shortening into the salt and flour using the whisking blades of a stand mixer until crumbs have pea-size. Use hand to stir in cold water just until the dough comes together. Split the dough in half then shape it into 2 disks. Enclose in plastic then refrigerate for 30 minutes to an hour until chilled through.
- Roll out 1 disk of dough into 11-inch circle. Line a 9-inch pie pan with pastry. Refrigerate until it is necessary. For the top crust, roll out the dough, move it to a baking sheet or plate, then refrigerate.
- Preheat the oven to 190 ° C (375 ° F). Put a baking tray in the oven for preheating.
- In a moderate-sized non-aluminum saucepan, put the cornstarch, sugar, and cherries. Let the mixture stand until the sugar draws out the cherries' juices, about 10 minutes. Boil over medium heat, continuously mixing. Reduce heat; simmer for a minute, until the juices thicken and become translucent. Take pan away from heat then mix in almond extract and butter. Let the filling cool to lukewarm. Distribute the filling in the pie shell. Cover with top crust then crimp edges to seal, and slice vents for steam.
- Bake in a preheated oven for 45 to 55 minutes at 190°C (375°F) on the baking tray, until crust is golden brown. Let cool for several hours prior to slicing.

Nutrition Information

- Calories: 506 calories;
- Protein: 3.6

- Total Fat: 27.5
- Sodium: 13
- Total Carbohydrate: 62.9
- Cholesterol: 4

88. Cherry Pie IV

Serving: 8 | Prep: 45mins | Cook: 55mins | Ready in:

Ingredients

- Crust:
- 2 cups all-purpose flour
- 1 cup shortening, chilled
- 1/2 cup cold water
- 1 pinch salt
- Filling:
- 1 1/8 cups white sugar
- 3 1/2 tablespoons cornstarch
- 2 pounds sour cherries, pitted
- 1 tablespoon butter
- 1/4 teaspoon almond extract

Direction

- Mix salt and flour in a big bowl. Slice in the cold shortening until pea-sized (you can use a stand mixer paddle for this phase, or pulse in a food processor, and move to a bowl). Mix in water until the blend shapes a ball. Split the dough in half, form it into balls. Enclose in plastic then refrigerate for a minimum of 1 hour or overnight.
- Roll out half the dough on a lightly floured work surface to fit a 9-inch pie plate. Put bottom crust in the pie plate, cover it loosely using plastic and refrigerate.
- In a saucepan, mix cornstarch and sugar together; put in cherries and stir to coat. Allow to stand for 10 minutes to draw out the cherry juices.
- Preheat the oven to 245 ° C (475 ° F). Put a baking sheet in the oven for preheating.
- Over medium heat, boil cherry filling, whisking constantly. Reduce heat and simmer

for a minute or until the juices thicken and become translucent (filling will thicken more as it cools). Take away from heat and mix in the almond extract and butter. Thoroughly stir then allow to cool to room temperature.
- Roll out the second crust then slice into lattice strips or decorative forms. Pour into the bottom pie shell when the filling is cool. Cover filling with cutouts or top crust then crimp edges.
- Lower the oven to 190 ° C (375 ° F) then put the pie on a hot baking sheet.
- Bake for 45 to 55 minutes, until the crust is golden brown and filling is bubbly in the preheated oven. Allow the pie to cool several hours prior to slicing.

Nutrition Information

- Calories: 532 calories;
- Total Fat: 27.7
- Sodium: 15
- Total Carbohydrate: 69
- Cholesterol: 4
- Protein: 4.4

89. Cherry Pie With Almond Crumb Topping

Serving: 1 | Prep: 20mins | Cook: 1hours15mins | Ready in:

Ingredients

- 1 1 (9 inch) unbaked pie crust (see footnote for recipe link)
- 1/2 cup slivered almonds
- 1/2 cup light brown sugar
- 1/3 cup rolled oats
- 1/3 cup all-purpose flour
- 3/4 teaspoon salt
- 6 tablespoons cold, unsalted butter, cut into pieces
- 2 pounds cherries, pitted

- 1/2 lemon, juiced
- 1/3 cup white sugar, or more to taste
- 1/4 cup cornstarch

Direction

- Start preheating the oven to 350°F (175°C). Use aluminum foil to line a cookie sheet.
- Roll pie crust out and put into a 9-in. pie pan.
- In a big bowl, mix together salt, flour, oats, brown sugar, and almonds. Use your fingers to work the butter into the almond mixture, crumbling any big chunks, until fully blended. Put a cover on and refrigerate for 15 minutes.
- Mix together cornstarch, white sugar, lemon juice, and cherries. Whisk for 3-4 minutes, or until the mixture thoroughly blends, and not remains any dry lumps. Pour into the prepared pie pan with cherries and any accumulated juices. Press down into the pan. Crumble over the top with the oat mixture. On the prepared cookie sheet, put the pan.
- Put in the preheated oven and bake for 75 minutes, or until the crumble topping and the crust turn brown, and the cherries are bubbly. Let fully cool.

Nutrition Information

- Calories: 3565 calories;
- Total Fat: 167.4
- Sodium: 3214
- Total Carbohydrate: 502.5
- Cholesterol: 183
- Protein: 42.7

90. Cherry Tart Pops

Serving: 18 | Prep: 30mins | Cook: 15mins | Ready in:

Ingredients

- 12 wooden pop sticks
- 1 cup pitted tart red cherries, chopped
- 3 tablespoons white sugar
- 2 tablespoons cornstarch
- 2 tablespoons water
- 1/2 teaspoon almond extract
- 1 (15 ounce) package prepared pie crusts
- 1/2 cup confectioners' sugar
- 1 tablespoon milk, or as needed
- 1/4 teaspoon vanilla extract
- 1 teaspoon multicolored candy sprinkles

Direction

- Preheat oven to 200°C or 400°F. Line parchment paper on a baking sheet. Place wooden pop sticks in water to soak.
- In a saucepan, add cherries and stir in almond extract, water, cornstarch, and white sugar. Bring to a boil over medium heat and cook for 2 minutes, or until thick, stirring constantly. Remove from heat and allow mixture to cool.
- Dust a work surface with flour and unroll each of the pie crusts to an 11-inch circle. Cut 18 rectangles out of each crust, around 1 1/2 x 2 inches.
- Arrange the 18 rectangles 1 inch apart on the baking sheet. Place a wooden pop stick onto each rectangle, leaving 1 in. of stick on the rectangle. In the center of each rectangle, place 1 teaspoon of the cherry filling. Place another rectangle of dough on top of each tart, crimping the edges together with a fork. Hold the stick in place by pressing the dough around the stick.
- Bake for 10 to 12 minutes, or until the edges are lightly browned. Let tarts cool.
- Stir vanilla extract, milk, and confectioners' sugar together until smooth and pourable, but not too thin. Spread glaze over each tart, sprinkle with candy sprinkles over the glaze. Before serving, let the glaze set for several hours.

Nutrition Information

- Calories: 142 calories;
- Total Fat: 7.3
- Sodium: 113

- Total Carbohydrate: 17.8
- Cholesterol: < 1
- Protein: 1.5

- Calories: 455 calories;
- Sodium: 325
- Total Carbohydrate: 46.3
- Cholesterol: 104
- Protein: 4
- Total Fat: 29.5

91. Chocolate Cherry Pie

Serving: 8 | Prep: 20mins | Cook: 8mins | Ready in:

Ingredients

- 1 1/3 cups vanilla wafer crumbs
- 1/4 cup butter, softened
- 1 (1 ounce) square unsweetened chocolate, chopped
- 1/2 cup butter, softened
- 3/4 cup white sugar
- 1/4 teaspoon salt
- 1 teaspoon vanilla extract
- 2 eggs
- 2 tablespoons chopped maraschino cherries
- 2 cups whipped cream, garnish
- 8 maraschino cherries, garnish

Direction

- Start preheating the oven to 375°F (190°C). Mix 1/4 cup softened butter and crumbs together in a medium-sized bowl. Press onto the sides and bottom of an 8-in. pie pan. Bake for 8 minutes in the preheated oven. Let cool.
- Microwave chocolate in a microwave-safe bowl until melted. Whisk sometimes until the chocolate is smooth. Put aside. Cream sugar and 1/2 cup butter in a big bowl until fluffy and light. Mix in vanilla, salt, and melted chocolate. Add eggs, 1 egg at a time, whisking for 5 minutes between each addition. Mix in chopped cherries. Spread into the cooled crust. Refrigerate for 4 hours.
- To serve, use maraschino cherries and whipped cream to garnish the pie.

Nutrition Information

92. Coconut Streusel Cherry Pie

Serving: 8 | Prep: 15mins | Cook: 25mins | Ready in:

Ingredients

- 1/4 cup white sugar
- 1/4 cup cornstarch
- 6 cups pitted Bing cherries
- 3 tablespoons almond-flavored liqueur (such as Disaronno®)
- 1 (9 inch) baked pie crust
- 1 1/2 cups all-purpose flour
- 3/4 cup white sugar
- 1/2 cup butter
- 3/4 cup flaked coconut

Direction

- Turn oven to 375°F (190°C) to preheat.
- Combine cornstarch and 1/4 cup sugar in a saucepan; add almond-flavored liqueur and cherries. Cook for 10 to 15 minutes over low heat, stirring, until thickened. Scoop filling into pie crust.
- In a bowl, combine 3/4 cup sugar and flour. Cut in butter until mixture resembles coarse crumbs; mix in coconut. Scatter topping over the filling to within 2 inches of center.
- Bake for 15 to 20 minutes in the preheated oven until topping is browned and coconut is toasted.

Nutrition Information

- Calories: 545 calories;
- Total Fat: 22.2

- Sodium: 220
- Total Carbohydrate: 81.2
- Cholesterol: 31
- Protein: 5.5

93. Drupey Pie

Serving: 8 | Prep: 1hours | Cook: 50mins | Ready in:

Ingredients

- 2 cups all-purpose flour
- 1 teaspoon salt
- 3/4 cup butter
- 7 tablespoons ice water
- 2 cups pitted sour cherries
- 3 nectarines, pitted and chopped
- 3 fresh apricots, pitted and sliced
- 5/8 cup turbinado sugar
- 1 pinch ground cinnamon
- 1 tablespoon cornstarch
- 2 tablespoons all-purpose flour
- 2 tablespoons butter, cut into pieces
- 1 teaspoon water
- 1 egg yolk

Direction

- Preheat an oven to 425 degrees Fahrenheit or 220 degrees C. In a colander, place apricots, nectarines, and cherries to drain any extra liquid.
- To make the dough: Combine salt and flour in a medium bowl and cut up 3/4 cup butter into the flour mixture until it looks like coarse crumbs. Pour 1 tablespoon water in at a time until the dough is stuck together, adding any additional water if needed. Divide the dough into two portions. Roll one half out into a circle that is 1/8th inches thick and place in a 9-inch pie pan. Roll the other half out and cut it into long strips about 1/2-inch-wide strips and set aside.
- To make the filling: Place the drained fruit mixture into a medium-sized bowl and stir in

flour, cornstarch, cinnamon, and sugar. Pour it into the prepped pie pan. Dot the filling with the remaining 2 Tbsp. butter. Arrange the pastry strips on top in a lattice pattern and crimp the edges. Whisk egg yolk and a teaspoon of water together in a small bowl. Use a pastry brush to coat the lattice strips, but not the edges.
- Bake in the oven until crust begins to brown, for 25 minutes. Reduce the heat to 350 degrees Fahrenheit or 175 degrees C and continue to bake for another 20 - 25 minutes.
- Remove the pie from the oven and let it cool a little before serving.

Nutrition Information

- Calories: 423 calories;
- Total Carbohydrate: 52.8
- Cholesterol: 81
- Protein: 5.1
- Total Fat: 22.3
- Sodium: 450

94. Freezer Pie Filling

Serving: 8 | Prep: | Cook: | Ready in:

Ingredients

- 4 cups cherries, pitted and halved
- 3 tablespoons tapioca
- 1 cup white sugar
- 1/4 teaspoon salt
- 2 tablespoons lemon juice

Direction

- Use freezer wrap or heavy foil to line an 8-in. pie plate and let it extend beyond the edge by 5-inch. Pour in 1-qt. filling
- Use paper or lining foil to loosely cover the filling. Freeze until firm. One firm, take out of the pie plate and tightly wrap. Put the frozen pie filling back into the freezer.

- To make pie for baking: Make a 2 crust pastry for each pie. Use the pastry to line a 9-in. pie plate. Unwrap the freezer wrap from the frozen shaped pie filling. Put in the 9-in. pan lined with the pastry. Dot with 1 tablespoon of butter and if you want, sprinkle cinnamon over. Modify the top crust and complete the pie as usual. Bake at 350°F (175°C) until the syrup boils with strong bubbles without popping, about 60 minutes.
- Note: If using other fruits like cherries, pears, or peaches, mix approximately 1/2 teaspoon ascorbic acid into the sugar before mixing with the fruit.

Nutrition Information

- Calories: 160 calories;
- Protein: 0.9
- Total Fat: 0.7
- Sodium: 73
- Total Carbohydrate: 39.9
- Cholesterol: 0

95. Fresh Cherry Pie

Serving: 8 | Prep: 20mins | Cook: 45mins | Ready in:

Ingredients

- Crust:
- 2 cups all-purpose flour
- 1 cup shortening
- 1/4 cup cold water, or as needed
- 1 pinch salt
- Cherry Filling:
- 2 pounds fresh Bing cherries, pitted
- 1 cup white sugar
- 2 tablespoons tapioca flour
- 1 teaspoon vanilla extract
- 1 teaspoon butter

Direction

- In a bowl, stir together the salt and flour. Cut in shortening using pastry blender or 2 knives until the blend looks coarse crumbs. Put in cold water, 1 tablespoon at a time, mixing using a fork, until the flour blend is moistened. Do not put in more water than you need: it should form a ball when you squeeze a handful of the moistened pastry blend.
- Split the dough in half then form into balls. Enclose in plastic wrap then refrigerate for minimum of 1 hour up to 3 days.
- Preheat oven to 190°C (375°F).
- In a saucepan, stir tapioca flour, sugar and cherries; allow to sit for 10 minutes, until the sugar pulls out the juices of the cherries. Heat the cherry blend over medium heat for 5 minutes, until the juices start to thicken and run clear. Take away from heat; stir in vanilla extract and butter. Allow to sit for 5 to 10 minutes, until filling has cooled to lukewarm.
- Roll out half the pastry to fit a 9-inch pie plate. Put bottom crust the pie plate. Spoon filling into the crust with a slotted spoon to drain excess syrup; dot using butter. Using a pastry wheel or sharp paring knife, slice the remaining dough into strips. Lay strips over the pie, pressing to seal the edges.
- Bake in the preheated oven for 40 to 50 minutes, until the crust is golden brown.

Nutrition Information

- Calories: 532 calories;
- Sodium: 24
- Total Carbohydrate: 69.4
- Cholesterol: 1
- Protein: 4.6
- Total Fat: 27.5

96. Fruit Pie

Serving: 24 | Prep: 30mins | Cook: 50mins | Ready in:

Ingredients

- 3 recipes pastry for a 9 inch double crust pie
- 1 (14.5 ounce) can pitted sour red pie cherries
- 1 (21 ounce) can cherry pie filling
- 4 cups dried currants
- 3 cups dried cranberries
- 2 (16 ounce) cans gooseberries
- 6 apples - peeled, cored, and sliced
- 2 1/4 cups white sugar
- 1 tablespoon ground cinnamon
- 1 tablespoon almond extract
- 3 tablespoons butter

Direction

- Set oven to 425°F (220°C) to preheat.
- Combine almond extract, cinnamon, sugar, apples, gooseberries, cranberries, currants, cherry pie filling and cherries in a big bowl. Let sit for 15 minutes.
- Into 3 pastry-lined 9-inch pie plates, scoop equal amounts of fruit mixture. Dot each pie with a tablespoon butter. Cover each pie with pastry. Close up edges and score steam vents in tops.
- Bake for 45 to 50 minutes in the prepared oven until golden brown.

Nutrition Information

- Calories: 505 calories;
- Total Fat: 16.6
- Sodium: 252
- Total Carbohydrate: 89.2
- Cholesterol: 4
- Protein: 4.3

97. Hawaiian Millionaire Pie

Serving: 8 | Prep: 15mins | Cook: |Ready in:

Ingredients

- 1 (9 inch) pie crust, baked
- 1 (15 ounce) can crushed pineapple, drained
- 1/4 cup lemon juice
- 1 (12 ounce) container frozen whipped topping, thawed
- 1/2 cup maraschino cherries, chopped
- 1 (14 ounce) can sweetened condensed milk
- 1 cup chopped walnuts

Direction

- Fold walnuts, condensed milk, cherries, whipped topping, lemon juice, and pineapple in a big mixing bowl. Transfer into pie shell and let it chill for a minimum of 1 hour prior to serving.

Nutrition Information

- Calories: 519 calories;
- Total Fat: 29.7
- Sodium: 176
- Total Carbohydrate: 59.6
- Cholesterol: 17
- Protein: 7.6

98. Healthy And Delicious Cherry Pie

Serving: 8 | Prep: 12mins | Cook: 12mins |Ready in:

Ingredients

- 1/4 cup margarine
- 1/4 cup brown sugar
- 1 teaspoon vanilla extract
- 3/4 cup rolled oats
- 3/4 cup all-purpose flour
- 3 tablespoons water
- 1/2 cup white sugar
- 2 cups fresh cherries, pitted

Direction

- Preheat the oven to 220 degrees C (425 degrees F).

- In the medium-sized bowl, cream the vanilla, brown sugar and margarine together. Whisk in the water, flour and oats. Then press the mixture into the 9-in. pie pan. In the medium-sized bowl, whisk the sugar and cherries together. Add to crust.
- Bake in the preheated oven till the crust turns golden-brown or for 12 minutes.

Nutrition Information

- Calories: 215 calories;
- Total Fat: 6.6
- Sodium: 68
- Total Carbohydrate: 37.2
- Cholesterol: 0
- Protein: 2.7

99. Holiday Cherry Pie

Serving: 6 | Prep: 10mins | Cook: 55mins |Ready in:

Ingredients

- 3/4 cup all-purpose flour
- 1/4 cup white sugar
- 1 teaspoon packed brown sugar
- 1/4 teaspoon ground nutmeg
- 1/4 teaspoon salt
- 6 tablespoons butter, softened
- 1 (9 inch) unbaked deep dish pie crust
- 1 (21 ounce) can cherry pie filling
- 1/4 teaspoon ground cinnamon
- 1/3 cup sliced almonds

Direction

- Set oven to 425°F (220°C) to preheat.
- In a bowl, combine salt, nutmeg, brown sugar, white sugar and flour. Use a pastry blender to cut softened butter into flour mixture until crumbly; put aside.

- Bake pie crust for 10 minutes in the preheated oven. Take pie crust out of the oven; lower oven temperature to 350°F (175°C).
- Combine cherry pie filling with cinnamon. Transfer filling to the baked pie crust. Scatter on top with crumb toppings, then drizzle with sliced almonds.
- Bake for about 45 minutes in the preheated oven until topping turns brown lightly. Let pie cool for about half an hour before cutting. Serve when still warm.

Nutrition Information

- Calories: 496 calories;
- Total Carbohydrate: 65
- Cholesterol: 31
- Protein: 4.5
- Total Fat: 24.4
- Sodium: 393

100.   Kevin's Cherry Tart

Serving: 8 | Prep: 30mins | Cook: 40mins |Ready in:

Ingredients

- 1 1/8 cups confectioners' sugar
- 7/8 cup butter
- 5 3/8 cups cake flour
- 3 eggs
- 1/2 teaspoon orange flower water
- 2 pounds sour cherries, pitted
- 3 eggs, room temperature
- 1/4 cup all-purpose flour
- 1 fluid ounce kirschwasser
- 2 cups heavy whipping cream
- 1 cup white sugar

Direction

- For dough: In a large bowl, cream 3 eggs and confectioners' sugar together. Add in the orange flower water and stir. Add margarine or butter then mix well. Slowly place in the cake flour and blend till just combined. Scrape onto a plastic piece and wrap. Let chill for at least 1 hour. Roll out the dough on a floured surface then fit into an 11-in. tart pan. Ensure that the dough has no hole.

- In the tart shell, place as many cherries as possible in 1 layer.
- For filling: Cream white sugar, cream, kirsch, 1/4 cup of flour and 3 eggs together using a mixer till smooth then pour over the cherries.
- Bake for 40 minutes at 175°C or 350°F to set the filling. Let cool. Serve at room temperature or warm.

Nutrition Information

- Calories: 1029 calories;
- Sodium: 224
- Total Carbohydrate: 135.6
- Cholesterol: 274
- Protein: 15.6
- Total Fat: 47.1

---

101. Million Dollar Pie I

Serving: 16 | Prep: 15mins | Cook: |Ready in:

Ingredients

- 1 (14 ounce) can sweetened condensed milk
- 1/2 cup lemon juice
- 1 (12 ounce) container frozen whipped topping, thawed
- 1 (20 ounce) can crushed pineapple, drained
- 1 (11 ounce) can mandarin oranges, drained
- 1 (21 ounce) can cherry pie filling
- 2 (9 inch) graham cracker crust

Direction

- Mix lemon juice and condensed milk in a medium bowl. Fold in whipped topping.

- Stir cherry pie filling, oranges and pineapple in a separate bowl. Lightly fold cherry pie filling mixture into condensed milk mixture.
- Put all the mixture into pie shells. Cover and chill overnight.

Nutrition Information

- Calories: 353 calories;
- Total Fat: 14
- Sodium: 195
- Total Carbohydrate: 54.8
- Cholesterol: 8
- Protein: 3.6

---

102. Millionaire Pie II

Serving: 16 | Prep: | Cook: | Ready in:

Ingredients

- 2 prepared 8 inch pastry shells, baked and cooled
- 3 tablespoons lemon juice
- 3/4 cup chopped pecans
- 1 (10 ounce) jar maraschino cherries, drained and chopped
- 1 (14 ounce) can sweetened condensed milk
- 1 (20 ounce) can crushed pineapple, drained
- 1 (16 ounce) package frozen whipped topping, thawed
- 2 tablespoons maraschino cherries, chopped (optional)
- 1/4 cup chopped pecans (optional)

Direction

- Mix pineapple, condensed milk, cherries, pecans and lemon juice in a big bowl. Stir well, then fold gently in the whipped topping until all the ingredients are well combined.
- Transfer the mixture into pie shells. Chill prior to serving. If desired, top with pecans and chopped cherries to garnish.

Nutrition Information

- Calories: 324 calories;
- Total Fat: 18.3
- Sodium: 120
- Total Carbohydrate: 38.5
- Cholesterol: 8
- Protein: 3.7

---

103.   Mock Cheese Cake Pie

Serving: 8 | Prep: 15mins | Cook: | Ready in:

Ingredients

- 1 cup plain yogurt
- 1 (3.5 ounce) package instant vanilla pudding mix
- 1 (16 ounce) can cherry pie filling
- 3 tablespoons white sugar
- 1 (9 inch) prepared graham cracker crust

Direction

- Mix well together instant vanilla pudding and yogurt in a big bowl, then stir in cherry pie filling. Transfer filling into the pie crust and refrigerate about 30-60 minutes.

Nutrition Information

- Calories: 277 calories;
- Total Fat: 7.1
- Sodium: 358
- Total Carbohydrate: 51
- Cholesterol: 2
- Protein: 2.9

---

104.   No Bake Dark Chocolate Cherry Tart

Serving: 8 | Prep: | Cook: | Ready in:

Ingredients

- Base:
- 3 tablespoons Ghirardelli® Unsweetened Cocoa Powder
- 1 1/2 cups graham cracker crumbs
- 1/2 cup butter, melted
- Filling:
- 1 (4 ounce) bar Ghirardelli® 100% Cocoa Unsweetened Chocolate Baking Bar
- 1 cup Ghirardelli® 60% Cacao Bittersweet Chocolate Baking Chips
- 1 cup heavy cream
- 2 tablespoons confectioners' sugar
- 1 cup morello (sour) cherries in syrup, drained thoroughly
- Topping and Decoration Options:
- 1 cup heavy whipping cream
- 2 tablespoons confectioners' sugar
- 1/2 cup cream cheese
- 16 fresh cherries with stems intact
- 1/2 cup Ghirardelli® 60% Cacao Bittersweet Chocolate Baking Chips

Direction

- To make the crust: combine graham cracker crumbs with cocoa powder and melted butter in a mixing bowl until well mixed.
- Press mixture firmly into the bottom and around the edges of a 13 3/4x 4 1/2 -inch rectangular or 9 1/2- inch circle tart tin. Chill the crust in the fridge.
- Cut unsweetened chocolate bars into small chunks and mix with chocolate chips in a bowl. Put aside.
- In a saucepan, heat 2 tablespoons confectioners' sugar and 1 cup heavy cream until just hot (no boiling). Transfer the hot cream mixture over chocolate bowl and allow to sit for a few minutes until melted, stirring gently until chocolate is dissolved.

- Take crust out of the fridge; scoop drained morello cherries all over the base.
- Pour chocolate over, smooth down. Put back into the fridge and chill for 2 hours until firm.
- Once it is chilled, slice to serve. Enjoy with a spoonful of whipped cream and garnish each slice with several fresh cherries on top.

Nutrition Information

- Calories: 714 calories;
- Total Carbohydrate: 48.5
- Cholesterol: 128
- Protein: 8
- Total Fat: 60.7
- Sodium: 245

---

105.   Old Time Mincemeat Pie

Serving: 8 | Prep: 45mins | Cook: 40mins | Ready in:

Ingredients

- 1 1/4 pounds round steak, cut into small pieces
- 1 cup apple cider
- 4 Granny Smith apples - peeled, cored and finely diced
- 1 1/3 cups white sugar
- 2 1/2 cups dried currants
- 2 1/2 cups raisins
- 1/2 pound chopped candied mixed fruit peel
- 1/2 cup butter
- 1 (16 ounce) jar sour cherry preserves
- 1 teaspoon ground ginger
- 1/2 teaspoon ground cloves
- 1/2 teaspoon ground nutmeg
- 1/2 teaspoon ground cinnamon
- 1/2 teaspoon salt
- 1 (16 ounce) can pitted sour cherries, drained with liquid reserved
- 1 recipe pastry for a 9 inch double crust pie
- 2 tablespoons heavy cream

Direction

- Combine beef and apple cider in a Dutch oven. Heat till boiling, then lower the heat to a simmer. Cover and cook until meat is tender, for about 20 minutes. Take the meat out and chop coarsely, then put it back into the pot.
- Stir cherry preserves, butter, currants, raisins, citrus peel, sugar and chopped apples into the mix. Add the salt, cloves, nutmeg, cinnamon and ginger into the mixture. Let them simmer on low heat, with no cover, until mixture is very thick, for about 90 minutes. Stir cherries into the mix and take off from heat.
- Tightly cover and refrigerate for no less than a week before using.
- Set oven to preheat at 350°F (175°C). Add the filling into the unbaked pie shell and put pastry on top. Crimp the edges together and poke a few holes in the pastry's top. Brush cream on top and sprinkle it with sugar.
- In preheated oven, bake until golden brown, for 40 minutes.

Nutrition Information

- Calories: 1106 calories;
- Sodium: 521
- Total Carbohydrate: 181.2
- Cholesterol: 80
- Protein: 20.7
- Total Fat: 37.5

---

106.   Perfect Cherry Pie

Serving: 10 | Prep: | Cook: | Ready in:

Ingredients

- 2 1/4 cups all-purpose flour
- 2 tablespoons sugar
- 1/2 teaspoon salt
- 8 tablespoons butter, cut into 1/2-inch cubes and frozen

- 4 tablespoons vegetable shortening, in small pieces, frozen
- 8 tablespoons very cold cream cheese, in small pieces
- 1/3 cup ice-cold water
- 3 (16 ounce) cans water-packed red, tart, pitted cherries, drained and juice reserved
- 1 cup sugar
- 1/4 cup potato starch
- 1/2 teaspoon almond extract
- 1 tablespoon butter, in small pieces
- 1 egg white, lightly beaten
- 1 1/2 tablespoons sugar

Direction

- In a food processor, mix salt, 2 tablespoons of sugar and flour. Put in 8 tablespoons of frozen butter. Pulse 4 times, one second long each time. Drop cream cheese and shortening into the flour mixture; pulse the other 4-5 times, one second long each, until fats are size of the fine gravel and peas.
- Dump the mixture into the medium bowl; then blend by rubbing through the clean fingertips. Using a rubber spatula to stir in the water until it forms dough clumps. Use your palm to press the dough to shape a ball, cut in 1/2. Cover each 1/2 with the plastic wrap, pressing to shape the thick disks. Place in the refrigerator at least 60 mins.
- Set the oven rack to the lowest position. Arrange the pizza stone or four 9-in. quarry tiles (from hardware store) on rack to form 18-in. square. Start preheating the oven to 400°.
- Cook a pinch of salt, potato starch, one cup of sugar and one cup of cherry juice in a large saucepan over medium-low heat. Use a rubber spatula to stir until it forms the very thick paste. In a bowl, scrape the paste into the cherries. Put in almond extract; combine by stirring.
- On a floured work surface, place the dough disk. Shape into a 14-in. circle. Then fold in 1/2 and lift into 9-in. Pyrex pie plate quickly (not a deep-dish). Then unfold. Fit the dough

into the pie plate so that it cannot be stretched in any way. Place in the refrigerator.
- Form the remaining dough disk into a 12-in. circle. Take out the pie shell from the refrigerator. Put in fruit filling. Dot with one tablespoon of butter. Fold the dough circle in 1/2; lift onto the filling quickly then unfold. Trim all around about 1/2-in. beyond the lip of the pie plate. Using the fingertips, roll overhanging dough under; then flute.
- On the pizza stone or tiles, place an 18-in. square of heavy-duty foil. Place the pie on foil. Bake for 20 mins or until the crust just begins to color. Take out from the oven, brush with the egg white. Add one and a half tablespoons of sugar. Bake for 20 more mins or until golden brown. Loosely cover the edges by bringing the foil up around the pie. Bake for 15-20 more mins, until the filling bubbles. Place on wire rack to cool.

Nutrition Information

- Calories: 436 calories;
- Cholesterol: 40
- Protein: 5.3
- Total Fat: 19.9
- Sodium: 240
- Total Carbohydrate: 61

---

107. Perfect Sour Cherry Pie

Serving: 16 | Prep: 25mins | Cook: 50mins |Ready in:

Ingredients

- 2 (15 ounce) packages double crust ready-to-use pie crust
- 2 pounds sour cherries, pitted
- 1 cup white sugar
- 2 tablespoons white sugar
- 3 1/2 tablespoons cornstarch
- 1 tablespoon butter
- 1/4 teaspoon almond extract

Direction

- Set oven to 375°F (190°C) to preheat. Pat the bottom pie crusts into 2 separate pie pans.
- Combine cornstarch, 1 cup + 2 tablespoons sugar, and cherries in a saucepan. Allow to stand for about 10 minutes or until sugar starts to draw out cherries' juices. Bring mixture to a boil, whisking frequently. Reduce heat; simmer for about 5 minutes or until juices are thickened and translucent. Turn off the heat; whisk in almond extract and butter until well incorporated. Transfer mixture to the bottom half of the pie crusts. Place the top crusts over filling, crimp to seal edges, and cut slits into top using a sharp knife.
- Bake for 45 to 55 minutes in the preheated oven until crust has a golden brown color.

Nutrition Information

- Calories: 342 calories;
- Total Fat: 17.1
- Sodium: 260
- Total Carbohydrate: 44.8
- Cholesterol: 2
- Protein: 3.6

108.   Rhubarb Cherry Pie

Serving: 8 | Prep: | Cook: | Ready in:

Ingredients

- 2 cups chopped rhubarb
- 1 (21 ounce) can cherry pie filling
- 3/4 cup white sugar
- 2 1/2 teaspoons quick-cooking tapioca
- 1 recipe Pastry for double-crust pie (9 inches)
- 1 tablespoon white sugar

Direction

- Mix tapioca, sugar, cherry pie filling, and rhubarb in a large bowl. Allow to stand about 15 minutes.
- Transfer the filling into unbaked pie shell, and cover with pie crust. Brush milk on top, and scatter with sugar.
- Bake at 400°F (200°C) about 40 to 45 minutes.

Nutrition Information

- Calories: 287 calories;
- Total Fat: 7.6
- Sodium: 132
- Total Carbohydrate: 53.5
- Cholesterol: 0
- Protein: 1.9

109.   Sour Cream Fruit Pie

Serving: 8 | Prep: 15mins | Cook: 45mins | Ready in:

Ingredients

- 2 cups sour cream
- 1 cup white sugar
- 1/4 teaspoon salt
- 3 tablespoons all-purpose flour
- 3 eggs, beaten
- 1 teaspoon vanilla extract
- 1 (21 ounce) can cherry pie filling
- 1 (9 inch) prepared graham cracker crust

Direction

- Set an oven to preheat to 175°C (350°F).
- Combine the flour, salt, sugar and sour cream in a big bowl. Put in vanilla and eggs, then mix until well blended. Pour the mixture on the graham cracker crust.
- Let it bake for 40-45 minutes in the preheated oven, until it becomes firm. Instantly scoop the pie filling on top. Let it cool a bit, then chill in the fridge for a minimum of 4 hours prior to serving.

Nutrition Information

- Calories: 474 calories;
- Total Fat: 20.5
- Sodium: 293
- Total Carbohydrate: 67.8
- Cholesterol: 95
- Protein: 5.9

110. Sweet Washington Cherry Pie

Serving: 6 | Prep: 40mins | Cook: 35mins | Ready in:

Ingredients

- 2 cups pitted fresh dark sweet cherries, such as Bing or Lambert
- 1/3 cup bottled cherry juice
- 1/4 teaspoon almond extract
- 1/3 cup brown sugar
- 1/3 cup white sugar
- 1/4 cup all-purpose flour
- 1 pastry for a double-crust 9-inch pie
- 1 tablespoon butter, cut into small chunks

Direction

- Turn oven to 425°F (220°C) to preheat.
- Combine cherries, flour, white sugar, brown sugar, almond extract and cherry juice in a bowl until sugar dissolves; allow to sit for about 15 minutes while you are preparing pastry dough.
- Line pastry crust into a 9-inch pie dish; pour in cherry filling to fill; scatter on top with small butter chunks. Place the leftover crust over. Crimp the edges to seal; use a sharp paring knife to cut several steam vents in the top crust.
- Bake for 35 to 40 minutes in the preheated oven until pie crust turns brown and filling is bubbly and thick. Let it cool before serving.

Nutrition Information

- Calories: 472 calories;
- Total Fat: 22.4
- Sodium: 331
- Total Carbohydrate: 64.5
- Cholesterol: 5
- Protein: 4.8

111. The Best Cherry Pie

Serving: 8 | Prep: 15mins | Cook: 48mins | Ready in:

Ingredients

- 1 (15 ounce) package double crust ready-to-use pie crust
- 3 cups cherries, pitted
- 3/4 cup white sugar
- 3 tablespoons cornstarch
- 1/4 teaspoon almond extract
- 2 tablespoons salted butter, cut into bits

Direction

- Start preheating the oven to 400°F (200°C). Use aluminum foil to line a cookie sheet. In a 9-in. pie pan, put bottom pie crust; use a fork to prick along the bottom.
- Put in the preheated oven and bake for 8 minutes, or until the crust turns light brown. Take the crust out of the oven and allow to cool for 5 minutes.
- In a bowl, mix together almond extract, cornstarch, sugar, and cherries. Pour into the prepared pie pan with the cherry mixture, dot with butter. Put on the top crusts to cover, seal by crimping the edges, and use a sharp knife to slice slits on the top. Put the pie on a cookie sheet lined with foil.
- Bake for 30 minutes in the preheated oven. Use an aluminum foil tent to cover the pie if it's browning too quickly. Keep baking for 10-

20 minutes, or until the filling is bubbling and the crust turns golden brown. Put on a wire rack to cool for 15 minutes.

Nutrition Information

- Calories: 395 calories;
- Total Carbohydrate: 52.7
- Cholesterol: 8
- Protein: 3.7
- Total Fat: 19.6
- Sodium: 274

Chapter 4: Cranberry Pie Recipes

***

112.   Apple Cranberry Tart

Serving: 4 | Prep: 30mins | Cook: 38mins | Ready in:

Ingredients

- 1/4 cup dried cranberries
- cooking spray
- 2 Granny Smith apples, peeled
- 1 teaspoon lemon juice
- 1/2 teaspoon vanilla extract
- 2 tablespoons white sugar
- 1 tablespoon cornstarch
- 1/2 teaspoon ground cinnamon
- 1/2 teaspoon ground nutmeg
- 1/4 teaspoon salt
- 1 (9 inch) prepared pie crust
- 1 egg white, beaten
- 1 tablespoon turbinado sugar, or to taste

Direction

- In a small bowl, put the cranberries. Pour boiling water on top to cover. Let soak for 15 minutes or until plump. Drain water.
- Start preheating oven to 350 deg F or 175 deg C. Use cooking spray to lightly grease a baking tray.
- In both sides of the apple, slice a vertical deep cut; make sure they do not cut through to core. Take a spiralizer with a straight-flat blade and attach 1 apple. Cut the apple into half-slices that are thin. Repeat process with remaining apple.
- In a bowl, mix apple slices, vanilla extract, cranberries, and lemon juice; mix to coat.
- In a bowl, combine cinnamon, salt, white sugar, nutmeg, and cornstarch. Mix into apple mixture.
- On a floured surface, roll the pie crust into a 10-in. circle. Move to the baking tray.
- Put the apple mixture in the middle of crust, leave 2-inch border. Lift the edges of crust and wrap around the apple mixture. Use egg white to brush edges. Sprinkle the turbinado sugar on top of tart.
- Bake in the oven for 38-40 minutes until crust turns golden brown and apples are soft. Put on a serving dish and cut.

Nutrition Information

- Calories: 333 calories;
- Total Fat: 15.1
- Sodium: 395
- Total Carbohydrate: 47
- Cholesterol: 0
- Protein: 3.9

113.   Bar Harbor Cranberry Pie

Serving: 8 | Prep: 10mins | Cook: 1hours | Ready in:

Ingredients

- 2 cups cranberries

- 1 1/2 cups white sugar, divided
- 1/2 cup chopped pecans
- 2 eggs, beaten
- 1 cup all-purpose flour
- 1/2 cup margarine, melted
- 1/4 cup shortening, melted

Direction

- Set oven to preheat at 325°F (165°C). Use butter to grease a 9-inch glass pie plate.
- Spread cranberries onto the buttered pie plate's bottom. Sprinkle 1/2 cup of sugar and pecans on top of the berries. Mix together the remaining sugar and eggs in a medium bowl till well incorporated. Stir flour, margarine and shortening into the mix, beat well after each increment. Add on top of the cranberries.
- In the preheated oven, bake for 1 hour until the filling sets, and the top is light brown.

Nutrition Information

- Calories: 441 calories;
- Protein: 4.1
- Total Fat: 24.4
- Sodium: 150
- Total Carbohydrate: 54
- Cholesterol: 46

---

114.   Buttery Cranberry Pie

Serving: 8 | Prep: 20mins | Cook: 40mins | Ready in:

Ingredients

- 1 recipe pastry for a 9 inch double crust pie
- 1 1/2 cups white sugar
- 1/3 cup all-purpose flour
- 1/4 teaspoon salt
- 1/2 cup water
- 1 (12 ounce) package fresh cranberries
- 1/4 cup lemon juice
- 1 dash ground cinnamon

- 2 teaspoons butter

Direction

- Preheat the oven to 220 degrees C/425 degrees F.
- Mix water, salt, flour and sugar in a saucepan; boil. Cook, constantly stirring, until smooth and thick. Add cinnamon, lemon juice and berries. Cook until berries pop and mixture is thick for 5 minutes. Take off from heat. Mix in butter.
- Roll 1 dough ball out to fit in a 9-in. pie plate. Put bottom crust into pie plate. Spoon filling in. Roll top crust out. Cut to strips for a lattice. Put lattice strips on the top. Seal edges.
- Bake for 40 minutes in preheated oven until crust becomes golden brown.

Nutrition Information

- Calories: 422 calories;
- Total Fat: 16.1
- Sodium: 315
- Total Carbohydrate: 67.9
- Cholesterol: 3
- Protein: 3.5

---

115.   Caramel Apple Cranberry Pie

Serving: 8 | Prep: 15mins | Cook: 1hours | Ready in:

Ingredients

- 1 pastry for a 9-inch double crust pie
- 2 tablespoons lemon juice
- 4 Granny Smith apples
- 1/2 cup butter
- 1 tablespoon all-purpose flour
- 2 tablespoons cornstarch
- 2 tablespoons water
- 1 tablespoon vanilla extract
- 1/2 cup white sugar

- 1/2 cup brown sugar
- 1 teaspoon ground cinnamon
- 1/2 teaspoon ground nutmeg
- 1 cup dried cranberries
- 1 tablespoon white sugar (optional)
- 1/2 teaspoon ground cinnamon (optional)

Direction

- Turn on the oven at 425°F (220°C) to preheat. Prepare a 9-inch pie plate and press 1 pie pastry in it. Save the remaining pastries.
- In a container which is large enough for the apples, put lemon juice and add cold water to fill halfway. Peel the apples; slice them into the lemon water and let them sit.
- Over medium heat, put a large saucepan and melt butter. Mix in cornstarch and flour; stir so that it forms a paste. Mix in nutmeg, 1 teaspoon of cinnamon, brown sugar, 1/2 cup of white sugar, vanilla extract and 2 tablespoons of water; let simmer. Drain the apples; stir them and the cranberries into the sugar mixture. Let cook for 5 minutes with stirs; take away from the heat and let cool slightly.
- Transfer the fruit to the pie plate; press on the top crust. Combine 1/2 teaspoon of cinnamon and 1 tablespoon of white sugar; drizzle over the pie.
- Put into the preheated oven to bake in 15 minutes. Lower the heat to 350°F or 175°C; bake for another 35-40 minutes until the top crust is golden brown in color.

Nutrition Information

- Calories: 530 calories;
- Sodium: 321
- Total Carbohydrate: 72.5
- Cholesterol: 31
- Protein: 3.3
- Total Fat: 26.5

116. Cassie's Frozen Cranberry Pie

Serving: 8 | Prep: 5mins | Cook: | Ready in:

Ingredients

- 1 (14.5 ounce) can prepared whole-berry cranberry sauce
- 1 (8 ounce) tub whipped topping, thawed
- 1 (8 ounce) package cream cheese, softened
- 1 graham cracker pie crust

Direction

- In a bowl, combine together cream cheese, whipped topping and cranberries, then spread the mixture into the bottom of prepped pie crust. Use plastic wrap to cover the pie, then freeze for a minimum of an hour.

Nutrition Information

- Calories: 367 calories;
- Cholesterol: 31
- Protein: 3.4
- Total Fat: 22.3
- Sodium: 223
- Total Carbohydrate: 40.3

117. Cranberry Apple Pie I

Serving: 8 | Prep: 30mins | Cook: 1hours | Ready in:

Ingredients

- 1 (9 inch) deep dish pie crust
- 6 apples - peeled, cored and chopped
- 1 (12 ounce) package fresh cranberries, roughly chopped
- 1 1/2 cups white sugar
- 1/3 cup quick-cooking tapioca
- 1 1/2 cups all-purpose flour
- 3/4 cup packed brown sugar
- 1 teaspoon ground cinnamon

- 1/2 teaspoon salt
- 2/3 cup unsalted butter
- 1 egg, lightly beaten

Direction

- Set oven to 325 degrees F or 165 degrees C. Turn the pie shell over another same sized pie pan to keep the crust from shrinking into the pan. Bake the pie shell in this position until partially baked, about 10 minutes. Turn the shell right side up and remove the extra pan from the inside of the crust.
- In a big bowl, combine sugar, cranberries, and apples, then cover and put aside for 20 minutes. Mix in the tapioca and put aside until the tapioca absorbs fruit juice, about 15-20 minutes. Spread the mixture onto the partly baked pie shell.
- In a medium-sized bowl, combine butter, salt, cinnamon, brown sugar, and flour. Use your fingertips to work the mixture until it becomes crumbly. Spread the mixture over the filling. Brush the exposed shell with a lightly beaten egg.
- Place onto a cookie sheet to get any of the drips. Bake on the bottom rack of the oven for 45-60 minutes, or until the apples become tender when tested using a wooden pick.

Nutrition Information

- Calories: 664 calories;
- Total Carbohydrate: 111.4
- Cholesterol: 64
- Protein: 4.9
- Total Fat: 23.9
- Sodium: 312

118. Cranberry Apple Pie II

Serving: 8 | Prep: 30mins | Cook: 1hours | Ready in:

Ingredients

- 6 apples
- 1 (16 ounce) can whole cranberry sauce
- 1/2 cup packed brown sugar
- 1/3 cup all-purpose flour
- 1 1/2 teaspoons ground cinnamon
- 1/2 teaspoon ground nutmeg
- 1 recipe pastry for a 9 inch double crust pie

Direction

- Set the oven at 1750C (350°F) and start preheating. Use pastry to line a pie dish.
- Peel the apples, removes the cores and cut them into slices.
- In a medium-sized mixing bowl, add cranberry sauce and apples and mix them together. Mix nutmeg, cinnamon, flour and brown sugar and put into the apple mixture; combine properly. Fill the pastry-lined pan with the filling. Put the top crust on top to cover. Fold edges. Slice slits into the top crust.
- Put the dish in the preheated oven and bake until the filling bubbles and the crust turns golden brown, or for 60 minutes.

Nutrition Information

- Calories: 435 calories;
- Total Carbohydrate: 73.5
- Cholesterol: 0
- Protein: 3.6
- Total Fat: 15.2
- Sodium: 251

119. Cranberry Apple Pie III

Serving: 8 | Prep: 30mins | Cook: 1hours | Ready in:

Ingredients

- 1 1/4 cups white sugar
- 1/4 cup all-purpose flour
- 1/4 teaspoon salt
- 2 cups cranberries

- 1/4 cup maple syrup
- 5 apples - peeled, cored and sliced
- 1/2 cup chopped walnuts
- 1 (9 inch) unbaked pie shell
- 1 cup dry bread crumbs
- 3/4 cup all-purpose flour
- 1/4 cup packed brown sugar
- 1/4 cup butter, melted

Direction

- To preheat: Set oven to 190°C (375°F).
- Put salt, 1/4 cup flour and white sugar in a large saucepan then whisk together. Stir in maple syrup and cranberries. Cook over medium-high heat, stir continuously. When mixture comes to a boil, lower heat, put a lid on and simmer for 5 minutes, remember to stir once in a while.
- Add apples to simmering mixture and stir, then keep cooking for 5 minutes or till apples become soft. Get the saucepan away from heat, stir in walnuts. Set aside and let saucepan cool to room temperature.
- Put melted butter, brown sugar, 3/4 cup flour and breadcrumbs in a medium bowl. Mix well. Spread cooled apple mixture into pie shell and use crumb topping to sprinkle over apple filling.
- Put into the preheated oven and bake for about half an hour till topping becomes golden brown and filling is bubbly. Serve warm.

Nutrition Information

- Calories: 553 calories;
- Total Fat: 19.1
- Sodium: 334
- Total Carbohydrate: 92.8
- Cholesterol: 15
- Protein: 6.3

120.   Cranberry Cherry Pie

Serving: 8 | Prep: | Cook: | Ready in:

Ingredients

- 1 (21 ounce) can cherry pie filling
- 1 (16 ounce) can whole cranberry sauce
- 1/2 cup golden raisins
- 2 tablespoons cornstarch
- 1/4 teaspoon ground ginger
- 1 recipe pastry for a 9 inch double crust pie
- 6 tablespoons orange juice
- 1 tablespoon milk
- 1 tablespoon white sugar

Direction

- In a large bowl, mix ginger, cornstarch, raisins, cranberry sauce and cherry pie filling together.
- Make piecrust dough, instead of orange juice, use water. Separate the dough 55%/45%. Roll the larger piece to 1.5 inches larger than a 9-in. pie pan. Add the crust in pie plate, leaving 1-in. overhang; then brush the crust with egg white. Scoop cherry filling into the pie crust.
- Roll the smaller crust to a 12-in. round. Slice into 14 strips to form a lattice top. Moisten the edge of bottom crust with water. Arrange 7 strips across the pie but not to seal the ends. Fold all the other strips back halfway from the middle. Add the middle cross strip on pie and replace folded part of strips. Then fold alternate strips back. Add the second cross strip in place. Keep weaving cross strips into lattice. Seal the ends. Turn bottom crust edge up over the strips' ends. Pinch to seal. Create high fluted edge. Brush milk onto the pastry; then slightly sprinkle with sugar.
- Bake at 400°F (205°C) until the crust turns golden brown and the fruit starts to bubble, or about 50 minutes. Cool slightly on wire rack.

Nutrition Information

- Calories: 469 calories;
- Total Carbohydrate: 76.6

- Cholesterol: < 1
- Protein: 3.8
- Total Fat: 16.9
- Sodium: 290

121. Cranberry Clafouti

Serving: 8 | Prep: 15mins | Cook: 45mins |Ready in:

Ingredients

- 1 tablespoon butter, or as needed
- 1 (12 ounce) package fresh cranberries
- 1 cup whole milk
- 1 cup heavy whipping cream
- 4 large eggs
- 2 large egg yolks
- 3/4 cup white sugar
- 1/4 cup brandy-based orange liqueur (such as Grand Marnier®)
- 2 teaspoons vanilla extract
- 1 pinch salt
- 3 tablespoons all-purpose flour
- 2 tablespoons confectioners' sugar, or as needed

Direction

- Set the oven for preheating to 375°F (190°C). Grease a 9x13-inch casserole dish using a butter.
- Scatter the cranberries in the bottom of the casserole dish.
- Stir together the cream, milk, eggs yolks, and egg, whisking it nicely in a bowl; put the white sugar, vanilla, salt and orange liqueur. Add the flour little by little while whisking the mixture continuously. Pour the egg mixture over a sieve on top of cranberries in casserole dish.
- Let it bake inside the oven for about 45 minutes until both cranberries and clafouti is set. Dust it off using the confectioners' sugar.

Nutrition Information

- Calories: 320 calories;
- Protein: 5.9
- Total Fat: 17.1
- Sodium: 72
- Total Carbohydrate: 33.7
- Cholesterol: 192

122. Cranberry Cream Pie II

Serving: 8 | Prep: 30mins | Cook: 1hours |Ready in:

Ingredients

- 1 1/4 cups graham cracker crumbs
- 2 tablespoons white sugar
- 1/3 cup chopped pecans
- 6 tablespoons butter, melted
- 1 (8 ounce) package cream cheese, softened
- 1/3 cup confectioners' sugar
- 1 teaspoon vanilla extract
- 2 tablespoons orange liqueur (optional)
- 1 cup heavy whipping cream
- 2 1/2 cups cranberries
- 1 cup white sugar
- 1 tablespoon water
- 3 tablespoons cornstarch
- 2 tablespoons water

Direction

- Preheat an oven to 175°C/350°F.
- Crust: Mix chopped pecans, 2 tbsp. white sugar and graham cracker crumbs in a medium bowl, blending well; mix in melted margarine/butter. Mix till ingredients are combined thoroughly. Press it into pan; in preheated oven, bake till lightly browned for 8-10 minutes. Cool to room temperature.
- Cream cheese filling: Whip cream cheese till fluffy in medium mixing bowl; mix in confectioners' sugar, then scrape bowl's sides. Add vanilla extract. If desired, add orange liqueur; stir well.

- Beat whipping cream till soft peaks form in another bowl; fold into the cream cheese mixture. Put filling into cooled crust. Use aluminum foil/plastic wrap to cover; chill for at least 3 hours.
- Cranberry topping: Mix together 1 tbsp. water, 1 cup white sugar and cranberries in a medium saucepan; cook on medium heat, constantly mixing, till cranberries start to pop and mixture reaches a full boil Take off heat. Mix 2 tbsp. water and cornstarch till smooth in a small bowl; mix into cranberry mixture. Put pan on heat; cook, constantly mixing, till it thickens and boils. Take off heat; cool to room temperature.
- Spread over cream cheese filling with cranberry topping; thoroughly chill pie before serving.

Nutrition Information

- Calories: 533 calories;
- Total Carbohydrate: 53.9
- Cholesterol: 94
- Protein: 4.3
- Total Fat: 34.1
- Sodium: 236

---

123.   Cranberry Crumb Pie

Serving: 8 | Prep: 20mins | Cook: 55mins | Ready in:

Ingredients

- 1 (9 inch) unbaked pie crust
- 1 (8 ounce) package cream cheese, softened
- 1 (14 ounce) can sweetened condensed milk
- 1/4 cup lemon juice
- 3 tablespoons light brown sugar
- 2 tablespoons cornstarch
- 1 (16 ounce) can whole berry cranberry sauce
- 1/4 cup butter, chilled and diced
- 1/3 cup all-purpose flour
- 3/4 cup chopped walnuts

Direction

- Set oven to 425°F (220°C) to preheat.
- Bake pie shell (unbaked) for 8 mins in the prepared oven. Take it off from heat. Turn down oven temperature to 375°F (190°C).
- Whip cream cheese in a big bowl until fluffy. Stir in sweetened condensed milk until smooth. Mix in lemon juice. Add to the pie shell.
- Stir a tablespoon light brown sugar with cornstarch in a small bowl. Stir in whole berry cranberry sauce. Scoop the mixture evenly on top of the cream cheese mixture.
- Combine leftover light brown sugar, all-purpose flour and butter in a medium bowl until crumbly. Mix in the walnuts. Scatter evenly on top of the cranberry mixture.
- Bake in the 375°F (190°C) oven for 45 minutes, or until lightly browned and bubbly. Let cool on a metal rack. Chill in the fridge or serve at room temperature.

Nutrition Information

- Calories: 619 calories;
- Total Carbohydrate: 71.4
- Cholesterol: 63
- Protein: 9.7
- Total Fat: 34.5
- Sodium: 317

---

124.   Cranberry Nut Pie

Serving: 6 | Prep: 15mins | Cook: 45mins | Ready in:

Ingredients

- 1 1/4 cups fresh or frozen cranberries
- 1/4 cup brown sugar
- 1/4 cup chopped walnuts
- 1 egg
- 1/2 cup white sugar
- 1/2 cup all-purpose flour

- 1/3 cup melted butter

Direction

- Preheat oven to 325 °F (165 °C.)
- In a pie plate of 9-inches in size, coat with butter; and on the bottom, layer cranberries. Have brown sugar and chopped walnuts to scattering over.
- In a large bowl, beat egg until thick. Add sugar gradually, beating until blended thoroughly. Mix in melted butter and flour. Blend well and pour over cranberries.
- In the preheated oven, bake for nearly 45 minutes or until it has the color of golden brown. Serve while it is still warm.

Nutrition Information

- Calories: 280 calories;
- Total Fat: 14.4
- Sodium: 88
- Total Carbohydrate: 36.8
- Cholesterol: 58
- Protein: 3.1

125.   Cranberry Nut Tarts

Serving: 24 | Prep: 20mins | Cook: 25mins | Ready in:

Ingredients

- 1/2 cup butter, softened
- 1 (3 ounce) package cream cheese, softened
- 1 cup all-purpose flour
- 1 egg
- 3/4 cup packed brown sugar
- 1 tablespoon butter, melted
- 1 teaspoon vanilla extract
- 3 tablespoons chopped walnuts
- 3 tablespoons chopped fresh cranberries

Direction

- Stirring cream cheese and butter together in a medium bowl. Mixing in the flour till blended well. Refrigerate, covered, for an hour.
- During the time the dough is chilling, preparing the filling. In a medium bowl, whisking vanilla, melted butter, brown sugar and egg together. Stirring in the walnuts and cranberries.
- Heat the oven to 160°C (325°F) beforehand. Rolling the dough into 1-inch balls. In the cups of mini muffin pans, pressing dough balls so that the dough covers sides and bottom. Fill a generous teaspoon of the filling into each one.
- In the preheated oven, allow to bake till edges of tarts turn browned lightly for 25-30 minutes.

Nutrition Information

- Calories: 106 calories;
- Total Fat: 6.4
- Sodium: 46
- Total Carbohydrate: 11.1
- Cholesterol: 23
- Protein: 1.3

126.   Cranberry Pecan Pie

Serving: 8 | Prep: 30mins | Cook: 1hours | Ready in:

Ingredients

- 1 (9 inch) deep dish pie crust
- 1 cup cranberries
- 3 eggs
- 2/3 cup white sugar
- 1 cup dark corn syrup
- 6 tablespoons unsalted butter, melted
- 1 teaspoon vanilla extract
- 1/4 teaspoon ground mace
- 1/8 teaspoon salt
- 1 cup pecan halves

Direction

- Preheat the oven to 175°C or 350°Fahrenheit.
- Chop the cranberries finely by hand or in a food processor; lay it out in a bottom of pie pan lined with pastry.
- Beat eggs in a big bowl until foamy; mix in salt, sugar, mace, corn syrup, vanilla, and margarine or melted butter. Transfer the mixture on top of the cranberry layer. Place the pecan halves neatly over the sugar mixture.
- Bake for 45-50mins in the preheated oven until the center sets and the pie is golden.

Nutrition Information

- Calories: 503 calories;
- Total Fat: 27.7
- Sodium: 275
- Total Carbohydrate: 63.6
- Cholesterol: 93
- Protein: 4.7

127. Cranberry Pie I

Serving: 8 | Prep: 30mins | Cook: |Ready in:

Ingredients

- 1 recipe pastry for a 9 inch double crust pie
- 3 cups cranberries
- 1 cup raisins
- 2 tablespoons all-purpose flour
- 1 1/4 cups white sugar
- 1/2 cup water
- 1 teaspoon vanilla extract

Direction

- Set oven to 450°F (230°C) to preheat. Line a 9 inch pie plate with pastry, and save leftover pastry for the top. Chill both while you prepare the filling.
- Coarsely chop the cranberries. Mix with vanilla, water, sugar, flour and raisins. Put

filling in cold pie crust. Cover with top crust, score top in a few places, and securely crimp edges together.
- Bake for 10 minutes in prepared oven. Turn down oven temperature to 350°F (175°C), and keep baking for half an hour. Let cool before serving.

Nutrition Information

- Calories: 438 calories;
- Protein: 3.8
- Total Fat: 15.1
- Sodium: 237
- Total Carbohydrate: 74.7
- Cholesterol: 0

128. Cranberry Pie II

Serving: 8 | Prep: 30mins | Cook: 1hours |Ready in:

Ingredients

- 1 1/3 cups white sugar
- 1/2 cup all-purpose flour
- 1 tablespoon grated orange zest
- 1 pinch ground cinnamon
- 1 pinch ground nutmeg
- 3 eggs
- 1/4 cup melted butter
- 1 1/4 cups cranberries
- 1 (9 inch) unbaked pie crust

Direction

- Set oven to 325°F (165°C) to preheat.
- Mix nutmeg, cinnamon, orange zest, flour and sugar in a big bowl. Whip in eggs. Mix in melted butter. Fold in cranberries, then add to shell.
- Bake for 35 to 40 minutes in the heated oven, or until filling is firm.

Nutrition Information

- Calories: 357 calories;
- Sodium: 185
- Total Carbohydrate: 51.8
- Cholesterol: 85
- Protein: 4.7
- Total Fat: 15.2

129.   Cranberry Streusel Pie

Serving: 8 | Prep: 30mins | Cook: 45mins |Ready in:

Ingredients

- 1 pound fresh cranberries
- 3/4 cup white sugar
- 1/4 cup all-purpose flour
- 1/2 cup packed brown sugar
- 1/2 cup walnuts
- 1/4 cup all-purpose flour
- 1 teaspoon shortening
- 1 recipe pastry for a 9 inch single crust pie

Direction

- Preheat an oven to 175°C/350°F.
- Smash berries; mix in 1/4 cup flour and sugar. Put filling into the pie crust.
- Smash walnuts to small pieces; use a pastry blender to mix in shortening, 1/4 cup flour and brown sugar. The mixture should be crumbly; sprinkle over pie with streusel.
- Put pie onto baking sheet; in preheated oven, bake for about 45 minutes till filling is bubbly and crust is golden.

Nutrition Information

- Calories: 339 calories;
- Protein: 3.4
- Total Fat: 12.3
- Sodium: 122
- Total Carbohydrate: 56.2
- Cholesterol: 0

130.   Cranberry Walnut Pie

Serving: 8 | Prep: 15mins | Cook: 50mins |Ready in:

Ingredients

- 2/3 cup light corn syrup
- 2/3 cup packed dark brown sugar
- 3 eggs
- 1/4 cup butter, melted
- 1 teaspoon vanilla extract
- 1/2 teaspoon salt
- 1 1/2 cups fresh cranberries
- 1 cup chopped walnuts
- 1 (9 inch) prepared pie crust

Direction

- Set oven to preheat at 350°F (175°C).
- Mix together the salt, brown sugar, eggs, butter, vanilla extract, and corn syrup in a large bowl; beat well. Fold cranberries and walnuts into the mix.
- Use the prepared crust to line a 9-inch pie plate. Pour the cranberry and walnut mixture into the prepared pie plate; smooth the top. Use thin aluminum foil strips to cover the rim of the crust to keep it from burning.
- In the preheated oven, bake until center is set, for about 50 to 60 minutes. Let it cool down before serving, for no less than 30 minutes.

Nutrition Information

- Calories: 444 calories;
- Total Fat: 24.6
- Sodium: 352
- Total Carbohydrate: 53.6
- Cholesterol: 85
- Protein: 6.1

131. Crustless Cranberry Pie

Serving: 8 | Prep: 15mins | Cook: 40mins | Ready in:

Ingredients

- 1 cup all-purpose flour
- 1 cup white sugar
- 1/4 teaspoon salt
- 2 cups cranberries
- 1/2 cup chopped walnuts
- 1/2 cup butter, melted
- 2 eggs
- 1 teaspoon almond extract

Direction

- Preheat the oven to 175 degrees C (350 degrees F). Coat one 9-inch pie pan with grease.
- Mix together the salt, flour, and sugar. Mix in the walnuts and the cranberries then stir to coat. Mix in the almond extract, butter, and beaten eggs. Mixture will be very thick if you're using frozen cranberries. Pour the batter in the prepared pan.
- Bake for about 40 minutes at 175 degrees C (350 degrees F) or until a wooden pick comes out clean when inserted near the middle. You can serve while still warm with whipped cream or ice cream.

Nutrition Information

- Calories: 335 calories;
- Sodium: 173
- Total Carbohydrate: 41.4
- Cholesterol: 77
- Protein: 4.5
- Total Fat: 17.7

132. Easy Apple Berry Crumble Pie

Serving: 8 | Prep: 20mins | Cook: 28mins | Ready in:

Ingredients

- 1 1/2 cups Quaker® Oats (Quick or Old Fashioned, uncooked)
- 1 cup all-purpose flour
- 1/2 cup firmly packed brown sugar
- 1/2 teaspoon baking soda
- 10 tablespoons butter or margarine, melted
- 1 (21 ounce) can apple pie filling
- 3/4 cup dried cranberries
- 1 1/2 teaspoons lemon juice
- 1/2 teaspoon ground cinnamon

Direction

- Heat oven to 375°F. Spray nonstick cooking spray lightly over 8- or 9-in. glass pie plate.
- Combine baking soda, brown sugar, flour and oats in medium bowl. Put in the melted butter, then mix well.
- Put aside 3/4 cup of the oat mixture for the topping.
- Firmly press the remaining oat mixture onto sides and bottom of the pie plate.
- Bake until light golden brown, about 10-12 mins. Place on wire rack to cool slightly.
- Stir cinnamon, lemon juice, cranberries and pie filling together using the same bowl.
- Add the filling over the hot crust, evenly spread. Evenly sprinkle the filling with the reserved oat topping.
- Bake until topping turns golden brown, about 18-22 mins.
- Enjoy at room temperature or warm.

Nutrition Information

- Calories: 402 calories;
- Sodium: 218
- Total Carbohydrate: 64.6
- Cholesterol: 38
- Protein: 3.9
- Total Fat: 15.7

133. Fall Flavors Cranberry Walnut Pie

Serving: 8 | Prep: 10mins | Cook: 25mins | Ready in:

Ingredients

- 1/2 cup dark corn syrup
- 2 eggs, lightly beaten
- 1 teaspoon vanilla extract
- 1/4 teaspoon salt
- 3/4 cup sweetened dried cranberries (such as Craisins®)
- 1 (9 inch) deep-dish pie shell
- 1/2 cup coarsely chopped walnuts

Direction

- Preheat an oven to 175°C/350°F.
- Beat salt, vanilla extract, eggs and corn syrup well in big bowl; mix cranberries in just till combined. Put in prepped pie shell; on top, scatter walnuts.
- In preheated oven, bake for 25-30 minutes till pie shell is golden brown and center is set.

Nutrition Information

- Calories: 278 calories;
- Cholesterol: 41
- Protein: 3.5
- Total Fat: 13.3
- Sodium: 267
- Total Carbohydrate: 37.7

134. Jen's Cranberry Apple Pie

Serving: 8 | Prep: 20mins | Cook: 50mins | Ready in:

Ingredients

- 2 pounds tart pink baking apples (such as Pink Lady®) - peeled, cored, and sliced
- 1 pound Granny Smith apples - peeled, cored, and sliced
- 1 1/2 cups fresh cranberries
- 1 cup firmly packed brown sugar
- 1/4 cup all-purpose flour
- 2 Meyer lemons, zested
- 1 1/4 teaspoons ground cinnamon
- 1/4 teaspoon freshly grated nutmeg
- 1 teaspoon vanilla extract
- 1 pie dough for a double-crust pie
- 2 tablespoons butter, cut into small pieces

Direction

- Set oven to 375 degrees Fahrenheit (190 degrees C) to preheat.
- In a bowl, combine vanilla, nutmeg, cinnamon, lemon zest, flour, brown sugar, cranberries, Granny Smith apples, and pink apples, then stir until the apples are coated completely.
- Roll out the dough and line 1/2 of it onto a pie dish, and then pour apple mixture over. Dot the mixture with pieces of butter. Roll the remaining 1/2 of the dough and place on top of the apple mixture, pinching the edges of the bottom and top crusts together, then tuck the dough in and crimp, forming a border. Cut vents on the top dough and place on a baking sheet.
- Bake pie in the prepped oven for 50 minutes until filling bubbles, the apples are soft, and the crust becomes golden brown. Transfer the pie onto a wire rack to cool.

Nutrition Information

- Calories: 355 calories;
- Total Fat: 10.6
- Sodium: 147
- Total Carbohydrate: 66
- Cholesterol: 8
- Protein: 2.4

135. Mincemeat II

Serving: 48 | Prep: | Cook: | Ready in:

Ingredients

- 3 pounds pork butt roast
- 2 (12 ounce) packages fresh cranberries
- 3 cups water
- 1 quart chopped apples
- 1 large orange
- 1 lemon
- 2 pounds raisins
- 3 (16 ounce) cans pitted sour red pie cherries
- 3 (16 ounce) cans gooseberries
- 2 cups brandy
- 2 cups distilled white vinegar
- 4 cups white sugar
- 1 tablespoon ground cloves
- 1 tablespoon ground nutmeg
- 2 tablespoons ground cinnamon
- 2 tablespoons ground allspice

Direction

- Preheat an oven to 175°C/350°F. Put meat in a roasting pan; cook for about 1 1/2 hours till tender. When done, remove meat; don't turn oven off.
- Simmer water and cranberries in a medium saucepan on low heat till cranberries start to split open as meat is cooking.
- When meat is finished, grind together with chopped apples; put aside.
- Grind up lemon and orange, peel and all; transfer into a big ovenproof pan. Add allspice, cinnamon, nutmeg, cloves, vinegar, sugar, brandy, gooseberries, cherries, raisins and cranberries; thoroughly mix together. Mix in meat mixture.
- Use aluminum foil to cover pan; put into oven. Heat mincemeat, occasionally mixing, for 30 minutes.
- Sterilize enough lids and canning jars to fit all the mincemeat.
- Put a wire rack inn bottom of a big stock pot; fill with water halfway. Put water onto a rolling boil.
- Into sterilized jars, pack mincemeat; be sure there aren't any air bubbles or spaces. Fill jars all the way to top; screw lids on. Lower the jars in boiling water carefully with a holder; be sure there's 2-in. minimum space between jars. If needed, add boiling water on jars to cover by 2-in. water. Cover the pot; process for 30 minutes.
- Lift jars from water carefully with a holder; put on a cloth-covered or wooden surface, 2-in. apart minimum. Cool; press on jar lid to check seal. If it doesn't move down or up at all, it's properly sealed. Before using, you should age mincemeat for 2 or 3 months.

Nutrition Information

- Calories: 231 calories;
- Sodium: 14
- Total Carbohydrate: 43.8
- Cholesterol: 11
- Protein: 4
- Total Fat: 2.7

136.	Mincemeat III

Serving: 64 | Prep: | Cook: | Ready in:

Ingredients

- 2 pounds cranberries
- 1 quart water
- 9 apples - peeled, cored and ground
- 2 pounds raisins
- 3 (16 ounce) cans gooseberries
- 3 (16 ounce) cans pitted sour red pie cherries
- 2 cups brandy
- 2 tablespoons lemon zest
- 2 tablespoons orange zest
- 2 cups distilled white vinegar
- 4 cups white sugar
- 1 tablespoon ground cloves
- 1 tablespoon ground nutmeg
- 2 tablespoons ground cinnamon
- 2 tablespoons ground allspice

Direction

- Preheat an oven to 175°C/350°F.
- Put water on cranberries in a big saucepan; simmer over low heat till cranberries start to split. Take off the heat; transfer into a big ovenproof baking dish.
- Add allspice, cinnamon, nutmeg, cloves, sugar, vinegar, orange rind, lemon rind, brandy, cherries, apples, raisins and gooseberries to the cranberries; thoroughly mix. Cover dish.
- In preheated oven, put dish; heat, occasionally mixing, for 30 minutes.
- To fit all mincemeat, sterilize enough lids and canning jars.
- Put a wire rack in the bottom of a big stock pot; fill with water halfway. Put water to a rolling boil.
- Pack mincemeat in sterilized jars; be sure there is no air bubbles or spaces. Fill jars all the way to the top; screw lids on. Lower jars into boiling water carefully with a holder; be sure there's 2-in. space minimum between jars. If needed, add more boiling water so they're covered by 2-in. water. Cover pot; process for 30 minutes.
- Lift jars from water carefully with a holder; put on a cloth-covered or wooden surface, 2-in. apart minimum. Cool; press on jar lid to check seal. Lid won't move down or up at all if properly sealed; before using, you should age mincemeat for 2-3 months.

Nutrition Information

- Calories: 155 calories;
- Cholesterol: 0
- Protein: 0.9
- Total Fat: 0.3
- Sodium: 5
- Total Carbohydrate: 34.5

---

137.   Mock Cherry Pie

Serving: 7 | Prep: | Cook: | Ready in:

Ingredients

- 1 1/2 cups cranberries
- 1 1/2 cups raisins
- 1 1/2 cups white sugar
- 1 cup water
- 1 tablespoon all-purpose flour
- 1 tablespoon butter
- 1 1/2 teaspoons vanilla extract
- 1 recipe pastry for a 9 inch double crust pie

Direction

- Prepare the oven by preheating to 450°F (230°C).
- Mix flour, water, sugar, raisins, and cranberries in a saucepan set on medium heat. Then the cooked mixture becomes thick and cranberries open. Let it cool and mix in vanilla and butter.
- Transfer in prepared pie crust and use top crust to cover.
- Trim slits at the top of the crust then place in the preheated oven and bake for 10 minutes. Minimize heat to 350°F (175°C) then bake for 35 more minutes or until the crust turns golden brown.

Nutrition Information

- Calories: 551 calories;
- Sodium: 283
- Total Carbohydrate: 94.7
- Cholesterol: 4
- Protein: 4.3
- Total Fat: 18.9

138.   Mom's Cranberry Apple Pie

Serving: 8 | Prep: 20mins | Cook: 45mins | Ready in:

Ingredients

- 2 prepared pie crusts
- 4 cups peeled and sliced apples
- 2 cups cranberries
- 3/4 cup white sugar
- 1 tablespoon cornstarch
- 1 teaspoon ground cinnamon
- 2 tablespoons butter, cut into small pieces

Direction

- Preheat an oven to 200°C/400°F>
- Fit pie crust in 9-in. pie dish; put sliced apples in crust. Spread cranberries on apples. Whisk cinnamon, cornstarch and sugar in small bowl; sprinkle mixture on cranberries. Distribute butter pieces on pie filling. Put leftover crust on filing then crimp both crusts together. Cut few slits in top crust to vent the steam.
- Bake for 45-60 minutes till fruit filling is bubbling and pie is browned.

Nutrition Information

- Calories: 373 calories;
- Cholesterol: 8
- Protein: 3.1
- Total Fat: 18
- Sodium: 255
- Total Carbohydrate: 51.9

139.   No Bake Cranberry Sauce Pie

Serving: 8 | Prep: 15mins | Cook: 10mins | Ready in:

Ingredients

- 1 (8 ounce) package cream cheese, softened
- 1 tablespoon margarine
- 1 teaspoon vanilla extract
- 1 cup confectioners' sugar
- 1 (9 inch) prepared graham cracker crust
- 1 (3 ounce) package raspberry flavored Jell-O® mix
- 1 cup boiling water
- 1 (14.5 ounce) can whole berry cranberry sauce
- 1/3 cup chopped walnuts (optional)

Direction

- In a mixing bowl, whip the vanilla extract, margarine and cream cheese together until fluffy and smooth. Sift in the confectioner's sugar and stir until well combined. Put evenly on top of the bottom of the graham cracker pie shell.
- In a small bowl, mix the gelatin with boiling water until dissolved. Mix in the walnuts and cranberry sauce. Add on top of the cream cheese layer in the pie shell. Chill for 3 to 4 hours until firm. Serve cooled.

Nutrition Information

- Calories: 446 calories;
- Total Fat: 20.9
- Sodium: 298
- Total Carbohydrate: 62.4
- Cholesterol: 31
- Protein: 4.9

140.   Pecan Cranberry Butter Tarts

Serving: 15 | Prep: 20mins | Cook: 20mins | Ready in:

Ingredients

- 1 cup brown sugar
- 1/2 cup chopped pecans
- 1/2 cup chopped dried cranberries

- 1/3 cup butter, melted
- 1/2 orange, zested and juiced
- 1 egg, beaten
- 1 teaspoon brandy, or to taste
- 15 (2 inch) sweetened pastry tart shells
- 15 pecan halves
- 15 fresh cranberries

Direction

- Set oven to preheat at 350°F (175°C).
- Mix together the brandy, egg, dried cranberries, butter, orange zest, orange juice, chopped pecans, and brown sugar in a bowl.
- Place the tart shells onto a baking sheet and scoop pecan-cranberry filling into each shell filling about 2/3 full. Into each tart, add 1 pecan half and 1 fresh cranberry.
- In the preheated oven, bake till filling bubbly and tart shells turn light brown, for about 18 to 20 minutes.

Nutrition Information

- Calories: 273 calories;
- Total Carbohydrate: 33.9
- Cholesterol: 23
- Protein: 2.8
- Total Fat: 14.6
- Sodium: 109

141.   Rustic Fall Fruit Tart

Serving: 8 | Prep: 20mins | Cook: 30mins | Ready in:

Ingredients

- 2 cups all-purpose flour
- 1/2 cup butter, chilled
- 1/2 cup cream cheese
- 1 tablespoon water, or as needed
- 4 apples - peeled, cored, and thinly sliced
- 2/3 cup fresh cranberries
- 1/4 cup brown sugar, or more to taste

- 1/4 cup white sugar, or more to taste
- 2 tablespoons all-purpose flour
- 3/4 teaspoon ground cinnamon
- 1/8 teaspoon ground nutmeg
- 1/3 cup roughly chopped walnuts, or more to taste
- 1 egg, beaten
- 1 tablespoon raw sugar

Direction

- Add 2 cups flour into a bowl. Use a knife or pastry blender to cut butter and cream cheese into the flour until mixture looks much like coarse crumbs. Mix the water into the flour mixture gently till dough shapes into a ball.
- Mix together the apples and cranberries with nutmeg, white sugar, 2 tablespoons flour, cinnamon, and brown sugar in a bowl till coated.
- Set oven to preheat at 375°F (190°C). Lightly grease a baking sheet.
- Onto a lightly floured work surface, roll the dough, forming about an 11-inch circle. Place the dough onto the prepared baking sheet. Decoratively place the mixture of apple-cranberry onto the dough, leave a 2-inch rim of the dough exposed. Sprinkle walnuts onto the mixture of apple-cranberry. Fold up the exposed crust over the fruit's edge.
- Brush egg onto the crust and around the tart's edge; sprinkle using raw sugar.
- In the preheated oven, bake till filling is tender and crust turn brown, for about 30 to 35 minutes.

Nutrition Information

- Calories: 402 calories;
- Sodium: 137
- Total Carbohydrate: 49.5
- Cholesterol: 70
- Protein: 6.4
- Total Fat: 20.8

142. Watermelon Harvest Pie

Serving: 8 | Prep: | Cook: | Ready in:

Ingredients

- 3 cups chopped watermelon rind
- 1 1/3 cups dried cranberries
- 3/4 cup chopped walnuts
- 1/3 cup distilled white vinegar
- 1/2 cup white sugar
- 2 teaspoons pumpkin pie spice
- 1 teaspoon all-purpose flour
- 1/4 teaspoon salt
- 1 recipe pastry for a 9 inch double crust pie
- 1/2 cup confectioners' sugar
- 2 teaspoons orange zest
- 1 teaspoon orange juice

Direction

- Set the oven to 220°C or 425°F to preheat.
- In a saucepan, add watermelon rind and water to cover, then bring to a boil. Lower heat and simmer without a cover until the rind is translucent and soft, for 10 minutes. Take away from the heat and drain.
- In a big bowl, add cooked watermelon rind, vinegar, walnuts and cranberries. Mix together salt, flour, pumpkin pie spice and sugar, then put flour mixture into the rind mixture, stirring well.
- Use bottom pastry to line a 9-in. pie plate, trimming the pastry equal with the edge. Put in the filling, then roll out the leftover pastry and create a lattice crust. Seal and flute edges.
- Use aluminum foil to cover pie and bake at 175°C or 425°F about 20 to 25 minutes. Take off the foil and bake until the crust turns golden brown, about 20 to 25 minutes longer.
- Mix together orange juice, orange rind and confectioners' sugar in a small bowl. Stir to mix and scoop over hot pie. Allow to cool on a wire rack.

Nutrition Information

- Calories: 459 calories;
- Sodium: 308
- Total Carbohydrate: 63.3
- Cholesterol: 0
- Protein: 4.9
- Total Fat: 22.4

Chapter 5:
Mincemeat Fruit Pie Recipes

***

143. Apple Mincemeat Pie

Serving: 8 | Prep: 20mins | Cook: 55mins | Ready in:

Ingredients

- 4 apples - peeled, cored and chopped
- 2 tablespoons butter
- 2 teaspoons lemon juice
- 1/2 cup white sugar
- 1/2 teaspoon ground cinnamon
- 1/8 teaspoon ground nutmeg
- 1 1/2 teaspoons vanilla extract
- 2 cups prepared mincemeat (such as None Such®)
- 1 cup chopped walnuts (optional)
- 1 package of refrigerated pastry for double-crust pie (such as Pillsbury®
- 1 egg yolk
- 1 tablespoon water

Direction

- Set the oven to 450°F (230°C).
- In a saucepan, cook lemon juice, butter and apples over medium heat, stir frequently for 8-

10 minutes until the apples are tender. Mix in vanilla extract, nutmeg, cinnamon and sugar. Stir in the walnuts and mincemeat until completely combined, then put aside the pie filling.

- Place a pie crust into a 9-inch pie dish to fit; pour in the filling. Dip a brush into water and make the edge of the bottom crust moist. Add the second crust on top of the pie, then use a fork to crimp together two crusts sides for sealing. Make 4 slits in the top crust to let steams vent. Whisk water and egg yolk in a small bowl, then brush the liquid over the top crust.
- Bake in the preheated oven for 15 minutes, then lower the oven temperature to 350°F (175°C). Take the pie out of the oven, and prevent over baking by wrapping cover the crust edges with strips of aluminum foil. Bake the pie again for 30-35 minutes longer until the crust turns golden brown and the filling is bubbly.

Nutrition Information

- Calories: 594 calories;
- Protein: 5.8
- Total Fat: 31.1
- Sodium: 430
- Total Carbohydrate: 78.4
- Cholesterol: 33

---

144. Blue Ribbon Mincemeat Pie Filling

Serving: 32 | Prep: | Cook: | Ready in:

Ingredients

- 3 1/4 pounds lean ground beef
- 12 cups apples - peeled, cored and diced
- 6 cups raisins
- 1 cup brandy
- 1 tablespoon ground cinnamon
- 1 tablespoon ground allspice
- 1 tablespoon ground nutmeg
- 3 1/2 cups white sugar

Direction

- In a large skillet, thoroughly cook the ground beef over medium heat. Make sure that it is not overbrowned.
- In a food processor, place cooked ground beef and chopped apples, then pulse to have the mixture in pea sized chunks.
- In a non-reactive skillet, mix the ground beef and apple mixture with the white sugar, ground nutmeg, ground allspice, ground cinnamon, brandy and raisins, then simmer for half an hour.
- Allow to cool to lukewarm and fill into freezer bags (2 cups each bag). Store in the freezer until ready to use. One bag will be used for one 8-inch double crust pie. Defrost it before using.

Nutrition Information

- Calories: 336 calories;
- Total Fat: 9.9
- Sodium: 36
- Total Carbohydrate: 50.3
- Cholesterol: 35
- Protein: 9.1

---

145. Christmas Mince Pies

Serving: 12 | Prep: 25mins | Cook: 17mins | Ready in:

Ingredients

- 2 1/4 cups all-purpose flour
- 1 pinch salt
- 1/2 cup butter, cubed
- 1/4 cup vegetable shortening, cubed
- 3/4 cup white sugar
- 2 oranges, zested

- 1 teaspoon vanilla extract
- 1/4 cup fresh orange juice, chilled
- 7 ounces prepared mincemeat filling, or as needed
- 1 tablespoon confectioners' sugar

Direction

- In a large bowl, mix salt and flour together. Put in shortening and butter; use cold finders to rub in until the mixture looks like fine bread crumbs. Stir in orange zest and sugar thoroughly. Stir in vanilla extract. Mix in enough amount of orange juice to bring the dough together.
- Briefly knead dough to make a smooth ball. Wrap in plastic wrap; place in the fridge till firm, at least 1 hour.
- Preheat oven to 350°F (175°C).
- On a lightly floured work surface, roll dough out to 1/8 inch thickness. Use a 2 1/2-inch cutter to cut out 12 circles and use a 1-inch cutter to make 12 circles.
- Line the 2 1/2-inch dough circles onto a muffin tin or12 mini tart pans. Cover the dough with about 1 tablespoon of mincemeat filling. Place circles of 1-inch on top.
- Bake in the prepped oven for 17 - 21 minutes, till the tops are pale golden brown. Slightly cool in about 10 minutes on wire racks. Dust with confectioners' sugar then serve.

Nutrition Information

- Calories: 277 calories;
- Total Carbohydrate: 39.2
- Cholesterol: 20
- Protein: 2.6
- Total Fat: 12.6
- Sodium: 104

146.   Classic Mincemeat Pie

Serving: 8 | Prep: 10mins | Cook: 30mins | Ready in:

Ingredients

- 1 (15 ounce) package refrigerated pie crusts, both crusts softened as directed on package
- 1 (29 ounce) jar Crosse & Blackwell® Mincemeat Filling & Topping or Crosse & Blackwell® Rum & Brandy Mincemeat Filling & Topping
- Vanilla ice cream (optional)

Direction

- Preheat oven to 425°F. Unfold pie crusts. Line ungreased 9-inch pie pan using one crust. Fill with mincemeat. Cover with another crust and enclose edges. Score slits in top crust to vent steam. Bake 25-30 minutes. Serve warm with vanilla ice cream (optional).

Nutrition Information

- Calories: 492 calories;
- Sodium: 551
- Total Carbohydrate: 80.6
- Cholesterol: < 1
- Protein: 3
- Total Fat: 16.3

147.   Green Tomato Mincemeat

Serving: 120 | Prep: 45mins | Cook: 3hours | Ready in:

Ingredients

- 8 quarts green tomatoes, minced
- 8 quarts minced, cored apples
- 1/2 pound beef suet
- 6 pounds brown sugar
- 1 cup distilled white vinegar
- 2 tablespoons salt
- 2 tablespoons ground cinnamon
- 2 tablespoons ground cloves
- 2 tablespoons ground allspice

- 2 pounds raisins
- 32 ounces candied mixed citrus peel (optional)
- 7 large orange, peeled, sectioned, and cut into bite-size
- 2 lemons, finely chopped

Direction

- Mix candied peel, raisins, chopped lemons, chopped oranges, vinegar, brown sugar, suet or oil, apples, and green tomatoes in a very large stockpot. Flavor with allspice, cloves, cinnamon, and salt. Put a cover on and cook for 3 hours on low heat.
- Following the manufacturer's directions, sterilize 30 canning jars (a pint) and lids.
- Fill the sterilized jars with the filling, leaving a 1/2 inch head space. Use a clean, damp cloth to wipe the jar. Put lids on jars to cover and screw on the jar rings.
- In a hot water canner, heat the water. Arrange the jars in the rack and lower the jars into the canner slowly. Cover the jars completely with water, and the water should be hot yet not boiling. Boil the water and pulse for 10 minutes.

Nutrition Information

- Calories: 179 calories;
- Sodium: 126
- Total Carbohydrate: 42.1
- Cholesterol: 1
- Protein: 0.9
- Total Fat: 2

---

148.   Green Tomato Mincemeat Fried Pies

Serving: 24 | Prep: 45mins | Cook: 1hours | Ready in:

Ingredients

- 2 pounds green tomatoes

- 3/4 cup distilled white vinegar
- 1 1/2 teaspoons ground cinnamon
- 3 cups cold water, divided
- 3 pounds tart apples - peeled, cored and chopped
- 1 1/2 pounds raisins
- 3 3/4 cups packed brown sugar
- 3 1/2 teaspoons salt
- 1 teaspoon ground nutmeg
- 1 teaspoon lemon zest
- 1 teaspoon ground cloves
- 1/4 cup lemon juice
- 1/2 cup butter flavored shortening
- 2 cups all-purpose flour
- 1 teaspoon salt
- 1/3 cup shortening
- 3 tablespoons ice water
- 3 cups shortening for frying

Direction

- Chop tomatoes coarsely; put in colander. Use your hand to press and squeeze out as much tomato juice as possible. Put tomatoes and 1 cup water in big saucepan; boil on medium high heat. Take off heat; drain well.
- Put 1 cup cold water and tomatoes in saucepan; boil. Drain.
- Put 1/2 cup butter-flavored shortening, vinegar, 3 1/2 tsp. salt, raisins, brown sugar, apples, leftover cup water and tomatoes; slowly cook on medium low heat, frequently mixing, for 30 minutes till tomatoes are transparent.
- Add juice, lemon rind, cloves, nutmeg and cinnamon at final 5 minutes of cooking. Take mincemeat off heat. Put aside; cool.
- Pastry: Mix shortening, 1 tsp. salt and flour in big bowl. 1 tbsp. at a time, add ice water till dough barely holds together. Use plastic to wrap; refrigerate for half an hour.
- Roll out dough to 1/8-in. thick on floured surface then cut to 5-in. circle. Put big spoonful of filling on 1/2 of circle then fold over. Use fork to press edges to seal; repeat with leftover dough.

- Heat shortening to 182°C/360°F in big heavy skillet; put 4 pies carefully in hot shortening. Fry till both sides are golden brown; drain over paper towels. Repeat with leftover pies.

Nutrition Information

- Calories: 383 calories;
- Total Fat: 10.5
- Sodium: 456
- Total Carbohydrate: 74.4
- Cholesterol: 0
- Protein: 2.6

---

149.   Green Tomato Mock Mincemeat Pie

Serving: 8 | Prep: 15mins | Cook: 1hours | Ready in:

Ingredients

- 2 cups chopped green tomato
- 2 cups peeled and chopped tart green apples
- 1 cup firmly packed brown sugar
- 1/2 cup chopped raisins
- 3 tablespoons cider vinegar
- 1 tablespoon butter
- 1 teaspoon ground cinnamon
- 1/2 teaspoon salt
- 1/4 teaspoon ground nutmeg
- 1/4 teaspoon ground cloves
- 1 pastry for a 9-inch double-crust pie

Direction

- In a large saucepan, combine cloves, nutmeg, salt, cinnamon, butter, vinegar, raisins, brown sugar, apples, and tomatoes; cook, stirring over medium-low heat for about 25 minutes, until bubbling and reduced slightly in volume. Remove the saucepan from the heat and allow to cool slightly for about 15 minutes.
- Set the oven at 230°C (450°F) to preheat. Press 1 pie crust into a 9-inch pie dish.

- Next, pour into the pie crust with the green tomato filling; lay the second pie crust on top, seal up by crimping the edges together.
- In the preheated oven, bake for 15 minutes. Then decrease the oven temperature to 190°C (375°F) and keep baking for 20-25 minutes more, until golden brown.

Nutrition Information

- Calories: 402 calories;
- Cholesterol: 4
- Protein: 3.8
- Total Fat: 16.6
- Sodium: 405
- Total Carbohydrate: 62.2

---

150.   Homemade Mince Pie With Crumbly Topping

Serving: 8 | Prep: 30mins | Cook: 1hours | Ready in:

Ingredients

- 1/2 cup cold butter
- 1 1/2 cups all-purpose flour
- 1/2 teaspoon salt
- 1/2 cup cold water
- 1 1/2 cups raisins
- 5 apples - peeled, cored and chopped
- 2 tablespoons finely chopped grapefruit peel without white layer
- 1/3 cup orange juice
- 1/2 cup apple cider
- 3/4 cup white sugar
- 1/2 teaspoon ground cinnamon
- 1/4 teaspoon ground cloves
- 1/2 graham cracker, crushed
- 1/3 cup white sugar
- 3/4 cup all-purpose flour
- 6 tablespoons butter
- 1/2 graham cracker, crushed

Direction

- Set oven to preheat at 425°F (220°C).
- Use a fork to mix 1/2 cup of cold butter, 1 1/2 cups flour and the salt in a bowl till mixture is extremely crumbly. Stir water into the mixture, 1 tablespoon at a time, just till the mixture comes together. Use a fork to mix again then turn it out onto a pastry cloth dusted with flour. Flatten dough to a round piece, and roll it out into a circle 10-inch in diameter. Flip a 9-inch pie dish onto the dough. Then flip the dough over, remove from the pastry cloth; if necessary, reposition the crust into the plate. Fold the dough on to pie dish's edge. Put the crust aside.
- Mix the apple cider, apples, grapefruit peel, orange juice, and raisins in a saucepan, and heat till simmering on medium heat. Cook, stir from time to time, till the apple pieces soften, for about 15 minutes. Stir half a crushed graham cracker, the cinnamon, cloves, and 3/4 cup of sugar into the mix, and combine thoroughly.
- Mix half a crushed graham cracker, 3/4 cup of flour, 6 tablespoons of butter, and 1/3 cup of sugar in a bowl, stir till the mixture resembles fine crumbs. Transfer the mince filling into the prepared pie crust, and evenly sprinkle the streusel topping on top.
- In the preheated oven, bake for 15 minutes, and lower the oven temperature to 350°F (175°C); bake till topping turn light brown, for about 30 more minutes. Let it cool down before serving.

Nutrition Information

- Calories: 559 calories;
- Cholesterol: 53
- Protein: 5.1
- Total Fat: 21
- Sodium: 306
- Total Carbohydrate: 92.2

151.   Meatless Mincemeat Pie

Serving: 8 | Prep: 30mins | Cook: 40mins | Ready in:

Ingredients

- 1 (18 ounce) jar prepared mincemeat pie filling
- 1 1/2 cups chopped walnuts
- 2 apple - peeled, cored, and chopped
- 1/2 cup packed brown sugar
- 1/4 cup rum
- 1 tablespoon lemon juice
- 1 recipe pastry for a 9 inch double crust pie

Direction

- In a bowl, mix rum, lemon juice, brown sugar, apples, walnuts and mincemeat. Stir well. Cover and chill overnight.
- Set oven to 425°F (220°C) to preheat.
- Get filling out of fridge and let it sit to room temperature. Make crusts. Mix filling well and put into shell. Put full crust over and create slits or form a lattice top. Crimp edges.
- Bake for 40 minutes in the prepared oven on low shelf or until golden brown.

Nutrition Information

- Calories: 463 calories;
- Total Fat: 23.5
- Sodium: 261
- Total Carbohydrate: 60.2
- Cholesterol: 0
- Protein: 4.8

152.   Mincemeat I

Serving: 16 | Prep: | Cook: | Ready in:

Ingredients

- 1 pound Golden Delicious apples - peeled, cored and chopped
- 1/2 pound golden raisins

- 1/2 pound dried currants
- 1/2 pound raisins
- 1/2 pound shredded beef suet
- 1/2 teaspoon ground allspice
- 1/2 teaspoon ground cinnamon
- 1/2 pound brown sugar
- 4 ounces candied mixed citrus peel
- 1/2 cup sliced almonds
- 2 lemon, juiced and zested
- 1/4 cup brandy
- 2 teaspoons ground ginger
- 1/4 teaspoon ground nutmeg

Direction

- In a big bowl, put nutmeg, ginger, brandy, lemon juice, lemon rind, almonds, citrus peel, brown sugar, cinnamon, allspice, suet, raisins, currants, golden raisins and apples and stir well. Cover and put in fridge for 2 days to let flavor mature.
- Sterilize canning jars and lids enough to put mincemeat in.
- Fill sterilized jars with mincemeat, ensure there are no air pockets or spaces. Pack jars all the way to top. Screw the lids on.
- In the bottom of a big stock pot, put a rack and pour boiling water to fill halfway. Lower jars carefully into pot with a holder. Leave a 2-inch space between jars. Put in more boiling water if need be, until tops of jars are covered by 2 inches of water. Heat water to a full boil, then cover and process for half an hour.
- Take out jars from pot and put on cloth-covered or wood surface, a few inches apart, until cool. When cool, push top of each lid with finger, making sure that it's tightly sealed (lid doesn't move up or down at all). Before using, mincemeat should be aged 2 or 3 months, you can also store it up to a year.

Nutrition Information

- Calories: 368 calories;
- Total Fat: 15.1
- Sodium: 11

- Total Carbohydrate: 58.4
- Cholesterol: 10
- Protein: 2.6

153. Mincemeat Pie Filling

Serving: 16 | Prep: 30mins | Cook: | Ready in:

Ingredients

- 1 1/2 cups diced cooked beef
- 4 cups chopped apples
- 1 1/2 cups raisins
- 1/4 cup sweet pickle juice
- 1/4 cup pineapple juice
- 1 large orange, peeled, sectioned, and cut into bite-size
- 1/2 teaspoon salt
- 1/2 teaspoon ground cloves
- 1 teaspoon ground cinnamon
- 1 teaspoon ground nutmeg
- 1 1/2 cups white sugar
- 1/2 cup sorghum
- 1 cup beef broth

Direction

- Mix 1 cup of beef broth, sorghum, sugar, nutmeg, cinnamon, cloves, salt, orange, pineapple, sweet pickle vinegar, raisins, apples and cooked beef together. Freeze or refrigerate until ready to use.

Nutrition Information

- Calories: 224 calories;
- Protein: 5.5
- Total Fat: 4.1
- Sodium: 136
- Total Carbohydrate: 43.7
- Cholesterol: 16

154.   Mincemeat And Pumpkin Layer Pie

Serving: 8 | Prep: | Cook: | Ready in:

Ingredients

- 1 1/2 cups prepared, meatless mincemeat
- 1 egg, beaten
- 1 cup pumpkin puree
- 1/2 cup white sugar
- 1/2 teaspoon ground cinnamon
- 1/4 teaspoon ground nutmeg
- 1/4 teaspoon salt
- 1 prepared 8 inch pastry shell
- 1 cup whipped cream

Direction

- Set the oven at 425°F (220°C) and start preheating.
- Using a rotary beater, beat salt, spices, sugar, pumpkin and egg together.
- Onto the bottom of a pastry shell, spread mincemeat. Transfer the pumpkin mixture on top of the mincemeat.
- Bake for 35-40 minutes. Enjoy with whipped cream. Serve cool or slightly warm, but not cold.

Nutrition Information

- Calories: 252 calories;
- Total Carbohydrate: 46.1
- Cholesterol: 29
- Protein: 1.9
- Total Fat: 7.9
- Sodium: 363

155.   Mincemeat/Pumpkin Chiffon Pie

Serving: 8 | Prep: | Cook: | Ready in:

Ingredients

- 1 cup solid pack pumpkin puree
- 1/2 cup packed brown sugar
- 3/4 teaspoon ground cinnamon
- 3/4 teaspoon ground nutmeg
- 1/2 teaspoon salt
- 3 eggs
- 1/2 cup heavy whipping cream
- 1 cup prepared mincemeat pie filling
- 1 (9 inch) pie shell

Direction

- Set oven to 425°F (220°C) to preheat.
- In a bowl, mix the salt, nutmeg, cinnamon, brown sugar and pumpkin, stirring well. Put in heavy cream and eggs. Whip until smooth with a rotary or electric mixer. Mix in the mincemeat and add to the unbaked pie crust.
- Bake for 35 minutes at 425°F (220°C) or until the filling is set. Let cool slightly on a wire rack and serve warm.

Nutrition Information

- Calories: 290 calories;
- Sodium: 435
- Total Carbohydrate: 40.5
- Cholesterol: 90
- Protein: 3.7
- Total Fat: 13.7

156.   Mini Orange Mince Pies

Serving: 18 | Prep: 25mins | Cook: 15mins | Ready in:

Ingredients

- 1 3/4 cups all-purpose flour
- 1/4 cup confectioners' sugar
- 2 teaspoons ground cinnamon
- 2/3 cup butter, softened
- 2 tablespoons grated orange zest
- 1/4 cup ice water

- 3/4 cup prepared mincemeat pie filling
- 1 egg, beaten
- 1/4 cup confectioners' sugar for dusting

Direction

- Heat oven to 200°C (400°F) beforehand.
- Sifting cinnamon, a quarter cup of confectioners' sugar and flour together. Mixing in the butter using 2 forks or a pastry cutter till mixture looks like fine bread crumbs. Stirring in the orange zest. Use ice water to scatter on and gather the dough into a ball. On a surface floured lightly, rolling out into 1/4 inch of thickness. Cutting out about 18 circles (2 inches) and 18 diameter circles (3 inch), reroll dough if necessary.
- Use 3-inch pastry circles to line tart tins or muffin cups. Fill approximately a tablespoon of mincemeat filling into each pastry cup. Place 2-inch pastry circles on top, to seal the edges, pinch circles together. Brushing egg on the top of every pie.
- In preheated oven, allow pies to bake for 15-20 minutes till tops turn golden brown. Place on wire racks for cooling down slightly. Before serving, use a quarter cup of confectioners' sugar to dust.

Nutrition Information

- Calories: 145 calories;
- Total Fat: 7.5
- Sodium: 79
- Total Carbohydrate: 18.4
- Cholesterol: 28
- Protein: 1.7

157.   Mock Mincemeat Pie

Serving: 8 | Prep: 20mins | Cook: 30mins | Ready in:

Ingredients

- 1 1/2 cups seedless raisins

- 4 Granny Smith apples - peeled, cored and sliced
- 1 tablespoon orange zest
- 1/3 cup orange juice
- 1/2 cup apple cider
- 3/4 cup white sugar
- 1/2 teaspoon ground cinnamon
- 1/2 teaspoon ground cloves
- 2 soda crackers, finely crushed
- 1 pastry for a 9 inch double crust pie

Direction

- Set oven to preheat at 425°F (220°C).
- Stir the apple cider, apples, orange zest, orange juice, and raisins in a pan. Simmer on medium heat, stir from time to time, till apples soften extremely, for about 20 minutes. Stir the sugar, cinnamon, cloves, and soda crackers into the mix till well incorporated. Refrigerate till ready to use, or add the apple mixture into the prepared pie crust. Place the second crust on top. To seal the crusts, pinch and crimp the edges. Use a fork to prick the top crust in several places.
- In preheated oven, bake for 15 minutes. Lower the oven temperature to 350°F (175°C), and bake till top turns golden brown, for about 30 minutes longer. Let it cool down before serving.

Nutrition Information

- Calories: 429 calories;
- Cholesterol: 0
- Protein: 4
- Total Fat: 15.2
- Sodium: 248
- Total Carbohydrate: 73.4

158.   Mum's Mincemeat

Serving: 50 | Prep: 45mins | Cook: | Ready in:

Ingredients

- 1 pound suet
- 1 pound brown sugar
- 1 pound sultana raisins
- 1 pound dark raisins
- 1 pound dried currants
- 4 ounces candied mixed fruit peel
- 4 ounces chopped almonds
- 1/4 cup ground allspice
- 3 tablespoons ground nutmeg
- 1 tablespoon salt
- 3 pounds apples, grated

Direction

- Melt suet in saucepan on medium low heat; through fine-mesh strainer, strain liquid into bowl. Discard solids; refrigerate liquid till solid again.
- Grate solid suet; get 12-oz. grated suet into bowl. Put aside.
- Mix salt, nutmeg, allspice, almonds, fruit peel, currants, dark raisins, sultana raisins and brown sugar in big bowl. Add grated suet; mxi. Fold grated apple through mixture.
- Loosely cover bowl with aluminum foil; sit, mixing once daily, at room temperature for 3-5 days till fermented. Refrigerate till needed.

Nutrition Information

- Calories: 226 calories;
- Total Fat: 10.1
- Sodium: 150
- Total Carbohydrate: 35.7
- Cholesterol: 6
- Protein: 1.6

Chapter 6: Peach Pie Recipes

***

159. 120 Calorie Peach Pies

Serving: 8 | Prep: 15mins | Cook: 10mins | Ready in:

Ingredients

- 1 recipe pastry for a single 9-inch pie crust
- 1 large fresh peach, sliced into 8 pieces
- 1 teaspoon white sugar
- 1 teaspoon ground cinnamon

Direction

- Set the oven at 450°F (230°C) and start preheating.
- Onto a cutting board, roll pie pastry. Using a cookie cutter, slice the crust into eight 4-in. circles. In the center of each circle, place 1 peach slice. To enclose each peach slice, fold the circle in half; seal the edges together. Arrange the mini pies on a baking sheet.
- In a small bowl, combine sugar and cinnamon; sprinkle on top of the mini pies.
- Bake in the preheated oven for 10-13 minutes, till the crust is browned lightly.

Nutrition Information

- Calories: 121 calories;
- Total Fat: 7.5
- Sodium: 118
- Total Carbohydrate: 12
- Cholesterol: 0
- Protein: 1.4

160. Apricot And Peach Fried Pies

Serving: 18 | Prep: | Cook: 30mins | Ready in:

Ingredients

- Dough:
- 4 cups all-purpose flour
- 2 teaspoons salt
- 1 cup shortening
- 1 cup milk
- Filling:
- 8 ounces dried apricots
- 1 (6 ounce) package dried peaches
- 3/4 cup white sugar
- water to cover
- 2 cups vegetable oil for frying

Direction

- Crust: Mix salt and flour in big bowl; cut shortening in till mixture is crumbly. Mix milk in; mix till dough becomes a ball. Roll dough out; cut to 18 6-in. circles. Put aside.
- Filling: Cover sugar, peaches and apricots with enough water in big saucepan; cover pan. Cook on low heat till fruit falls apart. Uncover; cook till water evaporates.
- Put shortening/oil in high-sided small skillet; put on medium heat. Put even filling amounts in each pastry circle; fold in half. Use fork dipped into cold water to seal pastry.
- A few pies at a time, fry pies in hot oil; brown both sides. Over paper towels, drain pies.

Nutrition Information

- Calories: 280 calories;
- Total Fat: 14.4
- Sodium: 266
- Total Carbohydrate: 34.8
- Cholesterol: 1
- Protein: 3.6

161.   Captain Jack's Peach Pie

Serving: 8 | Prep: 30mins | Cook: 45mins | Ready in:

Ingredients

- 1 (15 ounce) package double crust ready-to-use pie crust
- 1 cup white sugar
- 1/3 cup all-purpose flour
- 1 tablespoon cornstarch
- 1/4 teaspoon ground cinnamon
- 1/4 teaspoon ground cardamom
- 1/4 teaspoon ground allspice
- 1/4 cup butter, melted
- 8 fresh peaches - peeled, pitted, and sliced
- 2 tablespoons rum
- 2 tablespoons milk

Direction

- Preheat the oven to 200°C or 400°F. Lightly grease butter on a 9-in. pie dish.
- Press 1 pie crust into the prepped pie dish.
- In a bowl, mix together allspice, cardamom, cinnamon, cornstarch, flour and sugar. Stir the butter gradually into the sugar mixture to incorporate fully.
- In another bowl, toss rum and peaches together then place the sugar mixture into the peaches. Toss gently till peaches are coated. Transfer the peach mixture into pie crust. Place the leftover pie crust on top then seal 2 edges of the crust together. Make 4-5 slits in the top for ventilation. Brush milk over.
- Bake for 15 minutes in the preheated oven. Lower heat to 175°C or 350°F then bake for 30 minutes longer till it's golden brown on top. Turn off the oven and allow the pie to rest for at least 1 hour in the oven as it cools.

Nutrition Information

- Calories: 452 calories;
- Total Fat: 22.1
- Sodium: 300
- Total Carbohydrate: 58.5
- Cholesterol: 16
- Protein: 3.8

162. Chef John's Peach Pie

Serving: 10 | Prep: 30mins | Cook: 1hours15mins | Ready in:

Ingredients

- 3 pounds fresh freestone peaches, peeled and sliced
- 1 cup white sugar, divided
- 1 tiny pinch salt
- 1/4 cup all-purpose flour
- 1 tablespoon cornstarch
- 1 teaspoon lemon juice
- 1 pinch cayenne pepper
- 1 pinch ground cinnamon
- 1 pastry for a 10-inch double crust pie
- 1 1/2 tablespoons butter, cut into tiny pieces
- 1 tablespoon heavy whipping cream, or to taste
- 1 tablespoon white sugar, or to taste

Direction

- Set oven to preheat at 350°F (175°C).
- Stir together the peaches, 1/2 cup sugar, and salt in a bowl. Let them sit for 20 to 30 minutes. Strain the gathered juices into a saucepan and add the strained peaches back to the bowl.
- Heat the juices in saucepan to boil; lower the heat to medium-high, and cook till mixture thickens into the consistency of a syrup, for about 5 to 10 minutes.
- Whisk together 1/2 cup sugar, flour, and cornstarch in a bowl. Stir the cinnamon, cayenne pepper, and lemon juice into peaches; add in the flour mixture and toss the mixture to coat. Add the peach syrup on top of the peach mixture and stir.
- Unroll half of the pastry to fit a pie plate 10-inch in size. Put the bottom crust into the pie plate. Transfer the peach filling into the pie shell, tap the pie plate onto a surface for the filling to settle, and use butter to dot the surface.
- Unroll the leftover crust into a circle 11-inch diameter; use a pastry wheel or paring knife to cut into 1-inch strips.
- Place 5 pie crust strips on top of the pie. Weave the rest of the pastry dough strips through to create a lattice top. Fold the lattice strips' ends beneath the bottom crust then crimp the crust. Brush cream on top and sprinkle it with 1 tablespoon sugar.
- In the preheated oven, bake till bubbling and brown, for about 1 hour 15 minutes. Let it cool down fully then slice.

Nutrition Information

- Calories: 325 calories;
- Protein: 2.6
- Total Fat: 14.3
- Sodium: 223
- Total Carbohydrate: 47.2
- Cholesterol: 7

163. Chef John's Peach Tartlets

Serving: 8 | Prep: 15mins | Cook: 20mins | Ready in:

Ingredients

- 1/4 cup sugar
- 1/4 teaspoon Chinese five-spice powder
- 1 egg, beaten
- 1 teaspoon water
- 2 tablespoons butter
- 3 large peaches, each cut into 8 wedges
- 1 (15 ounce) package refrigerated pie pastry

Direction

- Set oven to 190°C (375°F) and start preheating. Use a silicone baking mat to line a baking sheet.

- In a small bowl, combine Chinese five-spice powder and sugar. In a separate bowl, beat water and egg.
- In a big skillet, heat butter over medium heat until melted. Once the butter becomes foamy, place one layer of peaches in the skillet. Spread sugar mixture on top of peaches; cook for 2 minutes, flipping peaches once, until syrup has a tan color and sugar melts and bubbles. Pour all into a bowl and let cool entirely.
- Cut pie crusts into eight 4 1/2-in. circles. Transfer to the lined baking sheet; make a 1/2-in. rim by folding up each crust's edges. Brush egg mixture over each crust.
- In the middle of each tart, put two peach slices, pit-sides facing each other. Put another peach slice in the middle of the previous 2 slices, skin-side facing up. Drizzle the excess syrup on top.
- Bake for 15 minutes at 190°C (375°F) until the tart bubbles and turn golden.

Nutrition Information

- Calories: 318 calories;
- Total Fat: 19.7
- Sodium: 284
- Total Carbohydrate: 31.6
- Cholesterol: 31
- Protein: 3.8

164. Creamy Peach Pie

Serving: 8 | Prep: | Cook: | Ready in:

Ingredients

- 1 recipe pastry for a 9 inch single crust pie
- 4 cups fresh peaches - peeled, pitted, and sliced
- 3/4 cup white sugar
- 1/4 cup all-purpose flour
- 1/4 teaspoon salt

- 1/4 teaspoon freshly grated nutmeg
- 1 cup heavy whipping cream

Direction

- Peel peaches; slice.
- Mix nutmeg, salt, flour and sugar. Put into the peaches; toss slightly. Turn out into a pie shell. Evenly pour whipping cream over the top.
- Bake at 400°F (205°C) in a preheated oven till golden brown on top and firm, 35-45 minutes. Chille for several hours. Serve.

Nutrition Information

- Calories: 320 calories;
- Cholesterol: 41
- Protein: 2.4
- Total Fat: 18.5
- Sodium: 204
- Total Carbohydrate: 36.8

165. Easy French Peach Pie

Serving: 8 | Prep: 10mins | Cook: 55mins | Ready in:

Ingredients

- 1 recipe pastry for a single 9-inch pie crust
- 1 (28 ounce) can sliced peaches, drained
- 1 cup white sugar
- 1 egg
- 1 tablespoon all-purpose flour
- 1 teaspoon butter
- 1/4 teaspoon ground cinnamon, or to taste

Direction

- Set the oven for preheating to 450°F (230°C). Press the pie pastry in a pan with a 9-inch diameter.
- Fill the pie crust with peaches. Stir together the egg, sugar, flour, cinnamon and butter together in a bowl then pour the mixture over the peaches.

- Let the pie bake inside the oven for about 15 minutes. Adjust the heat to 350°F (175°C) and continue to bake for roughly 40 to 45 minutes until the peach filling becomes bubbly and crust turns lightly browned.

Nutrition Information

- Calories: 271 calories;
- Sodium: 133
- Total Carbohydrate: 47.6
- Cholesterol: 25
- Protein: 2.9
- Total Fat: 8.6

---

166.   Easy Peach Pie

Serving: 10 | Prep: 30mins | Cook: |Ready in:

Ingredients

- 1 (9 inch) deep dish graham cracker pie crust
- 5 fresh peaches - peeled, pitted, and sliced
- 1 (18 ounce) jar peach glaze
- 1/4 cup white sugar
- 1 (12 ounce) container frozen whipped topping, thawed
- 2 (8 ounce) packages cream cheese

Direction

- In a mixing bowl, mix glaze and peaches. Let it rest for a few minutes.
- Mix cream cheese and sugar. With an electric mixer, blend on high speed for a minute. Put in the nondairy whipped topping gradually, beat on medium speed until you have a smooth mixture. Put mixture into pie crust. Put peach mixture over. Cover and refrigerate for an hour.

Nutrition Information

- Calories: 496 calories;

- Sodium: 373
- Total Carbohydrate: 49.5
- Cholesterol: 66
- Protein: 5
- Total Fat: 31.4

---

167.   Four Fruit Pie

Serving: 8 | Prep: 35mins | Cook: 35mins |Ready in:

Ingredients

- 1 (9 inch) pie shell
- 3 apples
- 3 fresh peaches
- 1 pear
- 1 cup raspberries
- 3/4 cup white sugar
- 1 teaspoon ground cinnamon
- 3 tablespoons all-purpose flour
- 1/3 cup packed brown sugar
- 3/4 cup all-purpose flour
- 6 tablespoons butter
- 1/2 cup chopped pecans

Direction

- Set oven to preheat at 400°F (205°C).
- Peel, core, and slice the pear, apples, and peaches. Add the fruit to a large bowl and put in the raspberries. In another bowl, mix together the 3 tablespoons flour, cinnamon, and white sugar. Put the mixture atop the fruit and toss gently to coat the fruit.
- Mound the fruit mixture into a 9-inch pie shell.
- Mix together 1/3 cup brown sugar and 3/4 cup flour in a medium bowl. Cut in the butter till the mixture looks like small peas. Mix in chopped pecans and sprinkle the crumble atop the fruit.
- Bake for 35 to 40 minutes at 400°F (205°C), or until the crust becomes golden brown and filling bubbles up. Allow to cool on wire rack.

Nutrition Information

- Calories: 422 calories;
- Total Fat: 19.1
- Sodium: 169
- Total Carbohydrate: 62.3
- Cholesterol: 23
- Protein: 3.3

168.   French Peach Pie

Serving: 8 | Prep: 15mins | Cook: 5mins | Ready in:

Ingredients

- 1 (9 inch) pie shell, baked
- 1 (15 ounce) can sliced peaches, juice reserved
- 1 (3.5 ounce) package instant vanilla pudding mix
- 1 cup milk
- 1 cup sour cream
- 1/4 teaspoon almond extract
- 1 tablespoon cornstarch
- 1 teaspoon lemon juice

Direction

- Strain water out of peaches, save up 2/3 cup syrup. Mix together almond extract, sour cream, milk and pudding mix for 2 minutes until really smooth. Put mixture into pie shell. Refrigerate for 10 minutes. Put peach slices on top of custard in pie shell in a nice pattern.
- Stir cornstarch and saved peach syrup in a small saucepan. Heat up to a boil, cook for 2 minutes. Take off from heat, mix in lemon juice. Put the glaze on top of peaches. Refrigerate until firm. Serve

Nutrition Information

- Calories: 268 calories;
- Total Fat: 14.5
- Sodium: 328
- Total Carbohydrate: 31.7

- Cholesterol: 15
- Protein: 3.7

169.   Fresh Fruit Custard Tart

Serving: 8 | Prep: 30mins | Cook: | Ready in:

Ingredients

- 1 (9 inch) refrigerated pie crust
- 1 cup Egg Beaters® Original
- 1/2 cup granulated sugar
- 1 teaspoon vanilla extract
- 2 cups fat free milk
- 2 cups assorted fresh fruit (such as blueberries, sliced strawberries, and/or peaches)
- Reddi-wip Original Whipped Light Cream

Direction

- Heat oven to 350°F to preheat. Put pie crust in 9-in. pie dish, firmly press the crust into sides and bottom of plate. Flute the edge.
- In a large bowl with wire whisk, whip vanilla, sugar and Egg Beaters until combined. Slowly whisk in milk until blended. Put pastry shell in heated oven. Gently put filling into prepped pastry. Bake until a knife inserted near center comes out clean, or 40 minutes. Let it cool totally on a wire rack.
- Let it rest in the fridge about 2 hours until set. Put fruit on top.
- Slice pie into 8 pieces. Decorate slices with a serving of Reddi-wip just before serving (optional).

Nutrition Information

- Calories: 234 calories;
- Total Fat: 8.2
- Sodium: 204
- Total Carbohydrate: 32
- Cholesterol: 4
- Protein: 7.4

170.   Fresh Peach Angel Pie

Serving: 8 | Prep: | Cook: | Ready in:

Ingredients

- 3 egg whites
- 3/4 cup white sugar
- 1 cup flaked coconut, toasted
- 1/2 cup toasted and sliced almonds
- 5 fresh peaches, pitted and sliced
- 1 cup heavy whipping cream, whipped
- 1/4 cup flaked coconut, toasted

Direction

- Whisk egg whites until forming soft peaks. Slowly put in sugar, whisking until very glossy and stiff. Fold in almonds and toasted coconut. Use a spoon to transfer to a 9-in. pie plate to make a shell.
- Bake for 30-35 minutes at 175° (350° F). Allow to cool.
- Fill with the sliced peaches. Arrange whipped cream and toasted coconut over top. Let chill until ready to serve.

Nutrition Information

- Calories: 250 calories;
- Sodium: 62
- Total Carbohydrate: 30.7
- Cholesterol: 20
- Protein: 4
- Total Fat: 13.3

171.   Fresh Peach Galette

Serving: 8 | Prep: 20mins | Cook: 15mins | Ready in:

Ingredients

- Dough:
- 2 1/2 cups all-purpose flour
- 1/2 teaspoon salt
- 1/2 cup iced water
- 1/4 teaspoon vanilla extract
- 2 sticks butter (such as Plugra®), cut into small cubes
- Fruit Filling:
- 3 peaches, cut into 1/4-inch slices, or more to taste
- 1/4 teaspoon salt
- 1/4 cup white sugar
- 1/2 teaspoon vanilla bean paste
- 1/2 teaspoon cornstarch

Direction

- In a medium bowl, mix salt and flour. Slowly add water and combine with bowl scraper until it is absorbed. Pour in vanilla extract. Gradually mash the butter into mixture with fingers until mixed well. Then flatten the dough to form a saucer and cover with plastic wrap. Chill for about one hour or up to overnight.
- In medium bowl, put the peaches and drizzle with salt. Add cornstarch, vanilla paste and sugar. Mix with wooden spoon and leave to rest for 5 to 10 minutes until the peach juices have been released.
- Preheat an oven to 175 degrees C (350 degrees F). Line parchment paper onto a baking sheet.
- Dust a work surface lightly with flour. Roll out the dough into a thickness of not more than 1/4 inch. Use the rim of a cereal bowl to chop out circles of dough. Transfer the rounds one inch apart into the baking sheet. Pour two spoonfuls of peach filling into the middle of each crust and leave approximately half inch of space around edges.
- Then fold in edges of crusts 1/4 inch towards the middle of each galette and make a short lip to keep filling at the center.
- Bake for 12 to 15 minutes in the oven until the bottoms are cooked through and the crusts are golden brown.

Nutrition Information

- Calories: 381 calories;
- Cholesterol: 61
- Total Fat: 23.4
- Protein: 4.3
- Sodium: 384
- Total Carbohydrate: 38.7

172.   Fresh Peach Pie

Serving: 8 | Prep: 30mins | Cook: 20mins | Ready in:

Ingredients

- 1 cup all-purpose flour
- 1/2 teaspoon white sugar
- 1/2 teaspoon salt
- 1/2 cup shortening
- 6 tablespoons ice water, or as needed
- 3 tablespoons cornstarch
- 1 cup white sugar
- 1 cup orange juice
- 1 cup water
- 1/2 lemon, juiced
- 10 fresh peaches - peeled, pitted, and sliced

Direction

- Set the oven at 450°F (220°C) and start preheating.
- Mix salt, 1/2 teaspoon of sugar and flour in a medium bowl. Between your fingers, rub in shortening, making evenly small lumps no larger than peas. Mix in water so that the dough forms a ball. Briefly knead to pull it together; allow to rest for a few minutes. Roll out the dough to around a 12-in. circle. Fit into a 9-in. pie plate; use a fork to prick. Place another pie plate on top; turn over. Thinner metal pans work better in this method rather than glass pans.
- Bake the crust in the preheated oven for 8-10 minutes, or till golden. Let it cool; turn back into the original pan. Without using pie weights, this process prevents the crust from sagging down into the pan.
- Meanwhile, in a saucepan, mix 1 cup of sugar and cornstarch. Mix in lemon juice, water and orange juice. Warm while stirring occasionally over medium heat till clear and thickened. Take away from the heat; keep chilled.
- To assemble the pie, arrange layers of fresh sliced peaches alternately with the chilled citrus sauce, starting and ending with the sauce. Serve accompanied with ice cream or whipped cream.

Nutrition Information

- Calories: 326 calories;
- Protein: 2
- Total Fat: 13
- Sodium: 152
- Total Carbohydrate: 51.3
- Cholesterol: 0

173.   Fresh Peach Pie I

Serving: 8 | Prep: | Cook: | Ready in:

Ingredients

- 1 (9 inch) pie shell, baked
- 1 cup white sugar
- 1/2 cup water
- 3 tablespoons cornstarch
- 1 tablespoon butter
- 2 cups fresh peaches, pitted and mashed
- 1/4 teaspoon ground nutmeg
- 1 teaspoon vanilla extract
- 4 cups fresh peaches - pitted, skinned, and sliced

Direction

- In a saucepan, mix nutmeg, mashed peaches, margarine or butter, cornstarch, water and sugar. Cook till thick and clear, on medium heat. Mix in vanilla.

- Put sliced fresh peaches to fill into pie shell alternately with glaze. Chill.

Nutrition Information

- Calories: 266 calories;
- Total Fat: 9.3
- Sodium: 136
- Total Carbohydrate: 44.4
- Cholesterol: 4
- Protein: 1.5

---

174. Fresh Peach Pie II

Serving: 16 | Prep: 20mins | Cook: 15mins | Ready in:

Ingredients

- 1 1/2 cups white sugar
- 1/4 cup cornstarch
- 2 cups water
- 1 (3 ounce) package peach flavored Jell-O® mix
- 4 cups fresh peaches - peeled, pitted, and sliced
- 2 (9 inch) pie shells, baked

Direction

- Mix cornstarch and sugar in a saucepan over medium heat. Pour in water and bring to a boil. Keep boiling for 3 minutes, mixing constantly. Mix in the peach gelatin mix. Take away from heat and let it cool.
- Mix the gelatin mixture with the chopped peaches in a large bowl. Slowly mix until peach pieces are coated with gelatin. Put into baked pie crusts. Chill until firm.

Nutrition Information

- Calories: 226 calories;

- Cholesterol: 0
- Protein: 1.9
- Total Fat: 7.8
- Sodium: 143
- Total Carbohydrate: 37.8

---

175. Fruity Tart

Serving: 8 | Prep: 20mins | Cook: 20mins | Ready in:

Ingredients

- 1 (9 inch) pie crust, baked
- 1 (4.6 ounce) package non-instant vanilla pudding mix
- 3 cups milk
- 1/2 cup fresh strawberries, sliced
- 1/2 cup fresh blueberries
- 1 cup fresh peaches, pitted and sliced
- 1/2 cup fresh raspberries
- 1 cup kiwi, sliced
- 1/4 cup any flavor fruit jam

Direction

- In a medium saucepan, mix milk and pudding mix. Cook it following package directions. Put pudding into pastry shell and place in the fridge until set and cool. Place the fruit on top of the pudding layer.
- Into a small saucepan over low heat, pour jam, mixing from time to time until the runny. Coat fruit with jam using a pastry brush. Now save the whole pie for yourself.

Nutrition Information

- Calories: 245 calories;
- Cholesterol: 7
- Protein: 4.3
- Total Fat: 7.3
- Sodium: 265
- Total Carbohydrate: 41.2

176. Georgia Peach Pie

Serving: 8 | Prep: 10mins | Cook: 30mins | Ready in:

Ingredients

- 3 egg whites
- 1 cup white sugar
- 14 saltine crackers, finely crushed
- 1 teaspoon vanilla extract
- 1/4 teaspoon baking powder
- 1/2 cup chopped pecans
- 7 fresh peaches - peeled, pitted, and sliced
- 2 cups sweetened whipped cream

Direction

- Preheat oven to 165 degrees C/325 degrees F.
- In a metal bowl or big glass, whip egg whites until they hold a peak. Sprinkle sugar in gradually while whipping egg whites to make stiff peaks. Fold in pecans, baking powder, vanilla and saltines. Evenly spread in a 9-in. deep, ungreased pie plate.
- Bake in preheated oven for 30 minutes until an inserted skewer in the middle exits clean. Take out of oven. Cool. Crust puffs and cracks while it cools.
- When crust cools completely, put sliced peaches on it. Use aluminum foil to cover to protect the color before serving time. Top sweetened whipped cream on it prior to serving.

Nutrition Information

- Calories: 238 calories;
- Cholesterol: 11
- Protein: 3
- Total Fat: 9.3
- Sodium: 115
- Total Carbohydrate: 37.1

177. Gingersnap Fresh Peach Pie

Serving: 10 | Prep: 30mins | Cook: 45mins | Ready in:

Ingredients

- 1/3 cup butter, melted
- 40 gingersnap cookies, crushed
- 3 fresh peaches - peeled, pitted, and mashed
- 1/4 cup all-purpose flour
- 2 tablespoons brown sugar
- 1/2 teaspoon ground cinnamon
- 1/2 teaspoon ground nutmeg
- 4 fresh peaches - peeled, pitted, and sliced
- 1/4 teaspoon lemon juice
- 1 1/2 tablespoons butter, melted
- 1/3 cup white sugar

Direction

- Set oven to preheat at 350°F (175°C).
- Mix 1/3 cup butter and gingersnaps in a bowl; pat the cookie mixture into a 9-inch baking dish to form a crust.
- Stir the mashed peaches together with nutmeg, brown sugar, cinnamon, and flour in a large bowl until thoroughly incorporated. Fold sliced peaches and lemon used gently into the mashed peach mixture. Transfer the peaches into the prepared crust, press the peaches down lightly.
- In the preheated oven, bake till bubbly, for about 40 minutes. Stir together the white sugar and 1 1/2 tablespoons butter in a small bowl; drizzle the butter syrup onto the peach filling.
- Set the oven's broiler to preheat.
- Take the pie back into the oven and broil till the syrup caramelizes, for about 5 to 10 minutes. Let the pie cool down before serving.

Nutrition Information

- Calories: 252 calories;
- Cholesterol: 21
- Protein: 1.5
- Total Fat: 12.3

- Sodium: 154
- Total Carbohydrate: 34.5

---

178. Gluten Free Almond Mini Tarts

Serving: 6 | Prep: | Cook: | Ready in:

Ingredients

- Crust:
- 1/2 cup gluten-free oat flour
- 1/2 cup almond flour
- 1/4 cup tapioca flour
- 1 tablespoon granulated sugar
- 1/2 teaspoon kosher or fine sea salt
- 4 tablespoons chilled unsalted butter, cut into 1/2-inch cubes
- 1/4 cup Mott's® Cinnamon Applesauce
- Filling:
- 1 large egg
- 1/2 cup gluten-free almond paste, broken into bite-size pieces
- 1/4 cup Mott's® Cinnamon Applesauce
- 1 tablespoon gluten-free oat flour
- 1 tablespoon powdered sugar
- 2 medium peaches
- 1 tablespoon apricot jam or other light-colored jam

Direction

- Preheat oven to 400°F.
- For making crust: Process together salt, sugar, tapioca flour, almond flour and oat flour in the food processor for 5 seconds to blend.
- Put in cubed butter and process till the moist and crumbly dough begins to form, about 8 to 10 additional times. Put in applesauce and blend till forming the soft dough.
- Split dough into 6 even portions and use fingers to press dough into 6 mini tart pans or a 9-in. tart pan in case no mini shell is available, ensure dough rises a bit above edges of each of the pans.

- Add tarts to the rimmed baking sheet and keep frozen for 15 minutes while oven heats.
- Bake tarts for 10 minutes, till they begin to brown at edges. Take out of oven and let crusts cool down to the room temperature.
- Lower the oven heat to 375°F.
- For making the filling: Whip together applesauce, almond paste and egg using the electric hand mixer on medium low speed till becoming smooth.
- Put in powdered sugar and oat flour and then whip on the low speed to blend completely.
- Split almond custard equally among cooled tart crusts.
- Pit and cut peaches into a-quarter-inch thick half-moons and fan slices of the peach across each tart crust. Stir 1 tbsp. of the water and jam to have the glaze. Brush peaches with glaze, using the pastry brush. Bring tarts back to oven and bake till custard becomes matte and puffy at edges, about 20 to 25 minutes longer. Serve right away.

Nutrition Information

- Calories: 332 calories;
- Total Fat: 19.9
- Sodium: 177
- Total Carbohydrate: 34.7
- Cholesterol: 51
- Protein: 6.4

---

179. Greg's Hot Peach Pie

Serving: 8 | Prep: 20mins | Cook: 50mins | Ready in:

Ingredients

- 1 1/2 cups all-purpose flour
- 1/2 teaspoon salt
- 9 tablespoons cold unsalted butter, cut into 1/4-inch cubes
- 3 tablespoons ice-cold peach nectar, or as needed

- 4 large fresh peaches - peeled, pitted and chopped
- 6 large fresh peaches - peeled, pitted, and sliced
- 3 habanero peppers, seeded and minced (wear gloves), or to taste
- 1/3 cup all-purpose flour
- 1 cup white sugar
- 1/4 cup unsalted butter, softened

Direction

- Briefly pulse salt and 1 1/2 cups flour 1-2 times to mix in a food processor's work bowl. Add 9 tbsp. chilled unsalted butter; pulse 4-5 times, several seconds each time, till it looks like coarse crumbs. 1 tbsp. at a time, drizzle peach nectar into dough till dough gathers itself to crumbly mass as machine runs. Put dough into bowl; shape to ball. Wrap in plastic wrap and refrigerate for 30 minutes to hydrate dough.
- Preheat an oven to 175°C/350°F.
- Pulse 4 chopped peaches to puree for 1 minute in the food processor. 1 tsp. at a time, add minced habanero peppers; puree till smooth. Put leftover 6 sliced peaches in bowl; lightly toss with habanero puree.
- Mix 1/4 cup softened unsalted butter, white sugar and 1/3 cup flour till it makes a crumbly mixture in a bowl; put aside streusel.
- Halve dough; roll every half to 10-in. diameter circle. Fit 1 dough circle in 9-in. pie dish. Put peach-habanero filing on bottom pie crust; sprinkle crumble sugar streusel. Onto pie, fit top crust; to seal edges, crimp with a fork. Cut few slices on top crust to vent steam.
- In preheated oven, bake for 50 minutes till filling is thick and bubbly and crust is golden brown.

Nutrition Information

- Calories: 412 calories;
- Protein: 3.3
- Total Fat: 19
- Sodium: 156

- Total Carbohydrate: 57.9
- Cholesterol: 50

---

180. Honey Peach Pie

Serving: 8 | Prep: 20mins | Cook: 1hours |Ready in:

Ingredients

- 6 fresh peaches - peeled, pitted and sliced into thin wedges
- 1/4 cup honey
- 2 fluid ounces peach schnapps, or more to taste
- 1 cup white sugar
- 1 teaspoon ground cinnamon
- 2 tablespoons all-purpose flour
- 2 prepared pie crusts

Direction

- Bring peach schnapps, honey and peaches to a saucepan on medium heat, then cook, occasionally mixing, for about 8 minutes till thickens and peaches soften; mix in cinnamon and sugar till combined. Mix in flour; bring to a simmer. Simmer for 10-15 minutes till flour thickens the filling. Take off heat; put filling into container. Refrigerate for 4 hours – overnight.
- Preheat an oven to 220°C/425°F.
- Into 9 1/2-in. pie pan, stretch out bottom pie crust; cut the other crust to 1-in. wide strips. Evenly spread peach filling on bottom crust; create a lattice crust from strips, weaving strips over and under each other. At both ends, pinch strips to bottom crust.
- In preheated oven, bake pie for about 15 minutes; remove. Use foil strips to cover crust edges. Put into oven; bake for about 30 minutes till top crust turns golden brown. Cool for a minimum of 2 hours on wire rack to set. Serve.

Nutrition Information

- Calories: 344 calories;
- Cholesterol: 0
- Protein: 1.7
- Total Fat: 10.4
- Sodium: 208
- Total Carbohydrate: 58.9

181.   Jump Rope Pie

Serving: 8 | Prep: 30mins | Cook: 50mins | Ready in:

Ingredients

- 1 recipe pastry for a double crust 9-inch pie
- 1 cup white sugar
- 3 tablespoons all-purpose flour, or more as needed
- 1/2 teaspoon ground cinnamon
- 1 pinch freshly grated nutmeg
- 2 cups peeled, cored and sliced apples
- 1 cup peeled, pitted and sliced peaches
- 1 cup peeled, cored and sliced pears
- 1 cup pitted and sliced plums
- 1 teaspoon grated fresh ginger root
- 1 tablespoon lemon juice

Direction

- Preheat an oven to 220 °C or 425 °F. Line pastry on a pie plate, 9-inch in size.
- In a small bowl, beat nutmeg, cinnamon, flour and sugar together; in pie plate, scatter a quarter cup sugar mixture on top of pastry.
- In a bowl, mix ginger, plums, pears, peaches and apples together; drizzle with lemon juice and mix to distribute. In pie plate, put the fruit mixture; scatter the rest of sugar mixture on top. Top with pastry to cover, pinch to seal bottom and top crusts together and using a sharp knife, slice several slits on the surface of pastry. Or, top with lattice crust to cover.
- In the prepped oven, bake for 15 minutes; lower temperature to 180 °C or 350 °F and

keep baking for 35 minutes till filling has thickened and crust turn golden. Cool fully prior to serving.

Nutrition Information

- Calories: 376 calories;
- Total Fat: 15.1
- Sodium: 235
- Total Carbohydrate: 58.4
- Cholesterol: 0
- Protein: 3.4

182.   No Skill Fruit Tart

Serving: 6 | Prep: 15mins | Cook: 30mins | Ready in:

Ingredients

- 2 cups all-purpose flour
- 1/2 teaspoon salt
- 1 cup shortening
- 1/2 cup cold water
- 3 tablespoons sugar
- 2 tablespoons cornstarch
- 2 cups sliced fresh peaches
- 1 cup fresh blackberries

Direction

- Preheat the oven to 450° F (220° C).
- In a medium bowl, stir salt and flour together. Rub between your fingers to cut in shortening till the mixture looks like oatmeal. Slowly mix in water till the dough just gets wet enough to hold together. Briefly knead just for the dough to hold together without crumbling. Arrange in the refrigerator while making the fruit.
- In a medium bowl, stir cornstarch and sugar together. Put in the blackberries and peaches, then gently toss to coat. Leave aside.
- Roll the crust dough out into a rough circle with a dinner plate size, then set on a flat baking sheet. Make a level mound by piling

fruit in the middle of the dough, keeping 1 to 2 inches of exposed dough around the edge. Discard any possible accumulated juices in the fruit bowl. Fold up the dough over the fruit - cover the edge over some berries and fruit, but do not reach the middle of the tart.

- In the preheated oven, bake for 25 to 30 minutes till the fruit becomes bubbly and the crust turns golden brown. Before cutting into wedges, allow to cool completely then serve.

Nutrition Information

- Calories: 509 calories;
- Total Fat: 34.7
- Sodium: 197
- Total Carbohydrate: 45.4
- Cholesterol: 0
- Protein: 4.7

183. Old Fashioned Peach Cream Pie

Serving: 8 | Prep: 20mins | Cook: 55mins | Ready in:

Ingredients

- 3/4 cup white sugar
- 2 tablespoons all-purpose flour
- 1/4 teaspoon salt
- 1 cup sour cream
- 1 egg, lightly beaten
- 1/2 teaspoon vanilla extract
- 2 cups sliced peaches
- 1 unbaked pie crust
- 1/3 cup all-purpose flour
- 1/3 cup white sugar
- 1 teaspoon ground cinnamon
- 1/4 cup butter, softened

Direction

- Set oven to 400°F (200°C).

- Beat together salt, the 2 tablespoons flour, and 3/4 cup sugar. Whip in the vanilla, egg, and sour cream. Mix in the peach slices. Add the mixture to the pie shell.
- Bake in the heated oven for 12 minutes. Turn down the oven temperature to 350°F (175°C) and keep baking about for 30 minutes until the filling is firm. Take it out of the oven.
- Turn up oven temperature to 400°F (200°C).
- In a small bowl, whip the cinnamon, 1/3 cup sugar, and 1/3 cup flour. Stir in the butter using a fork until mixture forms coarse crumbs. Scatter the crumb topping on top of the pie evenly.
- Put back the pie to the prepared oven and bake for about 10 minutes until golden on top. Let pie slightly cool before cutting.

Nutrition Information

- Calories: 376 calories;
- Total Fat: 19.9
- Sodium: 256
- Total Carbohydrate: 46.3
- Cholesterol: 51
- Protein: 3.9

184. Pamela's Peachy Meringue Tart

Serving: 8 | Prep: 45mins | Cook: 1hours30mins | Ready in:

Ingredients

- 1/4 cup egg whites
- 1/4 cup white sugar
- 1/4 cup sifted confectioners' sugar
- 10 peaches, peeled and cut into chunks
- 1 pinch ground cinnamon
- 1 cup heavy cream
- 1/2 teaspoon confectioners' sugar
- 1 teaspoon vanilla extract

Direction

- Turn on the oven to 300°F (150°C) to preheat. On a piece of parchment or wax paper, use pencil to draw a 9-inch circle. On a baking sheet, arrange the paper, pencil-side down. Use sugar and butter to grease the paper.
- In a large metal or glass mixing bowl, beat egg whites until it becomes foamy. Beat in white sugar gradually until it forms stiff peaks. The egg whites should hold its shape of a sharp peak when the whisk or beater is lifted straight up. Use the spatula to run through the center of the bowl and around the sides gently to fold in 1/4 cup of confectioners' sugar, repeating until well-blended.
- In a large pastry bag fitted with a 1/2-inch tip, add egg white mixture. On the paper, pipe a disk of 1/4-inch thickness inside the circle. Use a knife to smooth the meringue; create a wall by piping another layer along the outside of the disk.
- Put into the oven to bake for 1 1/2 hours for the meringue to be dry completely. Remove meringue shell onto a large plate.
- Collect peach juice by draining the cut peaches through a strainer set over a bowl. Use cinnamon to sprinkle onto the peach juices. In another bowl, add drained peaches. In a large metal or glass mixing bowl, beat heavy cream until it is foamy. Beat in vanilla extract and 1/2 teaspoon of confectioners' sugar until it forms stiff peaks. The whipped cream should hold its shape of a sharp peak when the whisk or beater is lifted straight up. On meringue shell, spread a thick layer of whipped cream. Top whipped cream with peach chunks; use peach juice to drizzle on top. Use more whipped cream to garnish. Ready for immediate serving.

Nutrition Information

- Calories: 179 calories;
- Total Fat: 11
- Sodium: 29
- Total Carbohydrate: 18.8
- Cholesterol: 41
- Protein: 1.5

185.   Peach Cream Pie I

Serving: 8 | Prep: | Cook: | Ready in:

Ingredients

- 1 cup white sugar
- 1/3 cup butter
- 1/3 cup all-purpose flour
- 1 egg
- 1 teaspoon vanilla extract
- 3 cups fresh peaches - pitted, skinned, and sliced
- 1 recipe pastry for a 9 inch single crust pie

Direction

- Prepare a crust-lined 9" pie pan. Set peaches in unbaked pie shell.
- Beat margarine (or butter) with sugar. Put in vanilla, flour and egg; blend thoroughly. Lather onto the top of the peaches.
- Bake for 60 minutes at 150°C (300°F).

Nutrition Information

- Calories: 320 calories;
- Total Carbohydrate: 42.3
- Cholesterol: 44
- Protein: 2.8
- Total Fat: 15.8
- Sodium: 182

186.   Peach Custard Pie I

Serving: 8 | Prep: | Cook: | Ready in:

Ingredients

- 6 fresh peaches - pitted, skinned, and sliced
- 1 (9 inch) pie shell
- 1/2 cup white sugar
- 1 tablespoon all-purpose flour
- 1 pinch salt
- 1 pinch ground cinnamon
- 1 egg

Direction

- Set oven to preheat at 400°F (200°C).
- Place the sliced peaches in an unbaked pastry shell.
- In a medium bowl, combine sugar, flour, salt, cinnamon and egg. Beat well and pour over peaches.
- Bake on bottom rack at 400°F (200°C) for approximately 30 minutes.

Nutrition Information

- Calories: 161 calories;
- Protein: 1.6
- Total Fat: 5.8
- Sodium: 114
- Total Carbohydrate: 25.7
- Cholesterol: 23

187.   Peach Custard Pie III

Serving: 8 | Prep: | Cook: | Ready in:

Ingredients

- 1 (9 inch) pie shell
- 3 tablespoons all-purpose flour
- 3 tablespoons brown sugar
- 5 large fresh peaches - peeled, pitted and halved
- 1 1/2 cups evaporated milk
- 1 egg, beaten
- 2/3 cup white sugar
- 2 tablespoons all-purpose flour
- 2 teaspoons ground cinnamon

- 1/4 teaspoon ground nutmeg

Direction

- Heat the oven to 220 ° C or 425 ° F to preheat.
- Stir brown sugar and three tablespoons of flour in a small bowl. Scatter the mixture into the bottom of pie pan lined with pastry. Place halves of peach over the mixture with cut side facing up.
- Whip egg and evaporated milk in medium-sized bowl. Transfer the mixture on top of peaches.
- Stir nutmeg, cinnamon, 2 tablespoons of the flour and white sugar in medium-sized bowl. Scatter top of peaches with mixture.
- Bake about half an hour in prepped oven, till an inserted knife an-inch from edge exits clean.

Nutrition Information

- Calories: 278 calories;
- Sodium: 166
- Total Carbohydrate: 43.5
- Cholesterol: 37
- Protein: 5.3
- Total Fat: 9.5

188.   Peach Finger Pie

Serving: 12 | Prep: 30mins | Cook: 45mins | Ready in:

Ingredients

- 4 cups all-purpose flour
- 2 tablespoons white sugar
- 1 pinch salt
- 1 1/2 cups vegetable shortening
- 1 egg
- cold water, or as needed
- 1 1/4 cups water, divided
- 1/4 cup cornstarch
- 3/4 cup white sugar

- 1/4 teaspoon salt (optional)
- 1 tablespoon lemon juice (optional)
- 4 cups fresh peaches - peeled, pitted, and sliced

Direction

- Mix pinch salt, 2 tbsp. sugar and flour in big bowl; cut shortening into flour mixture till it looks like coarse crumbs. Beat egg in small bowl; put in 1-cup measuring cup. Put enough cold water in to get 1 cup; mix egg and water into dough. Use your fingers to mix dough several times until it holds together; halve dough.
- Preheat an oven to 175°C/350°F.
- Whisk cornstarch and 3/4 cup water till smooth in bowl; put aside. Boil and mix 3/4 cup sugar and 1/2 cup water in big saucepan till sugar dissolves; whisk cornstarch mixture into boiling water, constantly whisking, for 1 minute till translucent and thick. Whisk lemon juice (optional) and 1/4 tsp. salt in; mix with sliced peaches.
- Roll 1/2 crust out to 12x20-in. rectangle on floured surface; fit pastry to 10x15-in. jellyroll pan. Roll 2nd crust half out to same size as 1st crust. Put peach filling in bottom curst; put top crust over pie. Crimp then fold edges to seal; slice several slits in top crust.
- In preheated oven, bake for 45-60 minutes till filling is bubbly and crust is browned. Completely cool to let filling set up. Slice to squares; serve.

Nutrition Information

- Calories: 462 calories;
- Total Carbohydrate: 51.6
- Cholesterol: 16
- Protein: 4.9
- Total Fat: 26.4
- Sodium: 58

189. Peach Pie

Serving: 8 | Prep: 1hours | Cook: 45mins | Ready in:

Ingredients

- 10 fresh peaches, pitted and sliced
- 1/3 cup all-purpose flour
- 1 cup white sugar
- 1/4 cup butter
- 1 recipe pastry for a 9 inch double crust pie

Direction

- Combine butter, sugar, and flour together until crumbly.
- At the base of a 9-in pie plate, put in 1 crust then line the shell with some peach slices; top with some of the butter mixture. Place more peach slices over the crumb mixture. Keep on layering until all the crumbs and peaches are gone.
- On the very top, place lattice strips of pie crust.
- Bake for 45mins in a 175°C or 350°Fahrenheit oven until the crust is golden. Let the pie cool then slice. Best served fresh.

Nutrition Information

- Calories: 425 calories;
- Total Fat: 20.7
- Sodium: 280
- Total Carbohydrate: 57
- Cholesterol: 15
- Protein: 3.4

190. Peach Pie The Old Fashioned Two Crust Way

Serving: 8 | Prep: 30mins | Cook: 45mins | Ready in:

Ingredients

- 1 (15 ounce) package pastry for a 9 inch double crust pie
- 1 egg, beaten
- 5 cups sliced peeled peaches
- 2 tablespoons lemon juice
- 1/2 cup all-purpose flour
- 1 cup white sugar
- 1/2 teaspoon ground cinnamon
- 1/4 teaspoon ground nutmeg
- 1/4 teaspoon salt
- 2 tablespoons butter

Direction

- Set the oven to 220°C or 450°F to preheat.
- Use one of pipe crusts to line the bottom and sides of a 9-in. pie plate, then use some of beaten egg to brush crusts to prevent dough from becoming soggy later.
- In a big bowl, add sliced peaches and sprinkle lemon juice over top and gently combine. Combine together salt, nutmeg, cinnamon, sugar and flour in a separate bowl. Drizzle mixture over peaches and blend gently. Transfer to the pie crust and dot with butter. Use the other pie crust to cover and fold edges under. Flute edges to seal or use the tines of a fork dipped in egg to press the edges. Brush top crust with leftover egg, then cut some slits in the top of crust to vent steam.
- In the preheated oven, bake about 10 minutes, then lower oven temperature to 175° or 350°F to bake about 30-35 minutes longer, until juice starts to bubble through the vents and crust turns brown. Use strips of aluminum foil to cover edges about halfway through baking in case edges is browned too quickly. Allow to cool prior to serving. Cake tastes better warm than hot.

Nutrition Information

- Calories: 428 calories;
- Total Fat: 19.8
- Sodium: 358
- Total Carbohydrate: 58.6
- Cholesterol: 31

- Protein: 4.7

191.   Peach Pie With Sour Cream

Serving: 8 | Prep: 20mins | Cook: 1hours15mins | Ready in:

Ingredients

- 1 1/4 cups all-purpose flour
- 1/2 cup butter, cut into chunks
- 1/2 teaspoon salt
- 2 tablespoons sour cream
- 4 fresh peaches - peeled, pitted, and sliced
- 3 egg yolks
- 2 tablespoons all-purpose flour
- 1/3 cup sour cream
- 1 cup white sugar

Direction

- Set the oven at 425°F (220°C) and start preheating. Coat a 9-in. pie dish with butter.
- In a food processor, place 2 tablespoons of sour cream, salt, butter and 1 1/4 cups of flour; pulse till the mixture comes together into a large ball. Press the dough into the prepared pie dish to make a crust.
- Bake in the preheated oven for around 10 minutes, till golden brown. Take the pie crust out of the oven.
- Turn the oven heat down to 350°F (175°C). Place peach slices into the pie crust.
- In a large bowl, beat egg yolks lightly. Put in 2 tablespoons of flour, 1/3 cup of sour cream and sugar; mix till well combined. Transfer the egg mixture on top of the peaches. Use aluminum foil to cover the pie.
- Bake for 50 minutes in the preheated oven; take the foil away. Keep baking for around 15 more minutes, till the peach filling is set.

Nutrition Information

- Calories: 337 calories;
- Total Fat: 16.1
- Sodium: 239
- Total Carbohydrate: 45.2
- Cholesterol: 113
- Protein: 3.8

192.   Peach Surprise Pie

Serving: 8 | Prep: 15mins | Cook: | Ready in:

Ingredients

- 1 (9 inch) pie crust, baked
- 2 (8 ounce) packages cream cheese, softened
- 1/4 cup white sugar
- 1/2 teaspoon vanilla extract
- 2 cups sliced peaches, drained
- 1/4 cup raspberry preserves
- 1 teaspoon lemon juice

Direction

- In a medium mixing bowl put vanilla extract, sugar and softened cream cheese together then mix. Combine until smooth. Spread the mixture onto bottom of baked pie shell. Let it chill overnight or for a few hours.
- Before serving, use drained peach slices to top cream cheese layer. Put lemon juice and raspberry preserves together and mix until everything is well mixed. Transfer on peaches. Use mint sprigs to garnish.

Nutrition Information

- Calories: 356 calories;
- Total Fat: 24.7
- Sodium: 270
- Total Carbohydrate: 29.8
- Cholesterol: 62
- Protein: 5.3

193.   Peach Tartlets With Apricot Glaze

Serving: 18 | Prep: 10mins | Cook: 12mins | Ready in:

Ingredients

- 1 (17.3 ounce) package frozen puff pastry, thawed
- 3/4 cup apricot preserves, divided
- 2 peaches - peeled, pitted, and thinly sliced, or more as needed
- 2 teaspoons hot water, or as needed

Direction

- Preheat the oven to 200 degrees C (400 degrees F). Use the parchment paper to line 2 baking sheets.
- Chop each sheet of the puff pastry into nine 3-in. squares. Dab a little of the apricot preserves to middle of each square. Fan 3 peach slices on top of the preserves, leaving a slim border of the pastry exposed. Scoop a little amount of the apricot preserves on top of slices of peach.
- Bake in the preheated oven, one baking sheet at a time, for roughly 10 minutes or till the puff pastry is golden.
- Thin the rest of apricot preserves with 2 teaspoons of hot water in the small-sized bowl to make a glaze.
- Scoop some glaze on top of each of the baked tartlet. Bring back to the oven and bake for roughly 2 minutes longer or till the tartlets turn golden brown. Repeat the process with the second baking sheet. Let the tartlets cool down on the wire rack prior to serving, for roughly 10 minutes.

Nutrition Information

- Calories: 185 calories;
- Total Carbohydrate: 21.5
- Cholesterol: 0
- Protein: 2.1

- Total Fat: 10.4
- Sodium: 74

194. Peach And Cream Cheese Torte

Serving: 8 | Prep: 25mins | Cook: 35mins | Ready in:

Ingredients

- 1/2 cup butter
- 1/3 cup white sugar
- 3/4 cup all-purpose flour
- 2/3 cup chopped pecans
- 1/2 teaspoon vanilla extract
- 1 (8 ounce) package cream cheese
- 1 egg
- 1/4 teaspoon almond extract
- 1/4 cup white sugar
- 1/2 teaspoon vanilla extract
- 1 (28 ounce) can peach slices, drained
- 1/2 teaspoon ground cinnamon

Direction

- Start preheating the oven to 450°F (230°C).
- Making the crust: In a bowl, mix half teaspoon of the vanilla extract, pecans, flour, 1/3 cup of the sugar and butter. Press into bottom of the 10-in. pie plate.
- Bake crust in the prepared oven 5 mins. Discard and let cool.
- In the meantime, in a bowl, beat half teaspoon of vanilla extract, a quarter cup of sugar, almond extract, egg and cream cheese, until they become smooth. Fold peach slices gently into cream cheese mixture. Spread cooled crust with filling over. Sprinkle top with cinnamon.
- Bake for 10 mins in the preheated oven. Lower the heat to 325°F (165°C) and keep cooking for another 20-25 mins.

Nutrition Information

- Calories: 422 calories;
- Cholesterol: 85
- Protein: 5.8
- Total Fat: 29.2
- Sodium: 178
- Total Carbohydrate: 37.4

195. Peach A Berry Pie

Serving: 8 | Prep: 25mins | Cook: 45mins | Ready in:

Ingredients

- 4 cups fresh peaches - peeled, pitted, and sliced
- 1 cup fresh raspberries
- 3/4 cup white sugar
- 3 tablespoons all-purpose flour
- 1 teaspoon ground cinnamon
- 2 (9 inch) pie crusts
- 2 tablespoons butter, softened and cut into pieces
- 1 tablespoon coarse granulated sugar

Direction

- Preheat an oven to 200°C/400°F.
- Drain extra fluid by putting berries and peaches in a colander for about 15 minutes; put into big bowl. Toss with cinnamon, flour and sugar gently; put into pie crust. Use butter to dot over; top with leftover crust. Cut vents into top crust; sprinkle coarse sugar over.
- In preheated oven, bake till crust is golden brown, 45 minutes.

Nutrition Information

- Calories: 301 calories;
- Total Fat: 13.4
- Sodium: 228
- Total Carbohydrate: 44.1
- Cholesterol: 8
- Protein: 1.9

196. Peaches 'n Cream Pie

Serving: 8 | Prep: | Cook: |Ready in:

Ingredients

- 3/4 cup all-purpose flour
- 1 (3 ounce) package non-instant vanilla pudding mix
- 3 tablespoons butter
- 1 egg
- 1/2 cup milk
- 2 1/2 cups canned sliced peaches, syrup reserved
- 1 (8 ounce) package cream cheese
- 1/2 cup white sugar
- 1 tablespoon white sugar
- 1 teaspoon ground cinnamon

Direction

- Preheat an oven to 175°C/350°F. Drain peaches; reserve syrup. Put aside.
- Mix together milk, egg, margarine, pudding mix and flour, beating well; put into 8-in. or 9-in. greased pie pan. Put drained peaches over mixture, just to the edges.
- Cream 3 tbsp. reserved peach syrup, sugar and softened cream cheese; put over peaches carefully, just to edges. Sprinkle cinnamon and sugar over.
- Bake at 175°C/350°F for 30-35 minutes; don't over bake.

Nutrition Information

- Calories: 353 calories;
- Cholesterol: 67
- Protein: 5.3
- Total Fat: 15.2
- Sodium: 214
- Total Carbohydrate: 49.6

197. Peaches And Cream Pie II

Serving: 24 | Prep: 45mins | Cook: |Ready in:

Ingredients

- 1 1/2 cups all-purpose flour
- 3/4 cup butter, softened
- 3/4 cup chopped pecans
- 1 tablespoon white sugar
- 1 (8 ounce) package cream cheese, softened
- 2 cups frozen whipped topping, thawed
- 1 cup confectioners' sugar
- 1 1/2 cups white sugar
- 4 tablespoons cornstarch
- 3 cups warm water
- 2 (3 ounce) packages peach flavored Jell-O® mix
- 5 fresh peaches - peeled, pitted, and sliced
- 1 (12 ounce) container frozen whipped topping, thawed

Direction

- Heat an oven to 175 ° C or 350 ° F. Oil a 9x13 inch baking pan lightly.
- Stir 1 tablespoon sugar, pecans, butter, and flour in a medium-sized bowl. Force the mixture in baking pan's bottom.
- Bake about 15 minutes in prepped oven. Take out of oven; cool down.
- Whip confectioners' sugar and cream cheese in a big bowl till smooth. Mix in 2 cups of whipped topping gently. Spread onto the cooled crust. Mix cornstarch and 1 1/2 cups of sugar in a small-sized bowl. Transfer the sugar mixture into a saucepan; mix in three cups of water. Cook on medium heat, mixing often till thick and clear. Mix in gelatin; take off from the heat.
- Mix peaches and gelatin mixture. Spread on top of the cream cheese layer with the entire mixture. Put 12 ounces container of whipped topping on top. Chill with cover about 1 hour.

Nutrition Information

- Calories: 296 calories;
- Sodium: 96
- Total Carbohydrate: 37.7
- Cholesterol: 26
- Protein: 2.5
- Total Fat: 14.8

198.   Quick And Easy Peach Pie Egg Rolls With Raspberry Sauce

Serving: 6 | Prep: 25mins | Cook: 20mins | Ready in:

Ingredients

- 1 (21 ounce) can peach pie filling
- 1/2 teaspoon ground cinnamon
- 1/4 teaspoon ground allspice
- 1/4 teaspoon ground cloves
- 1/4 teaspoon ground ginger
- 1/4 teaspoon ground nutmeg
- 1/4 teaspoon pumpkin pie spice
- 1 pinch salt
- 12 egg roll wrappers
- 1 (8 ounce) package cream cheese, softened
- 1/2 cup water
- 1 quart canola oil for frying
- 1/2 cup raspberry jam
- 1 tablespoon honey
- 1 quart vanilla ice cream
- 1/4 cup confectioners' sugar

Direction

- Mix the peach pie filling, salt, pumpkin pie spice, nutmeg, cinnamon, ginger, cloves, and allspice in a large bowl.
- Use about 1 tablespoon cream cheese to spread one side of each egg roll wrapper. Apply 1 tablespoon of the pie filling mixture on the top of the cream cheese. Next, fold the wrappers

over the mixture. Wet the ends with a small amount of water, then seal up.

- In a large skillet, heat the oil over medium-high heat. Next, drop the egg rolls a few at a time into the hot oil and fry until golden brown. Let drain on paper towels.
- Mix the remaining water, honey, and raspberry jam in a bowl. If necessary, pour more water to achieve a syrup-like texture. Finally, serve the warm egg rolls over ice cream, put the raspberry jam mixture on top, and dust with confectioners' sugar.

Nutrition Information

- Calories: 675 calories;
- Sodium: 290
- Total Carbohydrate: 78.8
- Cholesterol: 81
- Protein: 8.6
- Total Fat: 37.7

199.   Raspberry Peach Pie

Serving: 8 | Prep: 15mins | Cook: 45mins | Ready in:

Ingredients

- 1 (10 ounce) package frozen unsweetened raspberries, thawed
- 1 (10 ounce) package frozen unsweetened sliced peaches
- 1 1/3 cups white sugar, divided
- 6 tablespoons all-purpose flour
- 1 prepared double pie crust

Direction

- Set an oven to 450°F (230°C) to preheat.
- In a big bowl, stir flour, 1 cup sugar, peaches and raspberries.
- Push 1 pie shell into a pie pan; pour fruit mixture into pie shell. Scatter leftover 1/3 cup sugar on top of fruit.

- Cut designs in the second pie shell using a cookie cutter and put pie crust on top of fruit. Crimp the edges of the top and bottom crusts together to seal.
- Bake for 10 minutes in the prepared oven. Turn down oven temperature to 375°F (190°C) and keep baking about for 35 minutes more until fruit filling is bubbly and shell is golden brown.

Nutrition Information

- Calories: 406 calories;
- Total Fat: 15
- Sodium: 234
- Total Carbohydrate: 65.3
- Cholesterol: 0
- Protein: 4.1

200.   Single Crust Peach Pie

Serving: 8 | Prep: 30mins | Cook: |Ready in:

Ingredients

- 3/4 cup white sugar
- 2 tablespoons butter, softened
- 1/3 cup all-purpose flour
- 1/4 teaspoon ground nutmeg
- 6 fresh peaches - pitted, skinned, and sliced
- 1 recipe pastry for a 9 inch single crust pie

Direction

- Cream butter/margarine and sugar together. Add nutmeg and flour. Stir until mealy. Spread half of mixture into pie crust. Put peaches on crumb mixture. Sprinkle leftover crumb mixture on top of peaches.
- Bake for 10 minutes at 230 degrees C/450 degrees F. Lower heat to 175 degrees C/350 degrees F. Bake until brown for 40 minutes.

Nutrition Information

- Calories: 250 calories;
- Protein: 2
- Total Fat: 10.4
- Sodium: 140
- Total Carbohydrate: 37.5
- Cholesterol: 8

201.   Sour Cream Peach Pie

Serving: 8 | Prep: 10mins | Cook: 55mins |Ready in:

Ingredients

- 3/4 cup sour cream
- 1/2 cup white sugar
- 1/3 cup all-purpose flour
- 1/4 teaspoon almond extract
- 1 tablespoon all-purpose flour
- 1 (9 inch) unbaked pie crust
- 4 cups sliced fresh or frozen peaches
- 1/4 cup brown sugar

Direction

- Set the oven to 425°F (220°C).
- Mix the almond extract, 1/3 cup flour, white sugar and sour cream in a medium bowl until smooth. Dust 1 tablespoon of flour on top of the pie shell to avoid it from getting soggy. Layer peaches and the sour cream mixture alternatively, starting with a layer of peaches and ending with a layer of sour cream.
- Bake in the prepared oven for 20 minutes. Turn down the heat to 350°F (175°C). Keep baking for 35 minutes more. Take out the pie from the oven and dust brown sugar on top. Set the oven to Broil, and broil for 2-3 minutes, until caramelized.

Nutrition Information

- Calories: 273 calories;
- Sodium: 133
- Total Carbohydrate: 39

- Cholesterol: 9
- Protein: 2.7
- Total Fat: 12.1

Chapter 7: Pear Pie Recipes

***

202.	Autumn Apple And Pear Lattice Pie

Serving: 8 | Prep: 40mins | Cook: 1hours | Ready in:

Ingredients

- Pastry:
- 2 1/2 cups flour
- 1 tablespoon sugar
- 1/4 teaspoon salt
- 3/4 cup cold butter, cut into small pieces
- 6 tablespoons cold shortening, cut into small pieces
- 8 tablespoons ice water, or as needed
- Filling:
- 1 cup sugar
- 3 tablespoons flour
- 3/4 teaspoon ground cinnamon
- 1/4 teaspoon ground ginger
- 1/4 teaspoon nutmeg
- 1/4 teaspoon salt
- 1 2/3 pounds Granny Smith apples - peeled, cored and cut into 1/4-inch-thick slices
- 1 2/3 pounds firm ripe Anjou pears - peeled, cored and cut into 1/4-inch-thick slices
- 1 egg yolk
- 2 teaspoons water
- 1 tablespoon butter, cut into bits
- 1 tablespoon white sugar

Direction

- In a big bowl, mix together 1/4 teaspoon salt, 1 tablespoon sugar and 2 1/2 cups flour. Using 2 knives or a pastry blender, cut butter into mixture until coarse and crumbly. Mix in ice water, a tablespoon at a time, to form dough into a ball. Split into halves and make two 5-in. disks by flattening each piece. Wrap with plastic and refrigerate for no less than one hour or overnight (maximum 8 hours).
- In a big bowl, mix together 1/4 teaspoon salt, nutmeg, ginger, cinnamon, three tablespoons flour and one cup sugar. Put in pears and apples; stir until evenly coated.
- Set oven to 220°C (425°F) and start preheating. Place 2 oven racks in the lower third of oven. Place a foil sheet a few inches bigger than pie plate on the bottom rack, in case any liquid drips off.
- On a surface lightly dusted with flour, use a floured rolling pin to roll out one dough portion into a 12-in. round of 1/8-in. thickness. Line pastry onto a 9-inch pie plate; use a paring knife or kitchen shears to trim overhang to half an inch. Repeat with the remaining dough and slice into 10 dough strips of 3/4 – 1 in. width to make lattice crust.
- Spread filling into pastry crust. Brush some of egg wash on the rim. Dot the filling with butter. In parallel paths, place 5 dough strips across the pie, laying 1 inch apart and allowing the excess to hang over the rim. Place the rest of dough strips diagonally across the pie to create right angles with the first 5 strips. Firmly press ends to the pie's rim, cutting off the excess. Using fork tines or finger, crimp the edges. Brush remaining egg wash on top. Scatter the remaining tablespoon sugar over the crust.
- Bake on the lower third rack in preheated oven for 15 minutes; lower temperature to 190°C (375°F) and bake for 45 minutes longer, until liquid in the middle of the pie bubbles. (Use a sheet of foil to cover loosely to prevent overbrowning). Place on a wire rack for 2 hours to cool.

Nutrition Information

- Calories: 616 calories;
- Total Fat: 29.4
- Sodium: 282
- Total Carbohydrate: 86.9
- Cholesterol: 75
- Protein: 5.5

---

203. Autumn Spiced Apple And Pear Hand Pies

Serving: 16 | Prep: 1hours | Cook: 30mins | Ready in:

Ingredients

- 1 large Pink Lady apple - peeled, cored and diced
- 1 large Bartlett pear - peeled, cored and diced
- 1/4 cup brown sugar
- 1 tablespoon vanilla extract
- 2 teaspoons cornstarch
- 1 teaspoon ground cinnamon
- 1/2 teaspoon ground nutmeg
- 1/4 teaspoon ground cloves
- 1 pinch salt
- 1 egg
- 1 tablespoon water
- 1 recipe pastry for a 9-inch double crust pie
- 2 tablespoons coarse granulated sugar, or as needed (optional)
- 1/2 cup dark chocolate chips (optional)

Direction

- Set oven at 200°C (400°F) and start preheating. Use parchment paper to line a baking tray.
- In a bowl, combine salt, cloves, nutmeg, cinnamon, cornstarch, vanilla extract, brown sugar, pear and apple. In a small bowl, beat egg with water.
- Take the pastry to a light-floured surface, roll it out and use a 3-to 4-inch round cookie cutter to divide it into circles. Add a little of the apple mixture on the centre of each circle, foil it into half and press to seal the edges tightly. If preferred, use a fork to crimp. Put the pies on the prepared baking tray.
- Slit 3 small vents in the top of each hand pie using a sharp knife. Brush the egg mixture on top of the pies, dredge decorating sugar on top.
- Put them in the preheated oven and bake for about 25 minutes until the pies turn light golden. Let cool for 20 minutes to room temperature.
- Add chocolate chips to a microwave-safe ceramic or a glass bowl, put in a microwave and melt in 15-second intervals for 1 to 2 minutes, stirring after each interval. Drizzle melted chocolate on top of the pies.

Nutrition Information

- Calories: 125 calories;
- Total Carbohydrate: 18.1
- Cholesterol: 12
- Protein: 1.5
- Total Fat: 5.5
- Sodium: 75

---

204. Bartlett Pear Pie

Serving: 8 | Prep: 20mins | Cook: 30mins | Ready in:

Ingredients

- 1 (9 inch) pie crust pastry
- 1/2 cup unsalted butter, softened
- 1/2 cup white sugar
- 1/4 cup brown sugar
- 1 1/2 tablespoons all-purpose flour
- 1 teaspoon ground nutmeg
- 1/2 teaspoon ground allspice
- 1/4 teaspoon salt
- 1 pinch ground cinnamon
- 2 eggs

- 5 Bartlett pears, peeled and chopped

Direction

- Set oven to 375°F (190°C) to preheat. Push pie shell pastry into a 9-inch pie pan and chill while making filling.
- In a bowl, whip cinnamon, salt, allspice, nutmeg, flour, brown sugar, white sugar and butter with an electric mixer until smooth. Whip eggs, one by one, into butter mixture until combined; fold in pears. Add filling to cold shell.
- Bake 30 to 35 minutes in the prepared oven until filling is firm in the middle. Let cool completely about 1 hour before serving.

Nutrition Information

- Calories: 377 calories;
- Cholesterol: 77
- Protein: 3.7
- Total Fat: 20.5
- Sodium: 212
- Total Carbohydrate: 47.4

---

205.   Cheddar Pear Pie

Serving: 6 | Prep: 20mins | Cook: 45mins |Ready in:

Ingredients

- FOR THE CRUMBLE
- 1/2 cup all-purpose flour
- 1/2 cup brown sugar
- 1/2 cup shredded Cheddar cheese
- 1/4 cup butter
- FOR THE PIE
- 6 cups peeled and sliced pears
- 1 tablespoon fresh lemon juice
- 1/2 cup brown sugar
- 3 tablespoons cornstarch
- 3/4 teaspoon ground cinnamon
- unbaked pie crust

Direction

- Set the oven to 400°F or 200°C for preheating.
- Mix the Cheddar cheese, flour, and 1/2 cup of brown sugar. Cut in butter until the mixture looks like coarse crumbs.
- Toss the sliced pears and lemon juice together. In a separate bowl, mix the cornstarch, cinnamon, and a 1/2 cup of brown sugar. Mix the sugar mixture into the pear mixture, tossing well to coat.
- Pour the pears into the pie crust. Place the crumble mixture on its top. Let it bake inside the preheated oven for 45 minutes until the top is golden brown.

Nutrition Information

- Calories: 547 calories;
- Total Fat: 21.1
- Sodium: 281
- Total Carbohydrate: 87.3
- Cholesterol: 30
- Protein: 6

---

206.   Coffee Dusted Pear Galette

Serving: 4 | Prep: 30mins | Cook: 20mins |Ready in:

Ingredients

- Crust:
- 1 1/2 cups all-purpose flour
- 1 1/2 teaspoons white granulated sugar
- 1 teaspoon fine sea salt
- 1/2 cup unsalted butter, frozen
- 7 tablespoons ice-cold water, or more as needed, divided
- 1 large egg, beaten (for egg wash)
- 1 tablespoon turbinado sugar
- Reynolds Wrap® Aluminum Foil
- Reynolds® Parchment Paper
- Filling:

- 2 Bartlett pears, cored and thinly sliced
- 1/4 cup brown sugar
- 1 teaspoon cocoa powder
- 1 tablespoon finely ground coffee beans
- 1/2 teaspoon vanilla extract
- 1 pinch salt
- Whipped cream or vanilla ice cream, for serving

Direction

- Combine salt, sugar and flour in a big bowl. Grate cold butter with a box grater onto the flour mixture. With your hands, work rapidly to break butter bits into flour mixture until they look like the size of small peas and evenly distributed.
- Put in 4 tablespoon water and stir. At this stage, mixture will be shaggy. Put in water, one tablespoon at a time until the dough comes together (usually it will take 3 more tablespoons). On a floured work surface, turn out the dough. Knead several times until it hold together. Shape the dough into a disk. Use plastic wrap to wrap and refrigerate for at least an hour or overnight at best.
- Right before taking the dough out of the refrigerator, combine the filling. Stir salt, vanilla extract, coffee grounds, cocoa powder, brown sugar and pear slices in a medium bowl.
- Take out the dough from the refrigerator and let sit for 10 minutes until reaching room temperature. Liberally flour a rolling pin and work surface. Start rolling dough into a 16-in. circle, rotating occasionally to prevent sticking. Cut out 3 circles of dough with a 6-in diameter bottom of a plate or bowl. Roll the excess again to make another circle.
- In the center of each of the pie crust rounds, put the pear slices neatly following a circular pattern, remember to leave about 1 1/2 inch clear at the edges. Cover about 1/2 inch of the filling by folding over the edges. Repeat with the rest of rounds. Line Reynolds(R) Parchment Paper on a baking sheet; transfer the galettes to the lined baking sheet. Let it

chill in the freezer for 15 minutes. In the meantime, set the oven to 400°F to preheat.
- Brush egg wash onto the edges of crusts and scatter turbinado sugar over. Bake for 20-25 minute in the prepared oven until golden brown on the edges. Periodically check on the galettes. Cover the edges with Reynolds Wrap(R) Aluminum Foil if starting to overbrown. Once galettes turn golden brown on the edges, take out of the oven. Add your favorite vanilla ice cream to serve or you can serve warm a scoop of whipped cream.

Nutrition Information

- Calories: 515 calories;
- Total Fat: 25
- Sodium: 509
- Total Carbohydrate: 67.3
- Cholesterol: 108
- Protein: 7.1

---

207.   Creamy Pear Pie

Serving: 8 | Prep: 20mins | Cook: 55mins | Ready in:

Ingredients

- 1/3 cup white sugar
- 2 tablespoons all-purpose flour
- 4 cups peeled and sliced pears
- 1 cup sour cream
- 1/2 teaspoon vanilla extract
- 1/2 teaspoon lemon extract
- 1/2 teaspoon almond extract
- 1 (9 inch) unbaked pie shell
- TOPPING:
- 1/4 cup all-purpose flour
- 2 tablespoons brown sugar
- 2 tablespoons butter or margarine, melted

Direction

- Start preheating the oven to 400°F (200°C).

- Mix 2 tablespoons flour and white sugar together in a big bowl. Add pears, and toss to blend. Mix in vanilla and sour cream, almond and lemon extracts until evenly coating the pears. Put in the unbaked pie shell.
- Combine brown sugar and 1/4 cup flour in a small bowl. Stir in butter using your finger until the mixture is crumbly. Drizzle evenly over the pie top.
- Put in the preheated oven and bake for 10 minutes, and then lower the heat to 350°F (175°C). Bake until the pears are soft, about another 45 minutes.

Nutrition Information

- Calories: 317 calories;
- Total Fat: 16.5
- Sodium: 155
- Total Carbohydrate: 40.4
- Cholesterol: 20
- Protein: 3.2

---

208.   Frangipane Pear Tart

Serving: 8 | Prep: 30mins | Cook: 1hours15mins | Ready in:

Ingredients

- Pears:
- 4 cups water
- 1 cup white sugar
- 2 tablespoons honey
- 1 vanilla bean, split lengthwise
- 1 cinnamon stick
- 5 pods cardamom, crushed
- 4 Conference pears - peeled, halved, and cored
- Pastry:
- 1 1/2 cups all-purpose flour
- 1/2 cup confectioners' sugar
- 1/2 teaspoon salt
- 1/2 cup cold unsalted butter, cut into pieces

- 1 tablespoon cold unsalted butter, cut into pieces
- 1 egg yolk
- Frangipane:
- 2/3 cup white sugar
- 1/3 cup unsalted butter, at room temperature
- 3/4 cup ground blanched almonds
- 1 egg
- 1 egg white
- 2 teaspoons all-purpose flour
- 1 teaspoon cornstarch
- 2 teaspoons almond extract
- 1 teaspoon vanilla extract

Direction

- In big saucepan, mix cardamom, cinnamon stick, vanilla bean, honey, a cup of white sugar and water. Simmer on moderate heat. Put in pears; lower the heat and simmer for 10 minutes, till pears are clear or effortlessly prick with knife. Take off heat and let come to room temperature.
- In bowl, mix salt, 1 1/2 cup of flour and confectioners' sugar. Mash in half cup plus a tablespoon of butter till mixture become crumbly. Stir egg yolk in till dough gathers together in big lumps.
- Oil a tart pan, 9-inch in size, with detachable base. Evenly force the dough into pan. Freeze for half an hour. Set aside the rest of the dough to mend the cracks.
- Preheat an oven to 190°C or 375°F.
- Use butter to grease the glossy side of aluminum foil piece; put on pastry, butter-side facing down. Turn the tart pan onto baking sheet.
- In the prepped oven, bake for 20 minutes, use the reserved dough to mend any cracks, till dough seems dry and pale brown. Remove aluminum foil; cool the pastry.
- Lower the oven heat to 175°C or 350°F.
- In a big bowl, mix 1/3 cup of butter and 2/3 cup of white sugar; use an electric mixer to whip till fluffy and light. Stir ground almonds in. Put in cornstarch, 2 teaspoons flour, egg yolk and egg; whip till frangipane become

smooth. Whip vanilla extract and almond extract in.

- Evenly slather frangipane on pastry. Let pear halves drain and use paper towels to dry. Evenly slice lengthwise into pieces. Put on spatula with a half of pear and slowly fan slices out. Put on the frangipane. Redo with the rest of the pear halves.
- In the prepped oven, bake for 40 to 45 minutes, till frangipane becomes firm to touch. Let cool on the wire rack.

Nutrition Information

- Calories: 613 calories;
- Total Carbohydrate: 94
- Cholesterol: 104
- Protein: 8.9
- Total Fat: 24.1
- Sodium: 171

- Fill the bottom of a 9-inch pie dish with the pie crust. Cut in the butter, flour and brown sugar together in a bowl using a pastry cutter until the mixture is similar to crumbs. Scoop the pear mixture in the pie shell and scatter the surface with the brown sugar mixture.
- Let it bake inside the oven for 10 minutes. Adjust the oven temperature to 350°F (175°C) then continue to bake for roughly additional 35 minutes until the filling turns bubbly and crumble topping becomes lightly brown.

Nutrition Information

- Calories: 465 calories;
- Total Carbohydrate: 72.6
- Cholesterol: 31
- Protein: 3.8
- Total Fat: 19.4
- Sodium: 203

| 209. | French Pear Pie |

Serving: 8 | Prep: 45mins | Cook: 45mins | Ready in:

Ingredients

- 6 large pears, peeled and sliced
- 1 lemon, juiced
- 2/3 cup white sugar
- 1/2 teaspoon grated nutmeg
- 1 (9 inch) unbaked single pie crust
- 1/2 cup butter
- 1/2 cup brown sugar
- 1 cup all-purpose flour

Direction

- Set the oven for preheating to 450°F (230°C).
- Sprinkle the lemon juice over pears in a bowl. Combine the nutmeg and white sugar in another small bowl; scatter the mixture over pears and incorporate well.

| 210. | Fresh Pear Pie |

Serving: 8 | Prep: 40mins | Cook: 50mins | Ready in:

Ingredients

- 1 recipe pastry for a 9 inch double crust pie
- 1/2 cup white sugar
- 3 tablespoons all-purpose flour
- 1/4 teaspoon salt
- 1 teaspoon ground cinnamon
- 1 teaspoon lemon zest
- 5 cups peeled and sliced pears
- 1 tablespoon butter
- 1 tablespoon lemon juice

Direction

- Preheat the oven to 230°C or 450°F. Put baking sheet on lowest rack of oven.
- In mixing bowl, mix lemon zest, cinnamon, salt, flour and sugar. Unroll 1/2 pastry and line it on a pie pan, 9-inch in size.

- Place slices of pear in piles in the pan lined with pastry, sprinkle sugar mixture on top of every pile. Scatter bits of butter and drizzle lemon juice over.
- Unroll the rest of dough for top crust. Dipped your finger in small bowl with water to dampen rim of base crust. Put top crust on top of filling, and use a sharp paring knife or kitchen shears to clip edge. Fold the edge beneath the base crust, pinching to enclose. Crimp edge. Make slits in top crust to vent.
- In the prepped oven, bake for 10 minutes on baking sheet. Lower oven heat to 175°C or 350°F, and bake till filling bubbles and crust turn golden brown, for an additional of 35 to 40 minutes. Cool for a few hours prior to serving.

Nutrition Information

- Calories: 360 calories;
- Total Carbohydrate: 51.6
- Cholesterol: 4
- Protein: 3.5
- Total Fat: 16.5
- Sodium: 318

---

211.   Hasselback Pear Tart

Serving: 8 | Prep: 20mins | Cook: 35mins | Ready in:

Ingredients

- 1 sheet frozen puff pastry - thawed, unfolded, and lightly rolled
- 2 Bartlett pears, halved and cored
- 2 d'Anjou pears, halved and cored
- 1 red pear, halved and cored
- 2 tablespoons white sugar
- 1/2 lemon, juiced
- 1/2 (8 ounce) package cream cheese, softened
- 1/2 cup confectioners' sugar
- 1/2 teaspoon vanilla extract
- 1 tablespoon turbinado sugar

Direction

- Preheat the oven to 200 degrees C (400 degrees F). Fit the puff pastry into one 10-in. square tart pan with the removable sides.
- Add one pear half, with the cut-side facing downward, onto the working surface. Add one chopstick above and one below pear half, so pear is framed on top and bottom. Thinly chop pear half lengthwise, stopping when knife hits chopstick and leaving bottom a quarter in. of pear intact. Repeat the process with the rest of pear halves.
- Add the hasselbacked pears into the bowl; put in the lemon juice and white sugar and coat by lightly tossing. Allow the hasselbacked pears to rest for 5 minutes.
- Combine together vanilla extract, confectioners' sugar, and cream cheese in the bowl; spread on the puff pastry. Arrange the hasselbacked pears on the cream cheese layer, chopping some of the halves into quarters if necessary to fit in. Fan out each pear a bit and sprinkle any accumulated juices from pear bowl on the pears. Drizzle the turbinado sugar on the tart.
- Bake in preheated oven for roughly 35 minutes or till the juices become bubbly and the crust becomes puffed and brown a bit. Let the tart cool down for 15 minutes prior to slicing.

Nutrition Information

- Calories: 326 calories;
- Sodium: 118
- Total Carbohydrate: 43.2
- Cholesterol: 15
- Protein: 3.7
- Total Fat: 16.5

---

212.   Maple Pear Tarte Tatin

Serving: 8 | Prep: 15mins | Cook: 30mins | Ready in:

Ingredients

- 1/2 (17.3 ounce) package frozen puff pastry, thawed
- 1/4 cup butter
- 1/3 cup brown sugar
- 1/4 teaspoon ground cinnamon
- 1 pinch ground nutmeg
- 1/4 cup maple syrup
- 4 firm pears - peeled, cored, and halved, or more as needed

Direction

- Preheat the oven to 190°C or 375°F.
- On a slightly floured area, unroll puff pastry making quarter-inch thickness; refrigerate.
- In a cast iron skillet, 9-inch in size, liquify the butter on moderate heat; mix in nutmeg, cinnamon and brown sugar, and cook while mixing for 5 minutes, till sugar melts. Mix into mixture of brown sugar with maple syrup; cook and mix till mixture starts to become bubbly. Take skillet off heat.
- Put a pear half in the middle of skillet, cut side facing up. Halve the rest of pear halves once more; surround the middle pear with pear quarters, cut sides facing up.
- Set the skillet on moderately-low heat; let pears cook for 5 minutes, use syrup mixture to baste them, till they start to become tender. Take skillet off heat.
- Take puff pastry out of fridge; top pears with pastry, tuck pastry edges in pears surrounding inside the skillet.
- In the prepped oven, bake for 20 minutes, till pastry turn golden and puffed; cool for five minutes. Top skillet with a serving plate; flip over to take out the tart, skillet is still hot. Serve while warm.

Nutrition Information

- Calories: 329 calories;
- Total Carbohydrate: 42.4
- Cholesterol: 15
- Protein: 2.6
- Total Fat: 17.6
- Sodium: 122

| 213. | Pear Frangipane Tart |

Serving: 8 | Prep: 15mins | Cook: 50mins | Ready in:

Ingredients

- Crust:
- 6 tablespoons butter at room temperature
- 1/4 cup granulated sugar
- 1 large egg
- 1 1/3 cups all-purpose flour
- 1/3 cup seedless raspberry or strawberry jam
- Filling:
- 4 ounces almond paste
- 1/3 cup granulated sugar
- 1 large egg
- 1/2 cup butter at room temperature
- 1/2 teaspoon almond extract
- 1/3 cup all-purpose flour
- 1/4 teaspoon baking powder
- 1 (29 ounce) can pear halves, well drained

Direction

- Crust: Beat sugar and butter with a mixer on low speed till fluffy and light; add egg till blended. Add flour; beat till blended. Grease 9-in. tart pan that has removable bottom. Press dough up the sides and on the bottom of pan. Use fork to prick crust; spread jam on bottom. Refrigerate.
- Preheat an oven to 350°F. Filling: Beat egg, sugar and almond paste with a mixer on low speed. Add almond extract and butter; beat just till blended. Add baking powder and flour; beat well. Put mixture on jam in crust.
- Put pear halves on mixture in crust, cut side down; bake till filling is set, 50 minutes. Fully cool.

Nutrition Information

- Calories: 500 calories;
- Total Fat: 25.7
- Sodium: 182
- Total Carbohydrate: 63.9
- Cholesterol: 100
- Protein: 6.1

214. Pear Pie

Serving: 8 | Prep: 15mins | Cook: 45mins | Ready in:

Ingredients

- 1 (9 inch) unbaked pie crust
- 3 cups sliced Bartlett pears
- 1 cup sour cream
- 1/2 cup white sugar
- 2 tablespoons all-purpose flour
- 1 egg
- 1/2 teaspoon vanilla extract
- 1/2 teaspoon salt
- Topping:
- 1/2 cup all-purpose flour
- 1/2 cup butter
- 1/4 cup white sugar
- 1 teaspoon ground cinnamon

Direction

- Set oven to 400°F (200°C) to preheat. Push pie shell into a 9-inch pie pan.
- Place pear slices in the pie shell. In a bowl, mix salt, vanilla extract, egg, 2 tablespoons flour, 1/2 cup sugar and sour cream; add over pears.
- In a bowl, combine cinnamon, 1/4 cup sugar, butter and 1/2 cup flour together until topping looks much like coarse crumbs.
- Bake pie for 35 minutes in the prepared oven. Scatter topping onto pie and keep baking about 10 minutes more until topping is golden brown.

Nutrition Information

- Calories: 431 calories;
- Total Fat: 25.8
- Sodium: 369
- Total Carbohydrate: 47.6
- Cholesterol: 66
- Protein: 4.5

215. Pear Pie I

Serving: 8 | Prep: | Cook: | Ready in:

Ingredients

- 1/2 cup white sugar
- 2 tablespoons all-purpose flour
- 1/4 teaspoon ground ginger
- 1/8 teaspoon ground cinnamon
- 7 pears - peeled, cored and sliced
- 2 (9 inch) unbaked pie crusts
- 1 1/2 tablespoons lemon juice
- 1/4 teaspoon white sugar

Direction

- Set oven to 175° C (350° F) and start preheating.
- Combine cinnamon, ginger, flour and the first portion of sugar in a big bowl. Put in pears; toss together.
- In uncooked bottom shell, place the mixture. Sprinkle lemon juice over top and place unbaked pastry atop. Cut slits in top; sprinkle with the second portion of sugar.
- Place on the bottom shelf of the preheated oven and bake at 175° C (350° F) until crust is browned and pears are cooked, about 1 hour. Allow to cool; serve.

Nutrition Information

- Calories: 363 calories;
- Cholesterol: 0
- Protein: 2.7
- Total Fat: 14.4

- Sodium: 281
- Total Carbohydrate: 58.3

216.   Pear Pie II

Serving: 6 | Prep: 15mins | Cook: 50mins | Ready in:

Ingredients

- 1 (9 inch) unbaked pie crust
- 3 eggs
- 1/3 cup all-purpose flour
- 1 cup white sugar
- 1 teaspoon almond extract
- 1/4 cup melted butter
- 3 pears - peeled, cored and sliced

Direction

- Preheat the oven to 375°F (190°C.)
- In a large bowl, mix together melted butter, almond extract, sugar, flour and eggs. Add into an unbaked pie crust. Place the sliced pears in spokes radiating from the middle.
- Bake in the preheated oven for 15 minutes, and then lower the temperature to 350 degrees F (175 degrees C). Bake until the custard is firm, about 25-35 minutes longer. Allow to cool completely prior to serving.

Nutrition Information

- Calories: 472 calories;
- Total Fat: 20.3
- Sodium: 247
- Total Carbohydrate: 68.7
- Cholesterol: 113
- Protein: 6.2

217.   Pear Pie III

Serving: 8 | Prep: 15mins | Cook: 1hours | Ready in:

Ingredients

- 1 (9 inch) unbaked pie crust
- 2 pears - peeled, cored and cut in half
- 1 cup white sugar
- 1/4 cup butter
- 1/4 cup all-purpose flour
- 1 tablespoon vanilla extract
- 2 eggs, beaten

Direction

- Set the oven to 350°F (175°C).
- Push the pie pastry into up the sides and the bottom of a 9-inch pie pan. Flute the edges. Put the pear halves in the pie crust, cut side down, with the small ends toward the center.
- Stir the butter with sugar in a medium bowl until smooth, then whip in eggs, one by one, until fluffy and light. Mix in vanilla and flour. Add over the top of the pears.
- Bake in the prepared oven for an hour, until custard is set in the middle and pears are soft. Let cool completely before cutting and serving.

Nutrition Information

- Calories: 328 calories;
- Total Carbohydrate: 46.6
- Cholesterol: 62
- Protein: 3.6
- Total Fat: 14.6
- Sodium: 176

218.   Pear Sour Cream Pie

Serving: 6 | Prep: 25mins | Cook: 45mins | Ready in:

Ingredients

- FOR THE PIE
- 1 (9 inch) pie crust pastry
- 1/2 cup white sugar
- 1 cup sour cream
- 1/4 cup all-purpose flour

- 1 egg, beaten
- 1 teaspoon vanilla extract
- 1/4 teaspoon salt
- 4 large pears - peeled, cored and sliced
- FOR THE TOPPING
- 2/3 cup all-purpose flour
- 1/3 cup white sugar
- 5 tablespoons butter, melted
- 2/3 cup rolled oats

Direction

- Set the oven to 350°F or 175°C for preheating. Roll the pastry and transfer it into the 9-inches pie plate. Cut any extra dough and crimp its edges.
- In a bowl, mix the sour cream, salt, 1/4 cup of flour, 1/2 cup of sugar, vanilla, and egg until well-blended. Mix in the pears. Spread the mixture onto the pie plate. Let the pie bake for 15 minutes.
- Meanwhile, prepare the topping by mixing the melted butter, rolled oats, 1/3 cup of sugar, and 2/3 cup of flour in a bowl.
- Get the pie from the oven and sprinkle it with the crumble topping. Place the pie inside the oven and bake for 20 more minutes until the crust is brown and the filling is set. Let it cool until the pie is set. Serve.

Nutrition Information

- Calories: 624 calories;
- Total Fat: 29.4
- Sodium: 355
- Total Carbohydrate: 85.5
- Cholesterol: 73
- Protein: 7.9

219.   Pear And Almond Tart (Dairy And Gluten Free)

Serving: 8 | Prep: 15mins | Cook: 22mins | Ready in:

Ingredients

- 1 1/4 cups almond meal
- 1/4 cup gluten-free oat flour
- 1/2 teaspoon gluten-free baking powder
- 1 egg, beaten
- 1/4 cup maple syrup
- 2 tablespoons coconut oil, melted
- 1 teaspoon vanilla extract
- 1/4 teaspoon sea salt
- 1/4 teaspoon almond extract
- 1 1/2 (16 ounce) cans pear halves, drained and patted dry

Direction

- Set an oven to 175°C (350°F) to preheat. Grease the bottom of a tart pan with removable bottom and line it with parchment paper.
- In a bowl, mix together the baking powder, oat flour and almond meal.
- In a separate bowl, whisk together the almond extract, salt, vanilla extract, coconut oil, maple syrup and egg. Fold in the almond meal mixture to create a sticky dough.
- Press the dough into the prepped tart pan, then lay the pears on top.
- Bake for 22-25 minutes in the preheated oven until it turns golden brown in color.

Nutrition Information

- Calories: 234 calories;
- Total Fat: 14
- Sodium: 102
- Total Carbohydrate: 24
- Cholesterol: 23
- Protein: 5.6

220.   Pear And Hazelnut Frangipane Tart

Serving: 8 | Prep: 15mins | Cook: 50mins | Ready in:

Ingredients

- Dough:
- 1 1/4 cups all-purpose flour (or gluten-free flour mix)
- 1 teaspoon sugar
- 1/4 teaspoon salt
- 8 tablespoons cold unsalted butter, cut into 1/2-inch cubes
- 3 tablespoons cold water, or more as needed
- Reynolds® Parchment Paper
- Reynolds Wrap® Aluminum Foil
- Filling:
- 3 ounces hazelnuts
- 1/2 cup sugar
- 8 tablespoons unsalted butter, at room temperature
- 1 egg
- 1/2 cup all-purpose flour (or gluten-free flour mix)
- 1 tablespoon vanilla extract
- 1 tablespoon dark rum (optional)
- 1/2 teaspoon kosher salt
- 3 pears - peeled, cored and sliced

Direction

- Mix in food processor with salt, flour and sugar. Put in cold butter and pulse 10 times till butter is the size of big peas. Put in 3 tablespoons cold water and pulse till it gathers together. Transfer on a slightly floured work area and gather dough together, shaping into a disk. Use Reynolds® Parchment Paper to encase and chill for a minimum of 45 minutes.
- Roll dough on a slightly floured work area into 1/8-inch-thick. Fit the dough on a rectangle tart mold or tart mold, 9-inch in size. Slice off extra from top and chill for 15 minutes more.
- Preheat the oven to 400°F. Use Reynolds Wrap(R) Aluminum Foil to cover the dough top and weigh it down using dry beans or pie weights. Let bake for 15 minutes. Take off pie weights and foil and cool.
- In food processor, pulse sugar and hazelnuts into fine powder. Put in salt, rum, vanilla,

flour, egg and butter. Process till it gathers together into a paste.
- Scatter mixture on top of the par-baked tart. Place slices of pear in pattern on top. Let tart bake till golden brown, for 30 to 35 minutes. Cool for 10 minutes prior to cutting.

Nutrition Information

- Calories: 474 calories;
- Sodium: 206
- Total Carbohydrate: 45.6
- Cholesterol: 84
- Protein: 5.7
- Total Fat: 30.5

---

221. Pear, Almond, Frangipane Tartada

Serving: 10 | Prep: 20mins | Cook: 34mins | Ready in:

Ingredients

- 1 (9 inch) refrigerated unbaked pie crust
- 1/2 cup almond paste, or more to taste
- 1 egg
- 1 dash salt
- 3 pears, thinly sliced, or more to taste
- 1 tablespoon lemon juice
- 1 (3 ounce) package sliced almonds
- 2 tablespoons apricot preserves

Direction

- Preheat the oven to 175°C or 350°F. Unroll pie crust on baking sheet.
- In bowl, beat salt, almond paste and egg to incorporate. Smear on top of pie crust, keep space on the border to fold the crust.
- Sit in a bowl with lemon juice and pears. Place decoratively over the almond mixture. Fold the outer crust edges on top of pears.
- In the prepped oven, bake for 30 to 50 minutes, till crust turn golden.

- In skillet, put the almonds on moderate heat; cook for 3 minutes while mixing, till toasted. Put in the preserves; cook and mix for 1 minute or 2, till saucy. Put on top of tart.

Nutrition Information

- Calories: 240 calories;
- Protein: 4.7
- Total Fat: 14
- Sodium: 142
- Total Carbohydrate: 25.7
- Cholesterol: 19

222.   Pumpkin Figs Pie

Serving: 8 | Prep: | Cook: 30mins | Ready in:

Ingredients

- 1 (9 inch) unbaked pie crust
- 2 pears - peeled, cored and sliced
- 1 1/2 cups pumpkin puree
- 1/2 cup dried figs, soaked and chopped
- 1 tablespoon brown sugar (optional)

Direction

- Preheat an oven to 175°C/350°F.
- Put pie crust in pie plate; put pear slices in bottom. In preheated oven, bake for 20 minutes.
- As pears bake, process sugar, soaked figs and pumpkin in food processor/blender till smooth. Put on pears.
- In preheated oven, bake till pears are tender and crust is golden for 15 more minutes. Serve cold/warm.

Nutrition Information

- Calories: 192 calories;
- Total Fat: 7.8
- Sodium: 230

- Total Carbohydrate: 30.2
- Cholesterol: 0
- Protein: 2.4

223.   Rustic Autumn Fruit Tart

Serving: 8 | Prep: 15mins | Cook: 30mins | Ready in:

Ingredients

- 1/2 cup butter, chilled
- 1/2 cup cream cheese
- 1 1/2 cups all-purpose flour
- 2 apples - peeled, cored, and thinly sliced
- 1 pear - peeled, cored and sliced
- 1/4 cup orange juice
- 1/3 cup brown sugar
- 1/2 teaspoon ground cinnamon
- 1/4 teaspoon ground nutmeg
- 1/4 teaspoon ground cardamom
- 1 1/2 tablespoons cornstarch
- 1/2 cup apricot jam, warmed

Direction

- Use a knife or pastry blender to cut cream cheese and cold butter into flour until the mixture looks like coarse crumbs. You can also do this with a food processor by pulsing the cold butter with the flour until it resembles cornmeal, then add the cream cheese, pulsing until the mixture has the size of small peas. Mixture should form a ball when you squeeze a handful of it. Shape into a round disk and wrap in plastic, then refrigerate for a minimum of 1 hour.
- Toss pear and apple slices with orange juice. Whisk together cornstarch, cardamom, nutmeg, cinnamon, and brown sugar together, then toss with the sugar-spice mixture and set the mixture aside.
- Set oven to 375 degrees Fahrenheit (190 degrees C). Bring out an 8 inches tart pan or lightly grease a baking sheet if you're making a galette or free-form tart.

- On a lightly floured work surface, roll out the pastry into a 10 inches circle. Move the dough to the tart pan or baking sheet. Decoratively arrange the fruit in the tart pastry. If you're using a baking sheet, leave out a 2 inches rim of dough and fold it over the edge of the fruit (the folds will overlap).
- Bake tart for 30 minutes in preheated oven until filling bubbles and the crust turns brown. Remove tart and brush with apricot jam.

Nutrition Information

- Calories: 361 calories;
- Protein: 4
- Total Fat: 17
- Sodium: 136
- Total Carbohydrate: 50.5
- Cholesterol: 46

Stir the mixture gently until coated. Spread the mixture into the graham cracker crust.
- Let it bake inside the preheated oven for 25 minutes. In the meantime, prepare its topping in a medium bowl. Mix the flour and sugar, and then cut in the butter until the mixture looks like coarse crumbs. Sprinkle the pie with the topping.
- Let it bake for 30 more minutes. Allow it to cool completely before serving.

Nutrition Information

- Calories: 569 calories;
- Sodium: 308
- Total Carbohydrate: 74.3
- Cholesterol: 77
- Protein: 4.6
- Total Fat: 29.6

224.   Sour Cream Pear Pie

Serving: 8 | Prep: 15mins | Cook: 55mins | Ready in:

Ingredients

- 3/4 cup sugar
- 1 tablespoon all-purpose flour
- 1/4 teaspoon ground cinnamon
- 1 pinch salt
- 1 egg, beaten
- 1 cup sour cream
- 2 (15 ounce) cans pears, drained and chopped
- 1 (9 inch) graham cracker crust
- 1/2 cup sugar
- 2/3 cup butter
- 2/3 cup all-purpose flour

Direction

- Set the oven to 350°F or 175°C for preheating.
- Mix the cinnamon, 3/4 cup of sugar, salt, and 1 tbsp. of flour in a medium bowl. Stir in sour cream and egg until smooth. Add the pears.

225.   Spiced Pear & Apple Pie

Serving: 8 | Prep: 20mins | Cook: 40mins | Ready in:

Ingredients

- 1 Classic Crisco® Double Pie Crust
- 4 cups peeled, thinly sliced pears
- 2 cups peeled, thinly sliced apples
- 3/4 cup sugar
- 2 tablespoons Pillsbury BEST® All Purpose Flour
- 3/4 teaspoon ground cinnamon
- 3/4 teaspoon ground ginger
- 1/4 teaspoon salt
- 1 tablespoon lemon juice
- Milk
- Cinnamon sugar

Direction

- For double crust pie: Spread out dough to form bottom crust. Put in a 9-in. pie plate. Press to fit but do not stretch the dough. Trim to fit the pie plate. Set oven to 400 degrees F and start heating.

- In a big bowl, combine lemon juice, salt, ginger, cinnamon, flour, sugar, apples, and pears. Use a spoon to transfer to the prepared pie crust.
- Spread out dough to form top crust. Put onto filled pie or slice into strips to make a lattice top. Trim 1/2-in. beyond edge. Fold under the edge of bottom crust to seal. Crimp then flute edges. Prick the top crust with a fork or cut slits in top crust to let steam escape. Brush milk on crust and sprinkle cinnamon sugar on top.
- Bake until crust is golden brown and apples are tender, about 30-40 minutes.

Nutrition Information

- Calories: 418 calories;
- Sodium: 4920
- Total Carbohydrate: 62.7
- Cholesterol: < 1
- Protein: 3.9
- Total Fat: 18.5

---

226. Streusel Topped Cranberry Pear Tart

Serving: 8 | Prep: 20mins | Cook: 45mins | Ready in:

Ingredients

- Tart:
- 1 refrigerated pie crust, softened as directed on package
- 1/2 cup Stevia In The Raw® Bakers Bag
- 1 tablespoon cornstarch
- 1/4 teaspoon ground nutmeg
- 3 ripe but firm pears, peeled, cored, sliced 1/4 inch thick
- 1/2 cup fresh or frozen cranberries
- Streusel:
- 1/4 cup all-purpose flour

- 2 tablespoons Stevia In The Raw® Bakers Bag
- 2 tablespoons butter, cut into small cubes
- 1/4 cup chopped sliced almonds

Direction

- Heat the oven to 375 °F. Roll the crust into 11 inches. Fit in bottom and up the side of 9-inch tart pan with removable bottom. Clip surrounding edge. Bake till starting to brown or for 5 to 8 minutes. Gently press out any bubbles using back of a wooden spoon.
- In the meantime, stir nutmeg, cornstarch and half-cup Stevia in The Raw in a big bowl. Put in the cranberries and pears; coat by tossing. Scoop into partially baked crust. Using a fork or pastry blender, combine butter, 2 tablespoons Stevia in The Raw and flour in a small bowl, till crumbly. Scatter on top of pears. Scatter chopped almonds on top. Bake till crust turns golden brown and pears are soft or for 40 to 50 minutes. Cool for an hour. Take out of pan side. Serve cool or while warm.

Nutrition Information

- Calories: 214 calories;
- Sodium: 138
- Total Carbohydrate: 25.3
- Cholesterol: 8
- Protein: 2.7
- Total Fat: 12

---

227. D'Anjou Pear And Almond Tarts

Serving: 18 | Prep: 15mins | Cook: 45mins | Ready in:

Ingredients

- 18 (3 inch) unbaked tart shells
- 7 tablespoons brown sugar
- 2 tablespoons butter, melted

- 1 teaspoon pear-flavored white balsamic vinegar
- 1 teaspoon ground cinnamon
- 3 large ripe d'Anjou pears - peeled, cored, and diced
- 3 tablespoons chopped almonds

Direction

- Set oven to 175° C (350° F) and start preheating. Arrange tart shells over a baking sheet.
- In a bowl, mix together cinnamon, balsamic vinegar, melted butter and brown sugar. Mix in chopped almonds and pears until entirely coated. Use a spoon to transfer pear mixture to tart shells.
- Place in the preheated oven and bake 45 minutes until golden.

Nutrition Information

- Calories: 195 calories;
- Total Fat: 8.3
- Sodium: 101
- Total Carbohydrate: 29.7
- Cholesterol: 4
- Protein: 1.8

Chapter 8: Raspberry Pie Recipes

***

| 228. | Chocolate Raspberry Cloud |

Serving: 8 | Prep: | Cook: | Ready in:

Ingredients

- 1 1/2 cups finely crushed chocolate wafer cookies
- 3 tablespoons butter, melted
- 2 cups heavy cream
- 1/2 cup white sugar
- 1 teaspoon vanilla extract
- 1/2 cup raspberry syrup
- 1 (9 ounce) package thin chocolate wafers
- 1/4 cup fresh raspberries (optional)
- 1 tablespoon chopped fresh mint leaves (optional)
- 1/8 cup semisweet chocolate curls (optional)

Direction

- Prepare Crust: Stir together melted butter and crushed cookies in a small bowl. Push mixture into a 9-inch pie dish with the back of a spoon or your hands. Chill until set.
- Prepare Filling: Beat two cups of cream until it holds soft peaks. Keep whipping while gradually putting in sugar, then with vanilla extract. Beat until stiff, then mix in half cup raspberry syrup.
- Put a layer of whipped cream mix, 1/2-inch deep into bottom of pie shell. Top with a layer of chocolate cookies. Top with one more 1/2-inch layer of whipped cream mix, then with more cookies. Overlap the cookies a little (optional), coating them in whipped cream mix before putting them in pan. Keep layering until out of cookies, then top with a layer of whipped cream mix. Carefully cover it. Chill no less than 12 hours before enjoying. Pie will keep up to 3 days.
- Beat leftover half cup cream and top pie with a fresh layer just before serving. Garnish with chocolate curls, mint leaves, and fresh raspberries (optional).

Nutrition Information

- Calories: 591 calories;
- Total Fat: 34.7
- Sodium: 358

- Total Carbohydrate: 68
- Cholesterol: 94
- Protein: 5

229. Cream Cheese Raspberry Lemonade Pie

Serving: 8 | Prep: 10mins | Cook: |Ready in:

Ingredients

- 1 (8 ounce) package cream cheese, softened
- 1 (14 ounce) can sweetened condensed milk
- 1/2 (12 fluid ounce) can frozen raspberry lemonade, thawed
- 1 cup frozen raspberries
- 1 (9 inch) graham cracker crust
- 1/3 cup whipped topping, or to taste
- 1/2 cup frozen raspberries, thawed

Direction

- Whip the cream cheese with electric mixer till becoming fluffy. Put in the lemonade and condensed milk; combine well. Whisk in 1 cup of the frozen raspberries. Add the mixture to graham cracker crust. Keep chilled for 4 hours. Add several thawed raspberries and whipped topping on top of each slice.

Nutrition Information

- Calories: 498 calories;
- Cholesterol: 47
- Protein: 7.7
- Total Fat: 22.4
- Sodium: 318
- Total Carbohydrate: 69.4

230. Dutch Apple Berry Pie

Serving: 8 | Prep: | Cook: |Ready in:

Ingredients

- 2 cups sliced green apples
- 1/2 cup raspberries
- 1/2 cup fresh blueberries
- 1 (9 inch) deep dish pie crust
- 2/3 cup all-purpose flour
- 2/3 cup packed brown sugar
- 1/3 cup butter
- 1/2 teaspoon ground cinnamon
- 1/2 teaspoon ground allspice
- 1 pinch ground nutmeg

Direction

- Set an oven at 175°C (350°F) and start preheating.
- Combine blueberries, raspberries and apples; add the mixture into the pie shell.
- Mix nutmeg, allspice, cinnamon, margarine or butter, brown sugar and flour in a big bowl. Mix them together until the mixture turns into crumbs and dry. Dredge them on top of the fruit.
- Put the pie in the oven and bake until topping turns brown, or for 30 minutes.

Nutrition Information

- Calories: 319 calories;
- Total Fat: 15.4
- Sodium: 208
- Total Carbohydrate: 44
- Cholesterol: 20
- Protein: 2.4

231. Fresh Berry Tart With Chambord Sauce

Serving: 8 | Prep: | Cook: |Ready in:

Ingredients

- 1/2 (17.5 ounce) package frozen puff pastry, thawed
- 1 egg
- 2 cups milk
- 1 vanilla bean (optional)
- 6 egg yolks
- 6 tablespoons white sugar
- 1/4 cup all-purpose flour
- 1/2 cup white chocolate chips
- 2 tablespoons creme de cacao
- 1/2 cup raspberry jam
- 1 tablespoon Chambord (raspberry liqueur)
- 1/4 cup toasted and chopped almonds
- 2 cups fresh raspberries
- 2 cups fresh blueberries
- 2 cups fresh blackberries
- 1 (10 ounce) package frozen raspberries, thawed
- 3 tablespoons Chambord (raspberry liqueur)

Direction

- For Tart Shell: Roll out a puff pastry sheet; slice into a 6x14-in. rectangle. Transfer to a baking sheet. From the excess dough, cut out 1-in. strips to use for trimming edges. On each rectangle, brush cold water along 1-in of the edges; place strips on top to frame the edges. Whisk an egg; brush over the pastry's top. Refrigerate for 15 minutes until the pastry is firm (this step is important).
- Set oven to 205°C (400°F). Bake pastry in the oven for 10 minutes until it starts browning. Take out of the oven; turn down the heat to 190°C (375°F). Use the back of a fork to firmly press the shell until it collapses. Put back into the oven; bake for 8 minutes until it turns golden. Let cool on a wire rack. The shell can be made two days beforehand; keep in a tightly sealed container at room temperature to store.
- For White Chocolate Custard: In a heavy saucepan, heat milk over medium heat, stirring, until it starts boiling. Take away from the heat. Put in vanilla bean and allow to sit, covered, for 10 minutes. Discard vanilla bean. In the meantime, beat sugar and egg yolks until the mixture becomes light in color and has a thick consistency. Mix in flour. Mix in hot milk, a little at a time, whisking until smooth. Transfer to the saucepan. Over medium heat, boil the mixture until it becomes thick, stirring frequently. Reduce the heat. Keep cooking, stirring continuously, for 2 minutes until it becomes a little softer. Take away from the heat; fold white chocolate into the hot pastry cream. Place mixture in a small bowl and use plastic wrap to cover. Once cooled, remove the plastic wrap and put in creme de cacao. The custard can be made one day beforehand; chill while covered until needed.
- Chambord sauce can be made a maximum of two days beforehand. In a blender, blend defrosted raspberries until pureed. Strain puree to discard seeds; mix in 3 tablespoons of Chambord liqueur. Refrigerate the sauce.
- Just before assembling the tart, prepare the glaze. Heat preserves in a saucepan over low heat until melted. Take away from the heat; mix in a tablespoon of liqueur. Use while still warm.
- Tart is best enjoyed within 3-4 hours after done assembling. Brush the glaze onto the tart's bottom; scatter 1/2 chopped almonds over. Scoop custard into the crust and smooth out. Place fresh berries over and brush glaze over the top. Scatter the rest of the almonds over. Keep chilled until serving.

Nutrition Information

- Calories: 579 calories;
- Total Fat: 23.6
- Sodium: 130
- Total Carbohydrate: 79.3
- Cholesterol: 184
- Protein: 10.5

232. Key Lime And Raspberry Pies In Jars

Serving: 6 | Prep: 20mins | Cook: 22mins | Ready in:

Ingredients

- 12 graham crackers
- 2 tablespoons white sugar
- 6 tablespoons unsalted butter, melted
- 6 half pint canning jars
- 1 (14 ounce) can sweetened condensed milk
- 4 egg yolks
- 1/2 cup fresh lime juice
- 1 tablespoon grated lime zest, divided
- 1/2 cup heavy whipping cream
- 1 teaspoon white sugar
- 1 cup fresh raspberries

Direction

- Set the oven to 190 degrees Celsius or 375 degrees Fahrenheit, then use parchment paper to line a small pie pan.
- Use a food processor to pulse together 2 tablespoons of white sugar with graham crackers to form fine crumbs. Pour in the melted butter, pulsing to combine.
- Spoon 2 tablespoons graham cracker crumbles into each of the 6 1/2 pint jars and press the crumbles gently into the bottom. Put the jars on a big rimmed baking sheet. Press leftover graham mixture into the bottom of the pie pan.
- Bake the pie pan and jars until the graham cracker mixture turns golden brown, roughly 12-15 minutes. Take out of oven and place onto a wire rack to cool.
- Turn down the oven temperature to 175 degrees Celsius or 350 degrees Fahrenheit.
- In a big bowl, whisk egg yolks and condensed milk together until smooth. Add 1 1/2 teaspoons of lime zest and the lime juice, whisk to combine. Pour the lime mixture in the cooled jars.
- Bake jars just until the lime mixture sets, around 10-12 minutes. Move to a wire rack

and cool, then place in the refrigerator until ready to assemble.

- In a bowl, use an electric mixer to beat together 1 teaspoon of white sugar with heavy cream until it forms stiff peaks.
- Top the jars with lime zest, the leftover graham cracker crust, whipped cream, and fresh raspberries.

Nutrition Information

- Calories: 509 calories;
- Total Carbohydrate: 56.4
- Cholesterol: 216
- Protein: 8.7
- Total Fat: 29
- Sodium: 183

233. Lemon Raspberry Swirl Pie

Serving: 8 | Prep: 15mins | Cook: | Ready in:

Ingredients

- 3/4 cup boiling water
- 1 (3 ounce) package lemon flavored Jell-O® mix
- 1 (8 ounce) container low-fat lemon yogurt
- 1/2 cup creamy salad dressing (e.g. Miracle Whip)
- 1 cup frozen whipped topping, thawed
- 1 (9 inch) prepared graham cracker crust
- 2 tablespoons raspberry preserves, heated

Direction

- Put boiling water into gelatin in a medium bowl and mix until gelatin is dissolved completely, or for 1 to 2 minutes. Let it chill until slightly thick; mix constantly.
- With wire whisk, stir salad dressing and yogurt until smooth in a large bowl. Put in thickened gelatin and continue mixing until

smooth. Lightly fold in whipped topping. Put mixture into crust. Wrap it up and chill until firm or for a few hours. Drizzle preserves immediately on top of pie prior to serving.

Nutrition Information

- Calories: 291 calories;
- Total Fat: 13.2
- Sodium: 371
- Total Carbohydrate: 39.5
- Cholesterol: 6
- Protein: 3.6

---

234.   No Bake Coconut Fruit Tarts

Serving: 6 | Prep: 15mins | Cook: |Ready in:

Ingredients

- 1/4 cup almonds
- 12 Medjool dates, pitted
- 1 (11 ounce) bottle So Delicious® Dairy Free Culinary Coconut Milk
- 1/2 cup fresh raspberries
- 1/2 cup sliced fresh strawberries

Direction

- In a food processor, chop almonds and put medjool dates. Process until smooth.
- Save about 1/8 cup of date mixture and put aside.
- Line two individual-sized tart pans with parchment or grease with oil to prepare. Split the date mixture into the two pans and press along the sides and bottom.
- In a mixing bowl, use a hand mixer to whip the culinary Coconut milk for a minute or so then add about 5 berries and the reserved date mixture. Stir to incorporate.
- Scoop the coconut mixture into the tart crusts and freeze for at least 2 hours.

- Take the frozen tarts out of the pans. Top with sliced strawberries and raspberries to garnish.

Nutrition Information

- Calories: 183 calories;
- Total Fat: 12.4
- Sodium: 7
- Total Carbohydrate: 19.2
- Cholesterol: 0
- Protein: 2.5

---

235.   Phyllo Tarts With Ricotta And Raspberries

Serving: 6 | Prep: | Cook: |Ready in:

Ingredients

- 5 sheets phyllo dough
- 2 tablespoons unsalted butter, melted
- 1 cup low-fat ricotta cheese
- 1/4 cup white sugar
- 1 egg
- 1/2 teaspoon orange zest
- 1/2 teaspoon vanilla extract
- 1 pinch ground nutmeg
- 2 cups fresh raspberries
- 1 tablespoon confectioners' sugar for dusting

Direction

- Drain ricotta cheese for 20 minutes in a sieve; put aside.
- Preheat an oven to 175°C/350°F. Spray nonfat cooking spray on 6 3-in. loose-bottomed tart pans.
- Leave phyllo sheets in the stack; trace 6 5-in. squares on top sheet, 2 squares down and 3 squares across, using a ruler. Cut along traced lines using sharp knife, through all 5 dough sheets. Line each tart pan immediately using 5 dough sheets, brushing melted

margarine/butter lightly between every layer. Trim dough edges.

- Beat nutmeg, vanilla extract, orange rind, egg, sugar and ricotta using electric mixer till smooth in medium mixing bowl; put even mixture amount into every tart pan.
- In preheated oven, bake till golden brown for 25 minutes. Slightly cool tarts; put raspberries over. Serve: Remove the tarts from pans; sprinkle confectioners' sugar.

Nutrition Information

- Calories: 152 calories;
- Total Carbohydrate: 22.9
- Cholesterol: 41
- Protein: 2.6
- Total Fat: 5.9
- Sodium: 89

---

236.   Plum And Raspberry Tart

Serving: 8 | Prep: 20mins | Cook: 1hours5mins | Ready in:

Ingredients

- Crust:
- 1/4 cup coconut oil
- 1 egg
- 1 tablespoon honey
- 1 teaspoon vanilla extract
- 1 cup ground almonds
- 1 1/4 cups rolled oats
- Filling:
- 1 1/4 cups water
- 3/4 cup honey, divided
- 1 tablespoon ground cinnamon
- 1 teaspoon vanilla extract
- 4 plums, pitted and sliced
- 1 cup ground almonds
- 3 eggs
- 1/2 cup coconut oil
- 1/2 cup fresh raspberries

Direction

- Preheat an oven to 165 °C or 325 °F.
- In food processor bowl, mix together a teaspoon of vanilla extract, a tablespoon of honey, an egg and quarter cup of coconut oil; pulse till thoroughly blended. To the mixture, gradually put oats and a cup of ground almonds; pulse till thoroughly blended and dough forms into a ball.
- Roll out the dough to suit a pie dish, 9-inch in size.
- In the prepped oven, let it bake for 10 to 15 minutes till crust edge turn golden.
- In a saucepan, put a teaspoon of vanilla extract, cinnamon, 1/3 cup of honey and water; boil. Put in the plums; let it simmer for 20 minutes till softened over medium-low heat.
- In blender, mix together the rest of the honey, half cup coconut oil, 3 eggs and a cup of ground almonds; process till smooth. Transfer over the pastry. Cautiously put raspberries and plums on top.
- In the prepped oven, bake for half an hour till set.

Nutrition Information

- Calories: 598 calories;
- Cholesterol: 93
- Protein: 13
- Total Fat: 42.3
- Sodium: 39
- Total Carbohydrate: 49.8

---

237.   Raspberry Chiffon Pie I

Serving: 8 | Prep: | Cook: | Ready in:

Ingredients

- 1 1/2 (.25 ounce) packages unflavored gelatin
- 1/4 cup cold water

- 4 egg yolks, beaten
- 1 tablespoon lemon juice
- 1/2 cup white sugar
- 1 cup fresh raspberries, crushed
- 4 egg whites
- 1/4 cup white sugar
- 1/8 teaspoon salt
- 3/4 cup heavy whipping cream, whipped
- 1 (9 inch) vanilla wafer crust

Direction

- Soak gelatin in cold water to soften.
- In a saucepan, stir lemon juice, 1/2 cup sugar, and egg yolks. Cook until mixture coats the back of a spoon. Mix in gelatin, then stir in crushed raspberries. Refrigerate until partly set.
- Whip egg whites with 1/4 cup sugar and salt until stiff. Fold egg whites and whipped cream into raspberry mixture. Put filling into chilled pie crust and refrigerate 3 to 4 hours.

Nutrition Information

- Calories: 275 calories;
- Cholesterol: 126
- Protein: 5.5
- Total Fat: 14.4
- Sodium: 188
- Total Carbohydrate: 32.5

238.   Raspberry Chiffon Pie II

Serving: 8 | Prep: 30mins | Cook: 20mins | Ready in:

Ingredients

- 1 (9 inch) prepared graham cracker crust
- 3 cups raspberries
- 2/3 cup water
- 1 (.25 ounce) package unflavored gelatin
- 1/4 cup cold water
- 3 egg yolks, beaten

- 2/3 cup white sugar
- 3 egg whites
- 1/4 teaspoon cream of tartar
- 1/3 cup white sugar
- 1/2 cup heavy whipping cream
- 1/4 cup fresh raspberries

Direction

- Mix 2/3 cup water and 3 cups raspberries in a medium saucepan. Simmer over low heat until raspberries soften. Press mixture through a strainer or sieve to remove seeds and collect raspberry pulp.
- In a small bowl, put 1/4 cup cold water and gelatin. Put aside and let gelatin soften.
- Beat together 2/3 cup sugar, egg yolks, and raspberry pulp in a medium saucepan. Heat up to a full boil, mixing continuously. Take away from heat.
- Put gelatin into raspberry mixture and mix to dissolve. Put pan in a cold-water bath to cool completely.
- Whisk egg whites until foamy in a large glass or metal mixing bowl. Put in cream of tartar. Put in 1/3 cup sugar gradually, blending continuously until whites are glossy and stiff.
- Beat cream until stiff in a separate mixing bowl. Lightly fold together with meringue and cooled raspberry mixture. Scoop mixture into graham cracker shell. Refrigerate at least 2 hours prior to serving. Top with whole raspberries.

Nutrition Information

- Calories: 331 calories;
- Sodium: 182
- Total Carbohydrate: 48.7
- Cholesterol: 97
- Protein: 5
- Total Fat: 14

239.   Raspberry French Silk Pie

Serving: 8 | Prep: 30mins | Cook: 15mins | Ready in:

Ingredients

- Crust:
- 1 cup all-purpose flour
- 1/2 teaspoon salt
- 1/3 cup shortening
- 2 tablespoons beaten egg
- 1 tablespoon water
- 1 teaspoon lemon juice
- Filling:
- 3 ounces semisweet chocolate
- 3/4 cup butter, softened
- 1 cup white sugar
- 1/2 teaspoon vanilla extract
- 3 eggs
- 1/3 cup seedless raspberry jam
- Garnish:
- fresh raspberries
- fresh mint leaves
- whipped topping

Direction

- Creating crust, in a mixing bowl, combine salt and flour. Use a knife or pastry blender to cut in shortening until the mixture forms coarse crumbs. Mix together lemon juice, water and egg. Drizzle wet ingredients over the flour mixture and lightly toss using a fork until the flour mixture becomes moist. Use plastic wrap to wrap the dough and place inside the refrigerator for at least 1 hour or up to 3 days.
- Turn the dough out onto 9-inch pie plate to fit. Put the dough in the pie plate, form a 1inch overhang by trimming the edge. Turn the excess dough under itself and crimp the edges of the crust decoratively. Let the pastry-filled pie chill at least 20 minutes prior to baking to avoid shrinkage.
- Prepare the oven by preheating to 400 degrees F (205 degrees C). Then line pastry using a double thickness of foil and a layer if pie weights or dried beans. Place inside the preheated oven and bake for 10 minutes until edge of crust is golden in color. Gently detach the foil and weights and bake for about 5 more minutes until the crust has set. Let it fully cool before adding the filling.
- To create filling, in a double broiler, melt the chocolate. Cool to room temperature but remains fluid. In the meantime, use an electric mixer to beat butter until turns smooth. Slowly mix in the sugar, whisking until mixture is fluffy and light. Should be visibly lighter in color. Mix in the vanilla extract and cooled chocolate. One at a time, add the eggs, whisking for 2 minutes at high speed and pushing down sides of the bowl well after every addition.
- On the bottom of cooled pie crust, spread a thin layer (about 1/4-inch) of raspberry jam. Scoop the chocolate filling on top of the jam and smooth surface. Place inside the refrigerator overnight.
- Prior to serving, decorate each slice with a mint leaf, 3 fresh raspberries and a dollop whipped topping.

Nutrition Information

- Calories: 547 calories;
- Cholesterol: 121
- Protein: 5.1
- Total Fat: 34.7
- Sodium: 306
- Total Carbohydrate: 57

240.   Raspberry Lemon Meringue Pie

Serving: 8 | Prep: 20mins | Cook: 30mins | Ready in:

Ingredients

- Pie Crust:
- 1 pastry for a 9-inch pie crust
- 1 egg white, or as needed

- Raspberry Layer:
- 1/2 cup frozen raspberries (optional)
- 1 tablespoon cornstarch (optional)
- Lemon Filling:
- 1 cup white sugar
- 1/4 cup cornstarch
- 1 cup cold water
- 3/4 cup lemon juice, divided
- 3 egg yolks, lightly beaten
- 1 tablespoon lemon pulp (including zest if desired)
- 1 tablespoon butter
- Meringue:
- 3 egg whites
- 1/3 cup white sugar

Direction

- Set oven to 190° C (375° F) and start preheating. Press pie crust into a 9-in. pie pan. Brush enough egg white on crust as long as it coats a thin layer.
- Place in the prepared oven and cook for 5-10 minutes until golden brown. Take the crust out of the oven and allow to cool. Reduce the oven temperature to 175° C (350° F).
- In a saucepan on medium heat, stir and cook raspberries for 5-10 minutes till they begin to break down. Mix 1 tablespoon cornstarch into the raspberries, about 2-3 minutes until the mixture is thickened and cornstarch is dissolved. Scoop raspberry mixture into the pie crust.
- In a saucepan, combine 1/4 cup cornstarch and 1 cup white sugar. Slowly mix in 1/2 cup lemon juice and water until smooth. Mix egg yolks into the sugar mixture and heat to a boil. Cook the sugar-egg mixture at a boil for 1 minutes until smooth, mixing continuously. Take the saucepan away from heat. Mix butter, the remaining 1/4 cup lemon juice, and lemon pulp into the sugar-egg mixture; pour it over raspberry mixture.
- With an electric mixture, on high speed, whisk 3 egg whites until foamy in a small bowl. Slowly whisk 1/3 cup white sugar into the egg whites until forming stiff peaks. Spread egg white mixture over the lemon filling, fully sealing egg mixture onto edges of the crust.
- Put into the preheated oven and bake for 15-20 minutes till meringue is golden brown. Place pie on a wire rack; allow to cool to room temperature for about 30 minutes. Chill pie in the fridge for 3 hours until fully chilled.

Nutrition Information

- Calories: 312 calories;
- Cholesterol: 81
- Protein: 4.4
- Total Fat: 10.6
- Sodium: 159
- Total Carbohydrate: 51.5

---

241. Raspberry Lemonade Pie

Serving: 16 | Prep: 15mins | Cook: | Ready in:

Ingredients

- 1 1/2 cups boiling water
- 1 (3 ounce) package JELL-O Brand Lemon Flavor Gelatin
- 4 ounces PHILADELPHIA Cream Cheese, softened
- 1/2 (12 ounce) can frozen lemonade concentrate, thawed
- 1 (8 ounce) tub COOL WHIP Whipped Topping, thawed
- 1 cup fresh raspberries
- 2 (6 ounce) HONEY MAID Graham Pie Crusts

Direction

- In a small bowl, mix gelatin mix and boiling water for 2 minutes until melted completely; put aside. In a big bowl, beat cream cheese with mixer till creamy. Beat concentrate in gradually then gelatin till blended.
- Mix berries and cool whip in. Put into crusts.

- Refrigerate a pie till firm for 4 hours. Freeze leftover pie for a max of 1 week. Thaw before serving.

Nutrition Information

- Calories: 210 calories;
- Total Carbohydrate: 29
- Cholesterol: 8
- Protein: 1.9
- Total Fat: 9.6
- Sodium: 178

longer. Let the pie cool down fully before serving.

Nutrition Information

- Calories: 270 calories;
- Sodium: 169
- Total Carbohydrate: 44.8
- Cholesterol: 6
- Protein: 2
- Total Fat: 10.1

242.   Raspberry Pie III

Serving: 8 | Prep: 30mins | Cook: 40mins | Ready in:

Ingredients

- 1 recipe pastry for a 9 inch double crust pie
- 4 cups raspberries
- 1 cup white sugar
- 2 1/2 tablespoons tapioca
- 1 tablespoon lemon juice
- 1/4 teaspoon ground cinnamon
- 1/8 teaspoon salt
- 4 teaspoons butter
- 1 tablespoon half-and-half cream

Direction

- Set oven to preheat at 425°F (220°C).
- Mix together the cinnamon, sugar, tapioca, lemon juice, raspberries, and salt till raspberries are coated thoroughly.
- Transfer the mixture into 9 or 10-inch pastry shell. Use butter to dot; place the top crust on and crimp the edge.
- Slice slits into the top crust and brush using cream. In the preheated oven, bake for 15 minutes till the crust sets. Lower the heat to 375°F (190°C) and bake till the crust is golden and filling bubbles up, for about 25 minutes

243.   Raspberry Sour Cream Pie

Serving: 16 | Prep: 20mins | Cook: 40mins | Ready in:

Ingredients

- 2 (9 inch) unbaked pie crusts
- 2 eggs
- 1 1/3 cups sour cream
- 1 teaspoon vanilla extract
- 1 cup white sugar
- 1 pinch salt
- 1/3 cup all-purpose flour
- 3 cups raspberries
- 1/2 cup brown sugar
- 1/2 cup all-purpose flour
- 1/2 cup chopped walnuts
- 1/4 cup butter, chilled

Direction

- Set an oven to preheat to 200°C (400°F).
- Beat the eggs in a big bowl, until it turns light and lemon in color. Whisk in vanilla and sour cream. Combine the salt, flour and sugar in another bowl, then mix into the egg mixture. Fold in the raspberries gently. Pour the filling on the two pie crusts that are unbaked.
- Let the pies bake for 30-35 minutes in the preheated oven without the topping or until the middle starts to set.

- As the pies bake, prepare the topping: Combine the chopped nuts, flour and brown sugar in a medium bowl. Slice in the butter until it becomes crumbly, then put aside.
- Sprinkle the topping on the pies and put it back into the oven for 10-15 minutes or until the topping turns golden brown in color. Let it cool prior to serving.

Nutrition Information

- Calories: 307 calories;
- Total Fat: 16.8
- Sodium: 167
- Total Carbohydrate: 36.1
- Cholesterol: 39
- Protein: 4.1

| 244. | Raspberry Streusel Tart |

Serving: 8 | Prep: 25mins | Cook: 35mins | Ready in:

Ingredients

- Streusel:
- 6 tablespoons unsalted butter
- 1 1/4 cups all-purpose flour
- 6 tablespoons white sugar
- 1/4 teaspoon ground cinnamon
- 1/8 teaspoon salt
- Custard:
- 1 3/4 cups light cream
- 1/3 cup white sugar
- 4 teaspoons cornstarch
- 4 egg yolks
- 1 tablespoon unsalted butter
- 1 teaspoon vanilla extract
- 1 tablespoon kirschwasser
- 1 (11 inch) shortbread tart crust, baked
- 2/3 cup apricot preserves
- 2 tablespoons water
- 2 1/2 pints fresh raspberries
- 2 1/2 tablespoons sifted confectioners' sugar

Direction

- Preheat an oven to 175°C/350°F.
- Bring 6 tbsp. butter in a saucepan; melt on medium low heat, then cool till barely warm.
- Mix salt, cinnamon, 6 tbsp. sugar and flour; add to melted butter. Use fork to toss till you form crumbs.
- Take a clump of crumb mixture in hand; gently squeeze to make a bigger clump. Break apart bigger clump.
- Sprinkle crumbs on big shallow pan; repeat till the mixture is thoroughly crumbled. Put crumbs in oven; bake till they are light brown, 15-18 minutes. Put aside streusel mixture to cool, then harden.
- Heat cream till just under a boil in 2-qt. saucepan. Mix cornstarch and 1/3 cup sugar in a small bowl. Beat egg yolks with a whisk till slightly thick in a mixing bowl; whisk in cornstarch-sugar mixture. Add in hot cream slowly, constantly whisking; put into saucepan. Slowly heat, constantly whisking using a wooden spoon, till it boils and starts to thicken; be sure to reach every part of the pot to release any custard sticks to the pot.
- Simmer for about 1 minute when custard reaches a boil; take off heat. Mix in framboise/Kirschwasser, vanilla and 1 tbsp. butter; use a buttered plastic wrap piece to cover custard. Cool for about 10 minutes.
- Preheat an oven to 190°C/375°F.
- Spread custard into prebaked tart shell; bake for 20-25 minutes till bubbly. Remove from oven; cool on rack to set for 10 minutes.
- Mix together water and preserves in a small saucepan, then heat till it boils; pass glaze through fine-mesh strainer then discard pulp.
- Brush 1/2 hot preserves on top of custard gently; generously sprinkle over hot custard with berries. Brush leftover preserves on tops of berries lightly; generously sprinkle streusel on tart, gently pressing crumbs into berries to adhere. Chill tart without a cover for about 2 hours. Sift confectioners' sugar over before serving.

Nutrition Information

- Calories: 657 calories;
- Total Carbohydrate: 88.1
- Cholesterol: 164
- Protein: 7.4
- Total Fat: 30.8
- Sodium: 225

245.   Raspberry Tart

Serving: 8 | Prep: 1hours10mins | Cook: | Ready in:

Ingredients

- 1 cup all-purpose flour
- 1/2 cup butter
- 2 tablespoons confectioners' sugar
- 4 cups fresh raspberries
- 1 (8 ounce) jar raspberry jam

Direction

- Combine together sugar, butter and flour in a medium bowl. Refrigerate the mixture for one hour.
- Preheat an oven to 190 degrees C (375 degrees F).
- Pat the chilled mixture in a tart pan of 9 inch.
- Bake for 10 minutes in preheated oven. Remove from oven and let to cool.
- Spread the raspberries in crust. Then microwave jar of jam until it starts to boil. Spread the jam over the fruit. Cover and chill the tart for about one hour.

Nutrition Information

- Calories: 266 calories;
- Total Fat: 12
- Sodium: 82
- Total Carbohydrate: 39.1
- Cholesterol: 31
- Protein: 2.3

246.   Raspberry Lemon Pie In A Toasted Coconut Crust

Serving: 8 | Prep: 15mins | Cook: 25mins | Ready in:

Ingredients

- 2 cups shredded coconut
- 1/2 cup unsalted butter, melted
- 1 1/2 cups white sugar
- 1/2 cup unsalted butter
- 1/4 cup fresh lemon juice
- 3 eggs at room temperature
- 2 egg yolks at room temperature
- 1 tablespoon grated lemon zest
- 1 1/2 pints fresh raspberries

Direction

- Set oven to preheat at 350°F (175°C).
- Onto a baking sheet, spread out the coconut and, bake in the prepped oven till golden and lightly toasted, for about 10 minutes. Keep an eye on them to prevent burning. Mix 1/2 cup melted butter and the coconut in a bowl, and refrigerate till it starts to firm up, for about 15 minutes. Pat the coconut mixture into a 9-inch pie dish's bottom and sides. Chill till set, for no less than 30 minutes.
- Add the egg yolks, 1/2 cup of butter, lemon juice, eggs, and sugar into a saucepan. Put on low heat, and whisk continuously till thicken, for about 15 to 20 minutes. Do not boil. Pass the custard through a fine-mesh strainer right into a bowl, and stir the lemon zest into the mix. Put a plastic wrap sheet directly onto the custard's surface, and chill thoroughly.
- Into the coconut crust, spoon the lemon custard, and add fresh raspberries on top.

Nutrition Information

- Calories: 504 calories;
- Sodium: 84
- Total Carbohydrate: 54.9

- Cholesterol: 182
- Protein: 4.4
- Total Fat: 31.5

- Protein: 1.5
- Total Fat: 6.3
- Sodium: 85
- Total Carbohydrate: 21.9
- Cholesterol: 4

247. Summer Fresh Raspberry Pie

Serving: 12 | Prep: 20mins | Cook: 10mins | Ready in:

Ingredients

- 1/2 cup water
- 4 cups fresh raspberries, divided
- 2 tablespoons cornstarch
- 1/4 cup cold water
- 1/2 cup white sugar
- 1 tablespoon lemon juice
- 1 (9 inch) baked pie crust
- 1 cup whipped cream for garnish
- 1 teaspoon lemon zest for garnish

Direction

- Heat 1/2 cup water and 1 cup raspberries in a saucepan on medium heat; mix and cook for about 5 minutes till raspberries soften. Strain raspberries through a fine mesh sieve into bowl; discard seeds. Put mashed berries into saucepan.
- Mix 1/4 cup cold water and cornstarch till dissolved in a bowl; mix into mashed berries, then add sugar.
- Heat raspberry mixture on medium heat, constantly mixing, for about 5 minutes till thick; mix in lemon juice. Cool raspberry sauce to room temperature.
- Line leftover 3 cups raspberries on prepared pie crust; put raspberry sauce on berries. Chill till set. Garnish with lemon zest and whipped cream; serve.

Nutrition Information

- Calories: 146 calories;

248. Tartelettes De Framboises Au Mascarpone (Raspberry Tartlets)

Serving: 6 | Prep: 30mins | Cook: 20mins | Ready in:

Ingredients

- 2/3 cup confectioners' sugar
- 1/4 cup ground almonds
- 1 7/8 cups sifted all-purpose flour
- 1/2 cup softened unsalted butter
- 1 egg
- 9 ounces mascarpone cheese
- 1/2 cup Greek yogurt
- 4 1/2 tablespoons confectioners' sugar
- 1 vanilla bean, slit lengthwise, seeds scraped
- 1 pound fresh raspberries
- 3/4 cup coarsely chopped unsalted pistachios

Direction

- Prepare the oven by preheating to 350°F (175°C). Get six 4-inch tart pans and grease with butter, then sprinkle with flour.
- Mix together in a bowl the ground almonds and 2/3 cup confectioners' sugar and mix well. Add in the flour, then mix in the egg and unsalted butter. Whisk a few times until the dough becomes pliable and smooth, then make into a ball and place inside the freezer for 15 minutes.
- Split the dough into six portions, then flatten each portion to a circle 5 inches in diameter. Push the dough into the prepared tart pans; put parchment paper on top of the dough. Put pie weights or a few tablespoons of dried beans into bottom of each shell.

- Place inside the preheated oven and bake for 20 minutes until golden brown in color. Reserve the shells in their pans to cool on a rack. Detach and get rid of paper; keep pie weights or beans for another use.
- Beat together in a bowl scraped vanilla beans, 4 1/2 tablespoons of confectioners' sugar, yogurt, and mascarpone cheese until the mixture becomes smooth and thick. Scoop about 2 tablespoons of mascarpone filling in each cool tart shell; in a beautiful low mound arrange raspberries on top. Drizzle with pistachios each tart. Place inside the refrigerator for at least 15 minutes prior to serving.

Nutrition Information

- Calories: 723 calories;
- Protein: 15.2
- Total Fat: 46.3
- Sodium: 117
- Total Carbohydrate: 66.6
- Cholesterol: 128

249.   Teenie's Accidental Rhubarb Raspberry Pie

Serving: 8 | Prep: 15mins | Cook: 45mins | Ready in:

Ingredients

- 1 (15 ounce) package frozen prepared pie crusts, thawed
- 3 tablespoons all-purpose flour
- 1 cup white sugar
- 1 egg, beaten
- 1 cup raspberries
- 4 cups chopped fresh rhubarb

Direction

- Preheat an oven to 220 ° C or 425 ° F. Force a pie crust into a deep dish 9-inches pie pan.

- Mix sugar and flour together in medium bowl. Stir in raspberries and egg. Mix in rhubarb till equally coated. Turn onto prepped pie crust. Put another crust on top, and flute surrounding of edges to enclose. Using small knife, cut several slits in crust top to vent steam.
- In the prepped oven, bake for 10 minutes, then lower the heat to 175 ° C or 350 ° F, and bake for 35 minutes more, or till juices thicken and rhubarb is soft.

Nutrition Information

- Calories: 377 calories;
- Total Fat: 16.2
- Sodium: 314
- Total Carbohydrate: 55
- Cholesterol: 23
- Protein: 3.8

250.   Vegan Raspberry Chocolate Tarts

Serving: 12 | Prep: 40mins | Cook: 5mins | Ready in:

Ingredients

- Crust:
- 1 cup firmly packed pitted dates
- 1/2 cup walnuts
- Ganache:
- 1 1/2 cups vegan chocolate chips
- 1 tablespoon coconut oil
- 1/2 cup coconut cream (mix solid and liquid creams together before measuring)
- 3 tablespoons unsweetened cocoa powder
- Raspberry Filling:
- 6 ounces fresh raspberries

Direction

- In the bowl of a food processor, mix walnuts and dates and then blend about 2 minutes until combined well. Into the bottom of 12 mini tart pans, press approximately two tablespoons of the mixture. Transfer into the freezer as you prepare ganache.

- Put coconut oil and chocolate chips at the top of a double boiler on simmering water. To prevent scorching, mix often while scraping down the sides using a rubber spatula for about 5 minutes until the chocolate has melted. Pour the melted chocolate into the bowl of food processor. Pour in cocoa powder and coconut cream and blend for about 1 minutes on high until smooth.
- Take out the crusts from freezer. Scoop approximately 1 1/2 teaspoons of ganache over each crust and spread to the edges. Pour in enough to reach halfway up the side of tart cup. Return the tarts into freezer for about 10 minutes until firm.
- Use a fork to mash the raspberries in a bowl until you get consistency of a sauce. Onto the hardened ganache layer, layer mashed raspberries and do not go all the way to the edges. Place in a freezer for about 20 minutes until the sauce becomes firm and doesn't collapse after topping with ganache.
- Take out the tarts from the freezer. Pour the rest of the ganache on top and spread all the way to the edges. Ensure you seal in raspberry sauce as much as you can. Place back in the freezer to firm up. Store the tarts in the fridge in case you're serving them within two hours.

Nutrition Information

- Calories: 173 calories;
- Sodium: < 1
- Total Carbohydrate: 14.2
- Cholesterol: 0
- Protein: 1.5
- Total Fat: 13.8

Chapter 9: Rhubarb Pie Recipes

***

---
251.   Breezy Key Lime Pie With Strawberry Rhubarb Glaze

Serving: 8 | Prep: 20mins | Cook: 35mins |Ready in:

Ingredients

- 3 cups vanilla wafer crumbs
- 3 tablespoons butter, softened
- 2 (14 ounce) cans sweetened condensed milk
- 1 cup fresh Key lime juice
- 6 egg yolks
- 1 teaspoon vanilla extract
- 1 teaspoon Key lime zest
- 2 stalks fresh rhubarb, diced
- 2 cups chopped fresh strawberries
- 1 cup white sugar
- 1/2 cup water
- 2 teaspoons powdered fruit pectin

Direction

- Set oven to preheat at 350°F (175°C).
- In a bowl, mix together butter and the vanilla wafer crumbs until well combined, and press the crust into the bottom and up the sides of a 10-inch pie dish.
- Beat the key lime zest, vanilla extract, egg yolks, key lime juice and sweetened condensed milk in a bowl using an electric mixer until it has a smooth texture; put the filling into the prepared cookie crust.
- Bake the pie in the preheated oven for about 15 minutes until the center of pie is slightly jiggly. Let it cool for 10 minutes, then chill in the fridge.
- In a saucepan over medium heat, combine the pectin, water, sugar, strawberries, and

rhubarb, and bring the mixture to a boil. Stir frequently and boil until the berries and rhubarb break down and the glaze starts to thicken and has the consistency of jam, for about 20 minutes. Take off the heat; Allow to cool to lukewarm. The glaze will thicken as it cools down. Spread the glaze over the pie, and leave in the refrigerator until chilled. Let pie chill for at least 8 hours before serving for best texture.

Nutrition Information

- Calories: 834 calories;
- Total Fat: 29.4
- Sodium: 370
- Total Carbohydrate: 133.3
- Cholesterol: 198
- Protein: 13.2

---

252.   Buffalochef's Strawberry Rhubarb Pie

Serving: 8 | Prep: 30mins | Cook: 1hours | Ready in:

Ingredients

- 1/2 cup white sugar
- 1/2 cup all-purpose flour
- 1 teaspoon ground cinnamon
- 1/4 cup chilled butter
- 1 recipe pastry for a 9-inch double crust pie
- 1 pint fresh strawberries, sliced
- 3/4 pound rhubarb, chopped
- 1 1/3 cups white sugar
- 3 tablespoons minced crystallized ginger
- 1/4 cup all-purpose flour
- 1/2 teaspoon freshly grated nutmeg
- 1/4 teaspoon ground cinnamon
- 1/8 teaspoon salt
- 3 eggs

Direction

- Set oven to preheat at 220 o C (425 o F). Roll one half of the pie crust pastry out into a circle about 11 inches in diameter, and press the crust into a pie dish 9-inch in diameter. Put the pie dish onto a rimmed baking sheet.
- In a bowl, whisk together 1 teaspoon of cinnamon, 1/2 cup of flour, and 1/2 cup of sugar. Chop in the butter using a pastry cutter until the topping becomes crumbly; put the topping aside.
- In another bowl, stir together the strawberries, rhubarb, 1 1/3 cup of sugar, crystallized ginger, 1/4 cup of flour, nutmeg, 1/4 teaspoon of cinnamon, and salt until thoroughly combined; beat in the eggs.
- Roll the remaining pastry out into a circle 11-inch in diameter, and cut the crust into strips 1/2-inch width. Scoop the rhubarb-strawberry filling into the bottom crust, and evenly sprinkle the crumb topping atop the filling. Use a bit of water to moisten the rim of the filled bottom crust, and arrange the two longest strips in a cross in the center of the pie. Gradually work your way down from the next longest to the shortest ones, alternating horizontal and vertical strips, weave the strips as you work. Seal the lattice strips by pressing them down onto the bottom crust's edge, and neatly cut off the excess from the top crust strips. Use a fork dipped in a bit of flour to push down the crust edges to crimp the edges.
- In the preheated oven, bake for 10 minutes, then lower the heat to 175 o C (350 o F) until pie bubbles and the crumb topping and crust are light brown, an additional 45 to 50 minutes. Allow pie to cool at least 1 hour before serving.

Nutrition Information

- Calories: 557 calories;
- Sodium: 341
- Total Carbohydrate: 83
- Cholesterol: 85
- Protein: 7.1
- Total Fat: 23

253. Chef Neal's Strawberry Rhubarb Sour Cream Pies

Serving: 16 | Prep: 20mins | Cook: 55mins |Ready in:

Ingredients

- 2 (9 inch) frozen pie crusts
- 2 cups sour cream
- 4 large eggs
- 3 cups white sugar
- 4 tablespoons all-purpose flour
- 2 teaspoons vanilla extract
- 1/2 teaspoon salt
- 3 cups sliced strawberries
- 3 cups chopped rhubarb
- 1/2 cup packed brown sugar
- 1/2 cup all-purpose flour
- 6 tablespoons butter

Direction

- Preheat an oven to 230 ° C or 450 ° F. Line pie crusts on 2 pie plates.
- In a big bowl, mix together the eggs and sour cream. Mix in salt, vanilla extract, 4 tablespoons of flour and sugar. Mix in rhubarb and strawberries. Into two pie crusts, add the filling. Cover in aluminum foil.
- In the prepped oven, bake for 15 minutes, till crust is browned slightly. Lower the heat to 175 ° C or 350 ° F; keep baking for an additional of 20 minutes, till filling is well thickened and soft. Keep oven on.
- In bowl, mix together half cup of flour and brown sugar. Mash in butter till mixture looks much like coarse crumbs. Scatter mixture on top of pie fillings.
- Put pies back to hot oven. Bake for 20 to 25 minutes, till filling is firm.

Nutrition Information

- Calories: 440 calories;
- Sodium: 256
- Total Carbohydrate: 63.8
- Cholesterol: 71
- Protein: 4.9
- Total Fat: 19.3

254. Crispy Rhubarb Pie

Serving: 8 | Prep: | Cook: |Ready in:

Ingredients

- 3 1/2 cups diced rhubarb
- 1 tablespoon all-purpose flour
- 1/2 cup white sugar
- 1 recipe pastry for a 9 inch single crust pie
- 1/4 cup butter
- 1/2 cup packed brown sugar
- 1/2 cup crushed cornflakes cereal
- 1/2 cup all-purpose flour

Direction

- Combine white sugar, rhubarb and one tablespoon of the flour. Mix well then put into pie shell.
- Melt margarine or butter and mix with half a cup of the flour, crushed corn flakes and half a cup of the brown sugar. Mix in the bowl then pat down on top of the pie. Bake for 40 mins at 350°F (175°C) in the oven. Turn off the oven and leave pie for another hour in the oven. Enjoy warm.

Nutrition Information

- Calories: 315 calories;
- Protein: 3
- Total Fat: 13.4
- Sodium: 177
- Total Carbohydrate: 46.9
- Cholesterol: 15

255. Dave's Rhubarb Custard Pie With Meringue

Serving: 8 | Prep: 20mins | Cook: 30mins | Ready in:

Ingredients

- 1 (9 inch) refrigerated pie crust
- 4 cups rhubarb, chopped
- 1 1/3 cups white sugar
- 3 tablespoons butter
- 3 drops red food coloring (optional)
- 3 eggs, separated
- 6 tablespoons light whipping cream
- 6 tablespoons white sugar
- 3 tablespoons cornstarch
- 1/8 teaspoon salt
- 6 tablespoons white sugar
- 3/4 teaspoon vanilla extract

Direction

- Turn the oven to 400°F (205°C) to preheat. Use aluminum foil with a double layer to line the pie crust and put on dried beans or pie weights in a layer.
- Put in the preheated oven and bake for 10 minutes until the crust turns golden around the edge. Gently remove the weights and foil; keep baking for another 5 minutes until the crust sets. Take the crust out and let cool.
- Lower the oven heat to 325°F (165°C) and position a rack in the middle.
- In a pot, combine food coloring, butter, 1 1/3 cups sugar, and rhubarb over medium heat. Simmer for 7-10 minutes until the rhubarb is just beginning to fall apart and soft.
- In a bowl, combine salt, cornstarch, 6 tablespoons sugar, cream, and egg yolks. Pour into the rhubarb mixture while whisking continually. Keep whisking; simmer for 3-5 minutes until the mixture begins to get thick. Take away from heat and keep warm.
- In a ceramic, metal, or glass bowl, beat egg whites until frothy. Slowly add the leftover 6

tablespoons sugar, keeping beating until forming stiff peaks. Add to the meringue with vanilla extract.

- Add the rhubarb mixture to the baked pie crust. Lightly top the filling with the meringue in a pile. Spread the meringue until reaching the crust, sealing in the filling. Make a pretty pattern with the top of the meringue; the edges and high points will turn brown while baking.
- Bake for 15-20 minutes until turning finely brown and firm. Let the custard cool for 2 hours until set. Keep chilled.

Nutrition Information

- Calories: 428 calories;
- Sodium: 217
- Total Carbohydrate: 68.4
- Cholesterol: 89
- Protein: 4.6
- Total Fat: 15.9

256. Evie's Rhubarb Pie With Oatmeal Crumble

Serving: 8 | Prep: 15mins | Cook: 45mins | Ready in:

Ingredients

- 4 cups sliced fresh rhubarb (about 1/2 inch thick)
- 1 1/2 cups white sugar
- 2 tablespoons quick-cooking tapioca
- 1 1/2 tablespoons butter, melted
- 1 (9 inch) refrigerated pie crust
- 1/2 cup regular rolled oats
- 1/4 cup white sugar
- 2 tablespoons all-purpose flour
- 1 tablespoon butter, melted
- 1 pinch ground cinnamon

Direction

- Start preheating the oven at 400°F (200°C).
- In a large bowl, mix tapioca, 1 1/2 cups of sugar and rhubarb. Sprinkle with the melted butter and toss once more to coat. Transfer the rhubarb into the pie crust, and put aside.
- Combine cinnamon, softened butter, four, 1/4 cup of sugar, and oats in a small bowl until evenly blended. Spread the oat topping over the rhubarb.
- Bake in the prepared oven for about 15 minutes, then lower the heat to 325°F (165°C), and keep baking for an extra 30 minutes, until rhubarb is fork-tender. Let cool to room temperature before using.

Nutrition Information

- Calories: 361 calories;
- Sodium: 145
- Total Carbohydrate: 63.5
- Cholesterol: 10
- Protein: 2.9
- Total Fat: 11.5

257. Fast Apple Rhubarb Pie

Serving: 8 | Prep: | Cook: | Ready in:

Ingredients

- 1 (9 inch) pie shell
- 6 apple - peeled, cored, and chopped
- 3 rhubarb, diced
- 1 cup white sugar
- 2 teaspoons ground cinnamon

Direction

- Turn on the oven at 440°F (220°C) to preheat.
- In a large bowl, mix together rhubarb and apples. In a small bowl, combine cinnamon and sugar; add it onto the fruit. Stir until well-coated. Pour the mixture into the pastry shell.
- Put into the oven to bake in 40 minutes.

Nutrition Information

- Calories: 237 calories;
- Sodium: 104
- Total Carbohydrate: 48.4
- Cholesterol: 0
- Protein: 1.2
- Total Fat: 5.4

258. Fresh Rhubarb Pie

Serving: 8 | Prep: 30mins | Cook: 1hours | Ready in:

Ingredients

- 4 cups chopped rhubarb
- 1 1/3 cups white sugar
- 6 tablespoons all-purpose flour
- 1 tablespoon butter
- 1 recipe pastry for a 9 inch double crust pie

Direction

- Set the oven to 450°F or 230°C for preheating.
- Mix the flour and sugar. Sprinkle the pastry in a pie plate with 1/4 of the flour mixture. Heap the rhubarb all over this mixture. Sprinkle it with the remaining flour and sugar. Dot small pieces of butter all over it and cover it with the top crust.
- Position the pie into the lowest rack inside the oven. Bake it for 15 minutes. Adjust the heat to 350°F (175°C). Bake it for 40-45 more minutes. Serve this either cold or warm.

Nutrition Information

- Calories: 290 calories;
- Total Fat: 9.1
- Sodium: 130
- Total Carbohydrate: 50.8
- Cholesterol: 4
- Protein: 2.6

259. Fresh Rhubarb Torte

Serving: 8 | Prep: 20mins | Cook: 1hours5mins |Ready in:

Ingredients

- 1 cup all-purpose flour
- 2 tablespoons white sugar
- 1/2 cup butter, melted
- 1 1/4 cups white sugar
- 2 1/2 cups diced rhubarb
- 2 tablespoons all-purpose flour
- 1/3 cup milk
- 3 egg yolks, beaten

Direction

- Preheat oven to 165 degrees C/325 degrees F. Use cooking spray to prep a 9x9-in. baking dish.
- Mix melted butter, 2 tbsp. sugar and 1 cup flour until combined well. Pat mixture to the bottom of prepped baking dish.
- Bake crust in preheated oven for about 25 minutes until very lightly browned; put aside. Slightly cool. Bring oven heat to 175 degrees C/350 degrees F.
- Mix beaten egg yolks, milk, 2 tbsp. flour, rhubarb and 1 1/4 cup sugar until combined well. Pour on crust.
- Bake in oven for 40-45 minutes until set. Serve warm.

Nutrition Information

- Calories: 332 calories;
- Total Fat: 13.6
- Sodium: 91
- Total Carbohydrate: 50.2
- Cholesterol: 108
- Protein: 3.6

260. Grammy's Favorite Rhubarb Custard Pie

Serving: 8 | Prep: 30mins | Cook: 1hours |Ready in:

Ingredients

- 1 double crust ready-to-use pie crust
- 3 cups diced rhubarb
- 2 eggs
- 1 1/2 cups white sugar
- 1/3 cup light cream
- 1/2 teaspoon vanilla extract
- 1 tablespoon all-purpose flour

Direction

- Heat the oven to 220°C or 425°F.
- Put rhubarb to a prepped pie crust. Whip flour, vanilla extract, cream, sugar and eggs till evenly incorporated; put on top of rhubarb. Make lattice with the rest of pie crust, and put over pie.
- Bake for 15 minutes in prepped oven, then lower heat to 175°C or 350°F, and keep baking for about 45 minutes. Cool fully prior to serving.

Nutrition Information

- Calories: 404 calories;
- Protein: 4.8
- Total Fat: 16.3
- Sodium: 253
- Total Carbohydrate: 61
- Cholesterol: 46

261. Grandma's Rhubarb Torte

Serving: 15 | Prep: 15mins | Cook: 1hours30mins |Ready in:

Ingredients

- 3/4 cup butter
- 1 3/4 cups all-purpose flour, divided
- 1 tablespoon white sugar
- 6 eggs, separated
- 1 cup evaporated milk
- 2 cups white sugar
- 8 cups diced rhubarb
- 3/4 cup white sugar
- 1 teaspoon vanilla extract

Direction

- Set oven to preheat at 350°F (175°C). Grease a 9x13 inch baking dish lightly.
- Mix 1 tablespoon sugar, 1 1/2 cups flour, and butter in a mixing bowl; use an electric mixer to beat till incorporated. Pat the mixture into the prepared baking dish's bottom.
- In preheated oven, bake the crust till firm, for about 15 minutes. Take out of the oven and let the crust cool.
- Mix rhubarb, remaining 1/4 cup flour, evaporated milk, 2 cups sugar, and 6 egg yolks in large mixing bowl. Stir together and pour over cooled crust.
- Bake pie in the oven until filling sets, for about 1 hour.
- To make meringue, use an electric mixer to beat 6 egg whites in a large bowl till the whites are foamy. Beat 3/4 cup sugar and vanilla extract into the egg whites till the mixture holds firm peaks. Spread meringue onto the rhubarb filling.
- Take the pie back into the oven and bake till the meringue is golden brown, for about 15 to 20 minutes.

Nutrition Information

- Calories: 345 calories;
- Total Fat: 12.7
- Sodium: 114
- Total Carbohydrate: 53.5
- Cholesterol: 104
- Protein: 5.8

262.   Maman's Fresh Strawberry Rhubarb Pie

Serving: 8 | Prep: 15mins | Cook: 5mins | Ready in:

Ingredients

- 1 1/4 cups crushed graham crackers
- 1/4 cup melted butter
- 1 pound fresh strawberries, halved lengthwise
- 1/2 cup diced rhubarb
- 3/4 cup white sugar
- 3/4 cup water
- 3 tablespoons cornstarch
- 1 tablespoon lemon juice

Direction

- Combine melted butter and the graham cracker crumbs then press the mixture into the bottom of a 9-inch pie dish. Halve strawberries then arrange 1 layer of strawberry halves on the bottom of the pie crust.
- Put the remaining strawberries in a saucepan then crush (you should get a cup of crushed berries); add cornstarch, water, sugar, rhubarb to the crushed berries and stir. Bring the mixture to a boil over medium-low heat, remember to stir regularly till the mixture gets thick and becomes translucent. Get the mixture away from heat and allow to stand for about 2 minutes until it cools slightly; pour in lemon juice in and stir. Transfer the mixture to the pie dish on top of the strawberry halves.
- Keep in the fridge for about an hour until the mixture is chilled completely.

Nutrition Information

- Calories: 211 calories;
- Sodium: 122
- Total Carbohydrate: 36.4
- Cholesterol: 15

- Protein: 1.4
- Total Fat: 7.3

263.   Mulberry Rhubarb Pie

Serving: 8 | Prep: 15mins | Cook: 45mins | Ready in:

Ingredients

- 2 1/2 cups mulberries
- 1 1/2 cups finely chopped rhubarb
- 1 1/4 cups white sugar
- 1/4 cup all-purpose flour
- 1 tablespoon butter
- 1 recipe pastry for a 9 inch single crust pie

Direction

- Combine flour, sugar, rhubarb and mulberries.
- Pour into unbaked 9 inch pie crust. Dot filling with margarine or butter and put top shell on.
- Bake for 15 minutes at 400°F (205°C). Turn down oven temperature to 350°F (175°C). Bake about half an hour until pie is done.

Nutrition Information

- Calories: 285 calories;
- Cholesterol: 4
- Protein: 2.6
- Total Fat: 9.2
- Sodium: 132
- Total Carbohydrate: 49.8

264.   My Own Strawberry Rhubarb Pie

Serving: 8 | Prep: 30mins | Cook: 40mins | Ready in:

Ingredients

- 3 cups strawberries, cut into 1/2-inch pieces

- 3 cups chopped rhubarb
- 1/2 cup brown sugar
- 1/2 cup white sugar
- 1 teaspoon ground cinnamon
- 1 teaspoon ground allspice
- 1 tablespoon cornstarch, or as needed
- 1/4 cup all-purpose flour
- 1 tablespoon butter, diced
- 1 recipe pastry for a 9 inch double crust pie
- 1 tablespoon milk
- 1 tablespoon white sugar

Direction

- In a bowl, combine the flour, cornstarch, allspice, cinnamon, 1/2 cup of white sugar, brown sugar, rhubarb, and strawberries; stir to combine the flour and cornstarch until smooth. Let the filling sit for 30 minutes. If the filling is too juicy, add 1 more tablespoon of cornstarch.
- Set oven to preheat at 200 o C (400 o F).
- Split the pie pastry in half; on a floured work surface, roll one half out into a circle, and line bottom crust on a 9-inch pie dish. On a floured work surface, roll out the last half into a 10-inch circle, and put aside.
- Pour the filling into the pie dish lined with the crust. Sprinkle diced butter on top.
- Cut the saved crust into strips of 3/4-inch width (for a more beautiful crust, use a scalloped edge pastry cutter). Use a bit of water to moisten the rim of the filled bottom crust, and arrange two longest strips in a cross in the pie's center. From the next longest down to the shortest strips, arrange horizontal and vertical strips alternately, weave the strips as you work. Push down the lattice strips onto the edge of the bottom crust to seal, and neatly trim the strips of the top crust. Use milk to brush the crust, and sprinkle 1 tablespoon of sugar on top. Use aluminum foil strips to cover pie edges.
- In preheated oven, bake pie for 15 minutes; reduce temperature to 190 o C (375 o F), and bake until the filling bubbles and the crust turns golden brown, about 40 minutes. Take

out aluminum foil about 15 minutes before the baking finishes. Turn oven off, and with the door open, let pie sit for 15 minutes, then close the door and let sit for another 15 minutes. Let cool completely on wire rack overnight or for at least a few hours; as it sits, filling will thicken.

Nutrition Information

- Calories: 397 calories;
- Total Fat: 16.8
- Sodium: 251
- Total Carbohydrate: 59.3
- Cholesterol: 4
- Protein: 4.1

265.   Nicki's Summer Strawberry Rhubarb Pie

Serving: 8 | Prep: 30mins | Cook: 55mins | Ready in:

Ingredients

- 2 1/2 cups all-purpose flour
- 1 teaspoon salt
- 1/2 cup vegetable shortening, chilled
- 1/2 cup unsalted butter, chilled
- 1/4 cup ice water, or as needed
- 2 1/2 cups chopped fresh strawberries
- 2 1/2 cups chopped fresh rhubarb
- 1 1/4 cups white sugar
- 2 tablespoons quick-cooking tapioca
- 2 tablespoons all-purpose flour
- 1 teaspoon vanilla extract
- 1/2 teaspoon orange juice
- 1/4 teaspoon grated orange zest
- 1/2 teaspoon ground cinnamon
- 2 tablespoons butter, chilled and cut into small pieces
- 1 egg white, beaten

Direction

- In a big bowl, beat 2 1/2 cups of flour with salt. Cut the vegetable shortening and unsalted butter into the flour using a pastry cutter until the mixture forms coarse crumbs with several pea-sized pieces of fat; mix in ice water, a tablespoon at a time, just until the mixture sticks together when squeezed. Split dough in half and roll each half into a ball; cover the balls in plastic wrap and chill for at least an hour or up to overnight.
- Set oven to 375°F (190°C) to preheat. On a floured surface, shape a dough ball into an 11-inch circle; fit the shell into a 9-inch pie plate. Chill while preparing filling.
- In a bowl, combine cinnamon, orange zest, vanilla extract, 2 tablespoons of flour, tapioca, 1 1/4 cup of sugar, orange juice, rhubarb and strawberries. Put the filling into the pie pan lined with crust. Scatter 2 tablespoons of butter pieces on top of the filling. On a floured surface, shape second dough ball into a 10-inch circle and put the top crust onto the filling gently. Crimp the edges together using a fork to seal. Brush the pie using beaten egg white and score a few slits into the top using a sharp knife.
- Bake for 55 minutes to 1 hour in the prepared oven until golden brown on top and the filling is bubbling. Cover the pie edges using strips of aluminum foil if they begin to brown too quickly. Let cool completely prior to serving.

Nutrition Information

- Calories: 546 calories;
- Total Fat: 27.8
- Sodium: 323
- Total Carbohydrate: 70.2
- Cholesterol: 38
- Protein: 5.6

266. Orange Kissed Strawberry Rhubarb Pie

Serving: 8 | Prep: 30mins | Cook: 40mins |Ready in:

Ingredients

- 1 pastry for a 10-inch double crust pie
- 1 1/2 cups white sugar
- 1/4 teaspoon salt
- 1/2 teaspoon grated orange peel
- 1/4 cup quick-cooking tapioca
- 1/4 teaspoon ground nutmeg
- 4 cups rhubarb, cut into 1/2 inch pieces
- 2 cups fresh strawberries, quartered
- 1/4 cup fresh orange juice
- 2 tablespoons butter, cut into small chunks
- 1 tablespoon milk
- 1 tablespoon white sugar

Direction

- Set oven to preheat at 200°C (400°F). Split the pie pastry in half, roll out one half out to a round pie crust about a 12 inches diameter, and transfer the crust to a 10-inch pie dish's bottom. Chill the other half of the pie pastry in the refrigerator until needed.
- In a bowl, mix together nutmeg, tapioca, orange peel, the salt, and the 1 1/2 cups of sugar until well incorporated. Stir in gently the orange juice, strawberries, and rhubarb, be careful not to smash the strawberries; transfer into the prepared pie crust. Use butter pieces to dot the filling. Roll out the reserved pie pastry to about a 12-inch circle shape and cover the fruit filling with the top crust.
- Seal the two crusts together by folding the edges of the bottom and top crust together. To create a rounded indentation on the edge of pie crust, place your left index finger against the outer edge of the crust, and pinch the crust against it using the right index finger and thumb. Move around the edge of the pie, make a fluted crust by pinching the edge of the crust against the index finger of your left hand. Brush the top crust of the pie with milk and

sprinkle 1 tablespoon of sugar on top. Slice some vent holes in the top crust.
- In the preheated oven, bake until the filling is bubbling and thickened and the crust becomes brown, for 40 to 50 minutes. Check after 30 minutes baking, if the crust edges are browning too fast, use strips of aluminum foil to cover them. Allow the pie to cool before serving.

Nutrition Information

- Calories: 450 calories;
- Total Fat: 18.2
- Sodium: 331
- Total Carbohydrate: 70.1
- Cholesterol: 8
- Protein: 3.8

267. Pineapple Rhubarb Pie

Serving: 8 | Prep: 20mins | Cook: 45mins |Ready in:

Ingredients

- 1 pastry for a 9 inch double crust pie
- 1 pound fresh rhubarb, cut into 1 inch pieces
- 2 (8 ounce) cans pineapple chunks, drained
- 1 1/8 cups white sugar
- 2 tablespoons tapioca
- 1 tablespoon milk

Direction

- Turn the oven to 400°F (200°C) to preheat. On a surface lightly scattered with flour, roll 1 crust out and put in a 9-in. pie plate. Roll the top crust out and put aside.
- Combine tapioca, sugar, pineapple chunks, and rhubarb together in a big bowl. Add to the pie crust. Put on the top crust to cover, then seal and crimp the edge. Brush milk over and slice several vents in the top to release steam.

- Put in the preheated oven and bake until the liquid is bubbly in the middle and the crust turns golden, 45 minutes.

Nutrition Information

- Calories: 390 calories;
- Protein: 3.6
- Total Fat: 15.1
- Sodium: 237
- Total Carbohydrate: 61.9
- Cholesterol: < 1

268.   Pineapple Rhubarb Pie

Serving: 8 | Prep: 20mins | Cook: 45mins | Ready in:

Ingredients

- 1 (15 ounce) package refrigerated pie crusts
- 1 1/3 cups white sugar
- 1/3 cup all-purpose flour
- 1/2 teaspoon grated orange zest
- 1/8 teaspoon salt
- 3 cups chopped rhubarb
- 1 cup drained crushed pineapple
- 2 tablespoons butter

Direction

- Turn the oven to 425°F (220°C) to preheat. Press 1 of the pie crusts up the sides and into the bottom of a 9-in. pie plate. Chill the remaining crust until using.
- Combine salt, orange zest, flour, and sugar together in a medium-sized bowl. Mix together pineapple and rhubarb, then mix into the dry ingredients until evenly combined. Add to the prepared pie crust. Top with the other crust and seal in the filling by crimping the edges. Slice several holes in the top pastry to release steam.

- Put in the preheated oven and bake for 45-50 minutes until the rhubarb is fork-tender and the crust turns golden brown.

Nutrition Information

- Calories: 447 calories;
- Protein: 4.1
- Total Fat: 19.2
- Sodium: 312
- Total Carbohydrate: 66.3
- Cholesterol: 8

269.   Renee's Strawberry Rhubarb Pie

Serving: 8 | Prep: 30mins | Cook: 55mins | Ready in:

Ingredients

- 2 tablespoons cornstarch
- 1 tablespoon water
- 2 1/2 cups diced rhubarb
- 2 1/2 cups sliced fresh strawberries
- 1 1/4 cups white sugar
- 1/2 teaspoon lemon juice
- 3/4 teaspoon ground cinnamon
- 1 teaspoon vanilla extract
- 1 recipe pastry for a 9 inch double crust pie
- 1 egg white
- 1 teaspoon water
- 1 tablespoon turbinado sugar (such as Sugar in the Raw®)

Direction

- Whisk together 1 tablespoon of water and cornstarch in a bowl until well mixed. Mix in the vanilla extract, cinnamon, lemon juice, white sugar, strawberries, and rhubarb. Let the mixture sit for 30 minutes.
- Set oven to preheat at 220°C (425°F). Place bottom crust into a pie dish 9-inch in size. On

a floured work surface, roll the leftover crust out into a circle 10-inch in size, and put aside.

- Mix the filling, and add to the prepared pie dish. Cut the remaining crust into 1-inch wide strips (for a prettier crust, use a scalloped edge pastry cutter). Use a bit of water to moisten the filled bottom crust's rim, and arrange two longest strips in a cross in the pie's center. Using the second longest down to the shortest strips, arrange vertical and horizontal strips alternatively, weave the strips as you work your way down. Push the lattice strips onto the edge of the bottom crust to seal, and neatly trim the strips of the top crust. Beat 1 teaspoon of water and the egg white in a small bowl, and brush the beaten egg white atop the entire lattice top. Sprinkle turbinado sugar on top. Use aluminum foil strips to wrap around the pie's edges.
- In the preheated oven, bake for 15 minutes; lower heat to 190°C (375°F), and bake until the filling is bubbling and the crust is browned, for 40 to 45 more minutes. Take off the aluminum foil in the last 10 minutes of baking. Let pie cool thoroughly before serving.

Nutrition Information

- Calories: 391 calories;
- Sodium: 244
- Total Carbohydrate: 61.1
- Cholesterol: 0
- Protein: 3.9
- Total Fat: 15.2

270.   Rhubarb Cheese Pie

Serving: 8 | Prep: 15mins | Cook: 45mins | Ready in:

Ingredients

- 1 (9 inch) unbaked pie shell
- 1/3 cup white sugar
- 1 tablespoon all-purpose flour

- 2 cups chopped fresh rhubarb
- 1 (8 ounce) package cream cheese, softened
- 1/3 cup white sugar
- 2 eggs
- 1 cup sour cream
- 2 tablespoons white sugar
- 1 teaspoon vanilla extract

Direction

- Start preheating the oven at 425°F (220°C). Arrange the unbaked pie crust onto a 9-inch pie plate.
- In a medium bowl, blend 1/3 cup of sugar and flour. Include in rhubarb, toss to coat. Transfer into the pie shell.
- Bake about 15 minutes in the prepared oven. While baking, combine eggs, 1/3 cup of sugar, and cream cheese, until well-mixed and smooth. Add over the rhubarb once 15 minutes is done, and bring back to the oven.
- Lower the oven temperature to 350°F (175°C). Bake the pie once more for about 30 minutes. While baking, mix vanilla, 2 tablespoons of sugar, and sour cream until smooth. Scatter over the top of the pie right after coming out of the oven. Let cool, and then slice into wedges and enjoy.

Nutrition Information

- Calories: 379 calories;
- Protein: 6.4
- Total Fat: 24.6
- Sodium: 234
- Total Carbohydrate: 34.3
- Cholesterol: 90

271.   Rhubarb Cream Pie

Serving: 8 | Prep: | Cook: | Ready in:

Ingredients

- 1 (9 inch) deep dish pie crust
- 1 1/2 cups white sugar
- 1/4 cup all-purpose flour
- 3/4 teaspoon ground nutmeg
- 3 eggs, beaten
- 4 cups chopped rhubarb

Direction

- Turn the oven to 400°F (200°C) to preheat.
- Combine nutmeg, flour, and sugar in a big bowl. Mix in eggs. Add rhubarb and stir until completely coated. Add the filling to the pastry shell.
- Bake for 50-60 minutes in the preheated oven.

Nutrition Information

- Calories: 317 calories;
- Total Fat: 9.6
- Sodium: 176
- Total Carbohydrate: 54.8
- Cholesterol: 70
- Protein: 4.3

272.   Rhubarb Crumble Pie

Serving: 8 | Prep: 30mins | Cook: 40mins | Ready in:

Ingredients

- 1 cup all-purpose flour
- 1/4 teaspoon salt
- 1 cup rolled oats
- 1/2 cup white sugar
- 1/3 cup shortening, melted
- 3 cups diced rhubarb
- 1/2 cup white sugar
- 1/4 teaspoon ground cinnamon
- 1 tablespoon water
- 1 tablespoon butter

Direction

- Set the oven to 350°F (175°C) for preheating.

- Sift the salt and flour together in a medium bowl. Mix in 1/2 cup of sugar and oats. Cut in the shortening until the mixture is crumbly. Pat half of the mixture into the 9-inches pie pan. Put the remaining half for the topping aside. Spread the rhubarb onto the pie shell. Sprinkle rhubarb with 1/2 cup of sugar, water, and cinnamon. Dot the mixture with butter. Spread the filling with the remaining oat mixture.
- Bake it for 40 minutes inside the preheated oven until the rhubarb is tender.

Nutrition Information

- Calories: 290 calories;
- Total Fat: 10.9
- Sodium: 86
- Total Carbohydrate: 45.9
- Cholesterol: 4
- Protein: 3.4

273.   Rhubarb Custard Pie I

Serving: 8 | Prep: 20mins | Cook: 40mins | Ready in:

Ingredients

- 2 1/2 cups rhubarb, cut into 1/2 inch pieces
- 2 egg yolks
- 1 cup white sugar
- 2 1/2 tablespoons all-purpose flour
- 1 tablespoon butter
- 2 (9 inch) unbaked pie crusts

Direction

- Beat egg yolks until forming thick foams. Slowly beat in melted margarine or butter, flour, and sugar. Use 2 tablespoons flour for frozen rhubarb and 3 tablespoons flour for fresh rhubarb. Mix in rhubarb pieces.

- Add the rhubarb mixture to a chilled, unbaked pie shell. Put on the top crust to cover the filling. Flute and cut slits on the pie.
- Put on the bottom rack of the oven and bake for 10 minutes at 425°F (220°C), and then for 30 minutes at 375°F (190°C). Cool briefly before slicing.

Nutrition Information

- Calories: 361 calories;
- Total Fat: 16.8
- Sodium: 293
- Total Carbohydrate: 50.1
- Cholesterol: 55
- Protein: 3.2

274.   Rhubarb Custard Pie II

Serving: 8 | Prep: | Cook: | Ready in:

Ingredients

- 1 recipe pastry for a 9 inch double crust pie
- 3 eggs
- 2 cups white sugar
- 1/4 cup all-purpose flour
- 1 teaspoon vanilla extract
- 3 tablespoons milk
- 1 tablespoon butter
- 4 cups diced rhubarb

Direction

- To make bottom crust, roll out pastry, then transfer into a pie dish. Add rhubarb into the crust.
- Beat eggs lightly in a big bowl. Toss in margarine (or butter), milk, vanilla, flour and sugar. Transfer mixture onto rhubarb. Lay top crust to cover and seal the edges.
- Bake for 50-60 minutes at 205°C (400°F).

Nutrition Information

- Calories: 492 calories;
- Total Fat: 18.5
- Sodium: 275
- Total Carbohydrate: 76.7
- Cholesterol: 74
- Protein: 6.3

275.   Rhubarb Custard Pie III

Serving: 8 | Prep: | Cook: | Ready in:

Ingredients

- 1 (9 inch) pie shell
- 2 cups diced rhubarb
- 2 egg yolks
- 2 egg whites
- 3/4 cup white sugar
- 1 pinch salt
- 1 1/2 tablespoons all-purpose flour
- 1 3/4 cups scalded milk

Direction

- Set oven to 400°F (200°C) to preheat.
- Evenly spread rhubarb across bottom of pastry crust. Put aside.
- Whip egg yolks with egg whites in individual bowls. Add milk, flour, salt and sugar to yolks. Stir well, then fold in beaten egg whites gently. Add mixture over rhubarb layer.
- Put pie in the prepared oven. Bake for 10 mins, then turn down heat to 350°F (175°C). Bake for 40-50 minutes more. Let cool before serving.

Nutrition Information

- Calories: 209 calories;
- Total Fat: 7.4
- Sodium: 141
- Total Carbohydrate: 31.8
- Cholesterol: 55
- Protein: 4.4

276. Rhubarb Custard Pie V

Serving: 8 | Prep: | Cook: |Ready in:

Ingredients

- 1 (9 inch) pie shell
- 2 1/2 cups fresh rhubarb, cut into 1 inch pieces
- 1 cup white sugar
- 1/3 cup all-purpose flour
- 1 pinch ground cinnamon
- 2 eggs, beaten

Direction

- Start preheating oven to 190°C (375°F).
- Spread rhubarb into the pie shell evenly.
- Mix together cinnamon, flour and sugar in a medium bowl. Combine thoroughly; whisk in eggs. Transfer mixture onto rhubarb layer.
- Bake for 40-45 minutes in prepared oven until filling has set.

Nutrition Information

- Calories: 223 calories;
- Protein: 3.2
- Total Fat: 6.6
- Sodium: 121
- Total Carbohydrate: 38.7
- Cholesterol: 46

277. Rhubarb Custard Pie VI

Serving: 10 | Prep: 20mins | Cook: 50mins |Ready in:

Ingredients

- 2 1/2 cups all-purpose flour
- 1 teaspoon salt
- 1 cup shortening
- 1/4 cup water
- 1 tablespoon vinegar
- 1 egg, beaten
- 3 eggs
- 3 1/2 tablespoons all-purpose flour
- 1 1/2 cups white sugar
- 1/4 teaspoon salt
- 1/4 teaspoon ground nutmeg
- 2 tablespoons butter, softened
- 1/4 cup orange juice
- 4 cups diced rhubarb

Direction

- Set oven to 450°F (230°C) to preheat.
- Prepare Crust: Mix the 2 1/2 cups flour and 1 teaspoon salt in a medium bowl. Mash in shortening to form coarse crumbs. Mix in an egg, vinegar and water. Roll dough into ball and shape into 2 1/8 inch thick rounds. Cover sides and the bottom of a ten-inch pie plate with one.
- Prepare Filling: Whip leftover eggs in a large bowl until thick and light. Mix nutmeg, salt, sugar and flour. Fold into the eggs. Mix in orange juice and butter until the mixture is smooth. Fold in rhubarb. Add to pie crust; cover top of pie with leftover pie crust. Crimp edges together and score slits in top shell.
- Bake for 15 minutes in a prepared 450°F (230°C) oven. Turn down oven temperature to 350°F (175°C). Keep baking the pie for 35 minutes more at this temperature.

Nutrition Information

- Calories: 530 calories;
- Sodium: 336
- Total Carbohydrate: 72
- Cholesterol: 81
- Protein: 6.3
- Total Fat: 25.2

278. Rhubarb Meringue Pie

Serving: 6 | Prep: 15mins | Cook: 1hours |Ready in:

Ingredients

- 3 eggs, separated
- 1 (9 inch) unbaked single pie crust
- 3 cups chopped rhubarb
- 1 cup white sugar
- 1 cup half-and-half
- 2 tablespoons all-purpose flour
- 1 pinch salt
- 1/4 cup white sugar
- 1/4 teaspoon cream of tartar

Direction

- Set oven to 350°F (175°C) to preheat.
- Put egg yolks into a large bowl; put egg whites into a separate metal or glass bowl.
- Fit pie crust into a 9-inch pie dish. Spoon rhubarb into the bottom of the crust. Stir salt, flour, half-and-half, and 1 cup sugar into egg yolks until smooth; pour over rhubarb.
- Bake for 50 to 60 minutes in the preheated oven until filling is set and the crust is browned.
- Beat egg whites with an electric mixer until stiff; gradually beat in cream of tartar and 1/4 cup sugar until meringue becomes glossy. Spoon the meringue over the pie filling, covering all the filling and going right to the edge of the crust. Create decorative swirls in the meringue with a spatula or spoon.
- Put pie back into the oven and bake for 10 minutes longer until meringue turns brown lightly. Serve while slightly warm for the best flavor.

Nutrition Information

- Calories: 424 calories;
- Cholesterol: 108
- Protein: 7
- Total Fat: 17.2
- Sodium: 210

- Total Carbohydrate: 62.1

279. Rhubarb Orange Cream Pie

Serving: 8 | Prep: | Cook: |Ready in:

Ingredients

- 1 (9 inch) unbaked pie crust
- 1/4 cup butter, softened
- 3 tablespoons orange juice
- 3 egg yolks
- 1 teaspoon strawberry flavored Jell-O® mix
- 1 cup white sugar
- 1/4 cup all-purpose flour
- 1/4 teaspoon salt
- 3 cups diced rhubarb
- 3 egg whites
- 1/4 cup white sugar

Direction

- Insert rack to the lowest position in the oven. Set oven to 190°C (or 375°F) and begin preheating. Prepare a pastry-lined pie pan and create high fluted rim.
- Mix together strawberry gelatin, egg yolks, juice and butter in a big bowl. Whisk well. Pour in a cup of sugar, flour and salt; beat thoroughly. Mix in rhubarb.
- Beat egg white until stiff in a different bowl. Gradually add a quarter cup of sugar and keep beating. Fold meringue into the rhubarb mixture. Transfer filling into pastry shell.
- Bake for 15 minutes in prepared oven. Lower the heat to 165°C (or 325°F) and bake for another 45-50 minutes.

Nutrition Information

- Calories: 382 calories;
- Cholesterol: 92
- Protein: 4.4

- Total Fat: 14.9
- Sodium: 256
- Total Carbohydrate: 59.9

280. Rhubarb Pie

Serving: 8 | Prep: 10mins | Cook: 45mins | Ready in:

Ingredients

- 1 egg
- 1 1/2 cups white sugar
- 1 tablespoon all-purpose flour
- 1/4 teaspoon salt
- 3 cups chopped rhubarb
- 1 recipe pastry for a 9 inch double crust pie

Direction

- Turn the oven to 350°F (175°C) to preheat.
- In a mixing bowl, combine rhubarb, salt, flour, white sugar, and egg.
- In the bottom of a 9-in. pie plate, put 1 of the pie shells. Add the pie filling to the shell, then dot butter over. Put over the filling with the top crust and slice vents into the crust.
- Put in the preheated oven and bake for 30-45 minutes, or cook in a microwave for 7 minutes, and then in the oven for 10 minutes.

Nutrition Information

- Calories: 395 calories;
- Protein: 4.1
- Total Fat: 15.7
- Sodium: 317
- Total Carbohydrate: 60.9
- Cholesterol: 23

281. Rhubarb Pie Single Crust

Serving: 6 | Prep: 15mins | Cook: 45mins | Ready in:

Ingredients

- 1 tablespoon butter
- 2 eggs
- 1 cup white sugar
- 3 tablespoons all-purpose flour
- 3 cups diced rhubarb
- 1 (9 inch) prepared 9-inch single pie crust

Direction

- Set oven to 175°C (or 350°F) and start preheating.
- Heat butter for about 60 seconds in a 4-cup microwave-safe measuring cup in the microwave oven until melted but not hot. Using a fork, beat flour, sugar and eggs into butter until smooth. Spread rhubarb into unbaked pie crust and add liquid ingredients on top.
- Bake pie for about 45 minutes in prepared oven until filling is browned lightly.

Nutrition Information

- Calories: 348 calories;
- Total Fat: 13.7
- Sodium: 195
- Total Carbohydrate: 52.9
- Cholesterol: 67
- Protein: 4.9

282. Rhubarb Pie IV

Serving: 8 | Prep: 15mins | Cook: 40mins | Ready in:

Ingredients

- 4 cups chopped rhubarb
- 3/4 cup all-purpose flour
- 1 1/4 cups white sugar
- 2 (9 inch) unbaked pie crusts
- 1 egg, beaten

Direction

- Set oven to 350°F (175°C).
- Add rhubarb to the prepared pie shell. Mix flour with sugar; scatter on top of the rhubarb in the shell. Cover with top crust, be sure to score 4 steam slots in top. Brush the top with egg.
- Bake for 30 to 45 minutes in prepared oven.

Nutrition Information

- Calories: 407 calories;
- Total Fat: 15
- Sodium: 291
- Total Carbohydrate: 64.4
- Cholesterol: 23
- Protein: 4.4

---

283.   Rhubarb Rumble Pie Or Bars

Serving: 8 | Prep: 15mins | Cook: 5mins | Ready in:

Ingredients

- 3 cups chopped rhubarb
- 1 (3 ounce) package strawberry-flavored Jell-O® mix
- 1 1/2 cups cold skim milk
- 1 (3.4 ounce) package instant vanilla pudding mix
- 2 cups sliced fresh strawberries (optional)
- 1 prepared graham cracker crust

Direction

- In a large microwaveable glass bowl, mix strawberry gelatin mix and rhubarb. Cover and cook on high for 6 to 8 minutes until rhubarb has cooked down into threads and is very soft. Mix every 2 minutes. Let it cool.
- In a bowl, mix vanilla pudding mix and skim milk until moistened. Whip on low speed with an electric mixer for about 2 minutes until

thickened; mix prepared rhubarb mixture into pudding mixture.
- Arrange strawberry slices evenly into the bottom of prepped graham cracker crust. Scoop rhubarb pudding mixture on top of strawberries and chill about 1 hour until firm.

Nutrition Information

- Calories: 226 calories;
- Sodium: 358
- Total Carbohydrate: 41.6
- Cholesterol: < 1
- Protein: 4.1
- Total Fat: 5.6

---

284.   Rhubarb Sour Cream Pie

Serving: 8 | Prep: 15mins | Cook: 55mins | Ready in:

Ingredients

- 1 (9 inch) unbaked pie crust
- 4 cups chopped fresh rhubarb
- 1 egg
- 1 1/2 cups white sugar
- 1 cup sour cream
- 1/3 cup all-purpose flour
- 1/2 cup all-purpose flour
- 1/2 cup brown sugar
- 1/4 cup butter, melted

Direction

- Set oven to 450°F (220°C) to preheat.
- Line a 9-inch pie pan with the pie crust. Spread rhubarb in an even layer over the bottom of the crust. Whisk sour cream, 1/3 cup flour, white sugar, and egg together in a medium bowl until smooth. Pour mixture over the rhubarb.
- Combine brown sugar and 1/2 cup flour in a small bowl. Whisk in melted butter until crumbly. Sprinkle over top of the pie.

- Bake pie in the preheated oven for 15 minutes; lower temperature to 350°F (175°C); keep baking until topping turns golden, center is slightly jiggly, and edges have puffed, for 40 minutes. Allow to cool completely before cutting to serve.

Nutrition Information

- Calories: 493 calories;
- Total Fat: 20.1
- Sodium: 188
- Total Carbohydrate: 75.2
- Cholesterol: 51
- Protein: 5

---

285.   Rhubarb And Strawberry Pie

Serving: 8 | Prep: | Cook: | Ready in:

Ingredients

- 1 cup white sugar
- 1/2 cup all-purpose flour
- 1 pound fresh rhubarb, chopped
- 2 pints fresh strawberries
- 1 recipe pastry for a 9 inch double crust pie
- 2 tablespoons butter
- 1 egg yolk
- 2 tablespoons white sugar

Direction

- Turn oven to 400°F (200°C) to preheat.
- Combine sugar and flour in a large bowl. Add in chopped rhubarb and strawberries. Stir with flour and sugar; allow to sit for half an hour.
- Pour filling to the pie crust. Place dots of butter over the filling, and pour the top crust over to cover. Seal edges of bottom and top crust with water.

- Brush egg yolk over top of the pie with a pastry brush. Scatter top with sugar. Create small holes in the top to allow steam to release.
- Bake for 35 to 40 minutes in the preheated oven until bubbly and brown. Allow pie to cool on a rack.

Nutrition Information

- Calories: 437 calories;
- Total Fat: 18.8
- Sodium: 259
- Total Carbohydrate: 64.1
- Cholesterol: 33
- Protein: 5

---

286.   Rockin' Rhubarb Pie

Serving: 8 | Prep: 20mins | Cook: 45mins | Ready in:

Ingredients

- 1 (15 ounce) package pastry for a 9 inch double crust pie
- 4 cups chopped fresh rhubarb
- 3 tablespoons all-purpose flour
- 2 cups white sugar
- 4 egg yolks, beaten
- 1 cup half-and-half cream
- 1/2 teaspoon almond extract
- 1 tablespoon half-and-half cream
- 1 tablespoon white sugar

Direction

- Set the oven to 350°F (175°C) to preheat.
- Into the bottom of a 10-inch pie pan or 9-inch deep dish pie pan, put 1 of the pie shells. Place the rhubarb in the pie crust. Mix the flour with 2 cups of sugar in a small bowl. Beat together the almond extract, 1 cup half-and-half, and egg yolks in a medium bowl. Mix in the flour and sugar until well combined.

- Add the sauce on top of the rhubarb - throw any leftover mixture if all doesn't fit to the pan. Put the top pie shell on top of the filling, enclose the edges and flute. Brush the top crust with the leftover half-and-half, and scatter with leftover sugar. Score a few small slits in the top crust for ventilation. Put the pie onto a cookie tray to catch any drips.
- Bake in the prepared oven for 45 minutes, or until golden brown on top and puffed up in the middle. A tester should easily cut through the rhubarb. Let cool until just warm before serving to let the custard set.

Nutrition Information

- Calories: 538 calories;
- Protein: 6.1
- Total Fat: 22.2
- Sodium: 273
- Total Carbohydrate: 80.4
- Cholesterol: 114

---

287. Saskatoon (Serviceberry) Rhubarb Pie

Serving: 12 | Prep: 20mins | Cook: 50mins | Ready in:

Ingredients

- 2 (15 ounce) packages refrigerated pie crusts
- 2 cups chopped rhubarb
- 1/2 cup white sugar
- 1/4 cup cornstarch
- 2 tablespoons lemon juice
- 1 cup white sugar
- 4 cups fresh serviceberries

Direction

- Set oven to preheat at 400°F (200°C). Press two of the pie crusts into two 8-inch pie plates' bottom and sides.

- Mix rhubarb and 1/2 cup of sugar in a microwave-safe dish. Heat them in the microwave at full power till the rhubarb is soft and juice accumulates in the bottom of dish, for about 4 to 5 minutes. Drain the excess juice into a measuring cup and pour in enough water till it measures 2 cups. Dissolve cornstarch in the liquid.
- Stir together the remaining 1 cup of sugar, lemon juice and 2 cups of liquid in a saucepan. Add the saskatoon berries and rhubarb into the mixture; cook on medium-high heat till bubbly and thick, for about 5 minutes. Transfer into the two prepared pie crusts. Place the remaining crusts on top and slice holes into the top to ventilate the steam. Press edges together to enclose.
- In the preheated oven, bake for 15 minutes then lower the temperature to 350°F (175°C). Bake till the crust is golden brown and filling bubbles up, for about 30 more minutes.

Nutrition Information

- Calories: 468 calories;
- Cholesterol: 0
- Protein: 4.5
- Total Fat: 21.8
- Sodium: 339
- Total Carbohydrate: 65.2

---

288. Sour Cream Rhubarb Pie

Serving: 8 | Prep: 20mins | Cook: 1hours | Ready in:

Ingredients

- 1 1/4 cups white sugar
- 1 cup sour cream
- 3 eggs
- 2 tablespoons all-purpose flour
- 1/2 teaspoon vanilla extract
- 1/4 teaspoon salt
- 3 cups chopped fresh rhubarb

- 1 (9 inch) unbaked pie shell
- 1/3 cup white sugar
- 1/3 cup all-purpose flour
- 1 teaspoon ground cinnamon
- 1/4 cup butter, softened

Direction

- Begin preheating the oven to 190°C (or 375°F).
- In a big mixing bowl, beat 2 tablespoons of flour, eggs, sour cream and one and a quarter cups of sugar until smooth. Whisk in salt and vanilla. Fold rhubarb into the mixture. Fill into pie shell with rhubarb mixture.
- Bake in the prepared oven, 30 minutes. In the meantime, mix cinnamon, a third cup of flour and a third cup of sugar in a small bowl. Using a pastry blender or a fork, cut butter into the mixture until mixture looks like coarse crumbs. Put aside.
- Take pie out of the oven. Lower the oven temperature to 175°C (or 350°F). Scatter evenly over the pie with topping mixture. Bring the pan back into the oven and bake for another half an hour until topping and crust turn golden brown and filling is firm.

Nutrition Information

- Calories: 443 calories;
- Protein: 5.9
- Total Fat: 21.3
- Sodium: 274
- Total Carbohydrate: 59
- Cholesterol: 98

---

289. Strawberry Raisin Rhubarb Pie

Serving: 8 | Prep: 30mins | Cook: 40mins | Ready in:

Ingredients

- 1 recipe pastry for a 9 inch double crust pie

- 2 cups fresh strawberries, halved lengthwise
- 4 cups rhubarb, stalks only, sliced 1/2 inch thick
- 1/2 cup raisins, or to taste
- 6 tablespoons all-purpose flour
- 1 1/4 cups white sugar
- 1/4 teaspoon ground ginger
- 1 egg white, beaten
- 1 1/2 tablespoons unsalted butter, diced

Direction

- Preheat an oven to 220°C/425°F; line pastry crust on 9-in. pie dish.
- Mix ginger, sugar, flour, raisins, rhubarb and strawberries in bowl; stand mixture for 15 minutes. Meanwhile, roll leftover curst to 10-in. circle on floured work surface. Brush egg white on bottom crust; put filling in. evenly dot filling with butter.
- Cut leftover crust to 3/4-in. wide strips; for prettier crust, use scalloped edge pastry cutter. Use bit of water to moisten rim of filled bottom crust; lay 2 longest strips in cross in center of pie. Alternate horizon and vertical strips, working from next longest down to shortest strips, weaving strips as you go. Press lattice strips down on bottom crust edge so it seals; neatly trim top crust. Put pie in rimmed baking sheet.
- In preheated oven, bake for 20 minutes; reduce oven heat to 205°C/400°F. Bake for 20 minutes till golden brown; line aluminum foil on crust edges if it browns too quickly.

Nutrition Information

- Calories: 447 calories;
- Total Fat: 17.4
- Sodium: 245
- Total Carbohydrate: 70.2
- Cholesterol: 6
- Protein: 5

290. Strawberry Rhubarb Cream Pie

Serving: 10 | Prep: 15mins | Cook: 1hours | Ready in:

Ingredients

- 1 1/2 cups white sugar
- 1/4 cup all-purpose flour
- 3/4 teaspoon ground nutmeg
- 3 eggs, beaten
- 4 cups chopped rhubarb
- 3 cups halved fresh strawberries
- 1 recipe pastry for a 9 inch double crust pie
- 1 egg white

Direction

- Set oven to preheat at 200°C (400°F).
- Combine nutmeg, flour, and sugar in a large bowl. Mix in eggs. Fold in rhubarb, making sure it is coated thoroughly, then repeat the process with the strawberries. Add mixture into the pie crust. Put the second crust on top make sure to slice slits into it to make a vent for steam. Use egg white to brush on top crust.
- Bake in the preheated oven for 50 to 60 minutes, until crust is golden and rhubarb is tender.

Nutrition Information

- Calories: 314 calories;
- Total Fat: 7.7
- Sodium: 121
- Total Carbohydrate: 59.6
- Cholesterol: 56
- Protein: 4.2

291. Strawberry Rhubarb Custard Pie

Serving: 8 | Prep: 20mins | Cook: 1hours | Ready in:

Ingredients

- 1 (9 inch) unbaked pie crust (see footnote for recipe link)
- 3 cups rhubarb, sliced 1/4-inch thick
- 1 cup fresh strawberries, quartered
- 3 large eggs
- 1 1/2 cups white sugar
- 3 tablespoons milk
- 3 tablespoons all-purpose flour
- 1/4 teaspoon freshly grated nutmeg
- 1 tablespoon butter, diced
- 2 tablespoons strawberry jam
- 1/4 teaspoon water

Direction

- Prepare the oven by preheating to 350 degrees F (175 degrees C). In a 9-in pie plate, put rolled-out pie crust and set on a baking sheet that is lined with a silicone baking mat or parchment paper.
- In a bowl, mix together the strawberries and rhubarb; send to the pie crust, evenly spreading.
- In a medium bowl, whisk together the nutmeg, flour, milk and eggs. Gently put filling on top of rhubarb mixture until it achieves the top edge of the crust. Spread diced butter on top of the filling equally. Slightly shake and tap the baking sheet to get rid of any air bubbles.
- Send pie to the preheated oven and bake for about 1 hour, flipping halfway through, until custard is set and rhubarb is soft.
- In a small bowl, combine together the water, and strawberry jam; place inside the microwave for about 15 seconds to heat. Use the jam mixture to glaze the top of the pie. Let cool. Place inside the refrigerator until serving time.

Nutrition Information

- Calories: 342 calories;
- Sodium: 159
- Total Carbohydrate: 57.4

- Cholesterol: 74
- Protein: 4.8
- Total Fat: 11.1

---

292.   Strawberry Rhubarb Miniature Tarts

Serving: 12 | Prep: 20mins | Cook: 30mins | Ready in:

Ingredients

- 1 1/2 cups crushed pretzels
- 3/4 cup butter, melted
- 1/2 cup crushed walnuts
- 1/4 cup brown sugar, packed
- 2 tablespoons maple syrup
- 1 pinch ground cinnamon
- 1 pinch ground cardamom
- 2 egg whites
- 1 cup raw sugar
- 2 tablespoons self-rising flour
- 1 teaspoon vanilla extract
- 3/4 pound rhubarb, finely diced
- 2 cups finely chopped fresh strawberries

Direction

- Heat oven to 350°F (175°C). Grease twelve muffin cups.
- In a bowl mix cardamom, cinnamon, maple syrup, brown sugar, walnuts, butter and pretzel crumbs until mixture is well incorporated and loose. Into the bottom of the prepared muffin cups, scoop the pretzel mixture, fill them about 1/4 full. Push the crust down firmly.
- In a large mixing bowl, whip egg whites until foamy, and combine vanilla extract, self-rising flour, and raw sugar to create a batter; mix in strawberries and rhubarb. Scoop fruit mixture on top of pretzel crust, fill muffin cups up to the top.
- Bake in the heated oven for about 30 minutes until the fruit filling is bubbly and the top is

golden brown. Rest for 10 to 15 minutes to cool; serve warm.

Nutrition Information

- Calories: 285 calories;
- Total Fat: 15.2
- Sodium: 298
- Total Carbohydrate: 36.2
- Cholesterol: 31
- Protein: 3

---

293.   Strawberry Rhubarb Pie

Serving: 8 | Prep: | Cook: | Ready in:

Ingredients

- 2 1/4 cups all-purpose flour
- 1 teaspoon salt
- 1/2 cup vegetable oil
- 6 tablespoons milk
- 5 medium stalks rhubarb, cut into 1 1/2 inch pieces
- 1 1/2 cups sliced fresh strawberries
- 1 1/2 cups white sugar
- 3 1/2 tablespoons tapioca
- 1 pinch salt
- 1 1/2 teaspoons ground nutmeg

Direction

- Prepare Crust: Mix the salt and flour in a large bowl. Put a half cup of oil in a 1 cup sized measuring cup and cover with six tablespoons of milk. Remember not to mix! Distribute milk and oil over the flour and beat with a fork until a ball of dough is formed. Split dough into two balls. Put one on a sheet of waxed paper. Cover with another sheet of waxed paper and roll out to fit your pie plate. Keep rolling out the remaining ball of dough in the same way. Take top paper away from a crust and turn dough onto pie plate. Take off paper and push dough in. Put remaining dough aside for top crust.

- Heat oven to 425°F (220°C).
- Prepare Filling: Stir the nutmeg, salt, tapioca, sugar, strawberries and rhubarb until the fruit is evenly coated. Put filling into the shell and sprinkle with butter. Place top crust over the filling, seal the edges and score 3 1-inch slits in the top of crust.
- Bake for 20 mins at 425°F (220°C). Turn oven down to 375°F (190°C) and bake for 20 minutes more. Let rest to cool before slicing.

Nutrition Information

- Calories: 432 calories;
- Total Fat: 14.7
- Sodium: 298
- Total Carbohydrate: 71.9
- Cholesterol: < 1
- Protein: 4.6

---

294.   Strawberry Rhubarb Pie III

Serving: 8 | Prep: | Cook: |Ready in:

Ingredients

- 1 recipe pastry for a 9 inch double crust pie
- 1 teaspoon orange zest
- 4 cups diced rhubarb
- 3 cups sliced fresh strawberries
- 1 1/2 cups white sugar
- 6 tablespoons quick-cooking tapioca
- 1 tablespoon milk
- 1 tablespoon white sugar for decoration
- 1 cup all-purpose flour (optional)
- 1 cup white sugar (optional)
- 1 teaspoon salt (optional)
- 1/2 cup butter (optional)

Direction

- Turn the oven to 400°F (205°C) to preheat. Line bottom crust onto a pie pan.
- Combine tapioca, 1 1/2 cups sugar, orange zest, strawberries, and rhubarb. Put on the crust. Roll the second crust out and put over the filling. Enclose the edges. Brush milk over and sprinkle over the top with additional sugar.
- Bake for 10 minutes at 400°F (205°C). Lower the temperature to 350°F (175°C) and bake for another 35 minutes.
- To prepare the crumb topping, remove the top pie crust. Mix together salt, 1 cup sugar, and flour. Cut in margarine or butter until the mixture is crumbly. Put on the filling and bake following the instructions above.

Nutrition Information

- Calories: 688 calories;
- Sodium: 611
- Total Carbohydrate: 109.3
- Cholesterol: 31
- Protein: 5.6
- Total Fat: 27

---

295.   Summer Strawberry Rhubarb Pie

Serving: 8 | Prep: 30mins | Cook: 40mins |Ready in:

Ingredients

- 1 recipe pastry for a 9 inch double crust pie
- 2 cups diced rhubarb
- 2 1/2 cups hulled strawberries
- 1 cup white sugar
- 1/4 cup all-purpose flour
- 3 tablespoons butter, diced
- 1/4 teaspoon ground nutmeg
- 1 tablespoon white sugar
- 1 teaspoon ground cinnamon

Direction

- Heat oven to 450°F (230°C). Split the pastry in half; stretch out half into a circle on a floured surface, line a 9-inch pie pan with bottom crust. Stretch the other half out into a 10-inch circle on a floured surface, put aside.
- In a bowl, stir the nutmeg, butter, flour, 1 cup of sugar, whole strawberries and rhubarb together in a bowl. Put the filling into the prepared pie pan.
- Slice the leftover crust into 3/4-inch wide strips (for a nicer shell, use a scalloped edge pastry cutter). With a bit of water, moisten the edge of the filled bottom crust, put the 2 longest strips in a cross in the center. From the next longest down to the shortest strips, place alternately horizontal and vertical strips, weaving the strips as you place. Push the lattice strips down onto the bottom crust edge to seal and trim the top crust strips neatly. In a small bowl, stir cinnamon with a tablespoon of sugar and put aside.
- Bake in the heated oven for 10 minutes; turn heat down to 375°F (190°C). Take pie out. Drizzle the top with cinnamon-sugar mixture and bake again in the oven about 30 more minutes; until the crust is golden brown and the filling is bubbly.

Nutrition Information

- Calories: 406 calories;
- Cholesterol: 11
- Protein: 3.8
- Total Fat: 19.5
- Sodium: 266
- Total Carbohydrate: 55.4

---

296. Zendea's Strawberry Rhubarb Pie

Serving: 6 | Prep: 15mins | Cook: 45mins | Ready in:

Ingredients

- 1 cup white sugar
- 1 1/2 cups sliced fresh or frozen rhubarb, thawed
- 1/2 cup butter
- 1/2 cup frozen sliced sweetened strawberries, thawed
- 2 eggs
- 1 (15 ounce) package pastry for a 9 inch double crust pie
- 1 tablespoon milk
- 3 tablespoons white sugar

Direction

- Heat oven to 375°F (190°C).
- In a saucepan put a cup of sugar, then stir in the rhubarb; put butter, heat to a boil over medium-high heat. Cook, mixing frequently for about 10 mins until the rhubarb softens. Mix in the strawberries, put aside. Rest to cool until lukewarm. In a bowl, whip the eggs until foamy, stir into the rhubarb mixture.
- Roll out the pie shells, and line an 8-inch pie dish with a layer of crust; put the filling into the bottom shell. Put the next crust over the pie and crimp the edges together. Press the edge with a fork to seal. Score four 1-inch slits in the top crust with a sharp knife. In a small bowl, put milk and brush it on top of the pie; drizzle with three more tablespoons sugar.
- Bake in the heated oven 45 minutes to 1 hour until the crust is golden and the filling is firm. Let cool before cutting. Chill the leftovers.

Nutrition Information

- Calories: 669 calories;
- Cholesterol: 103
- Protein: 6.7
- Total Fat: 38.7
- Sodium: 473
- Total Carbohydrate: 76.3

Chapter 10: Strawberry Pie Recipes

***

Nutrition Information

- Calories: 418 calories;
- Cholesterol: 59
- Protein: 3.2
- Total Fat: 21.9
- Sodium: 156
- Total Carbohydrate: 52.9

---

297. 1970's French Strawberry Pie

Serving: 8 | Prep: 15mins | Cook: 10mins | Ready in:

Ingredients

- 1 (4 ounce) package cream cheese, softened
- 1 tablespoon heavy whipping cream
- 1 (9 inch) prepared shortbread pie crust (such as Keebler®)
- 2 cups fresh strawberries, quartered
- 2 cups fresh strawberries, mashed
- 1 cup white sugar
- 1/4 cup cornstarch
- 1 cup heavy whipping cream
- 2 tablespoons white sugar (optional)
- 1/4 teaspoon vanilla extract (optional)

Direction

- Beat 1 tbsp. heavy cream and cream cheese in bowl; spread in bottom of pie crust. Put 2 cups quartered strawberries over cream cheese layer.
- Cook cornstarch, 1 cup sugar and 2 cups mashed strawberries in saucepan on medium heat for 10 minutes till thick and slightly reduced; completely cool.
- In pie crust, put cooled strawberry mixture on strawberry layer; chill in the fridge for 2 hours till set.
- Beat vanilla extract, 2 tbsp. sugar and 1 cup heavy cream for 5 minutes till fluffy and light in bowl; spread on cooled pie.

---

298. Aunt Barbara's Strawberry Pie

Serving: 8 | Prep: 20mins | Cook: 15mins | Ready in:

Ingredients

- Crust:
- 1 cup graham cracker crumbs
- 1/4 cup white sugar
- 1/4 cup butter, melted
- Filling:
- 1 tablespoon unflavored gelatin
- 1/4 cup cold water
- 1 cup heavy whipping cream
- 1/2 cup chopped strawberries
- 1/3 cup white sugar

Direction

- Heat oven to 375°F (190°C).
- In a mixing bowl, stir together melted butter, 1/4 cup sugar, and graham cracker crumbs; stir until moistened evenly and press into the bottom and sides of a 9-inch pie pan.
- In the preheated oven, bake about 12 minutes until the crust is lightly browned and has a toasty smell. Take out of the oven and cool.
- Soak gelatin in cold water for 3 minutes. Cook the water and gelatin over a double boiler set on simmering water, mixing frequently until gelatin is completely dissolved.
- In a chilled glass or metal bowl, whip whipping cream until soft peak.
- In a bowl, mix 1/3 cup sugar and strawberries together. Add gelatin mixture over

strawberries. Gently fold in whipped cream until combined. Add mixture into baked pie shell and refrigerate at least 2 hours until set.

Nutrition Information

- Calories: 257 calories;
- Sodium: 116
- Total Carbohydrate: 24.2
- Cholesterol: 56
- Protein: 1.5
- Total Fat: 17.9

---

299.   Banana Kiwi Strawberry Tart

Serving: 8 | Prep: 25mins | Cook: 35mins |Ready in:

Ingredients

- 1/2 cup all-purpose flour
- 1 tablespoon light brown sugar
- 1/4 teaspoon ground cinnamon
- 1/8 teaspoon salt
- 2 tablespoons unsalted butter
- 1 1/2 tablespoons ice water
- 1 cup skim milk
- 3 egg whites
- 2 tablespoons white sugar
- 1/4 teaspoon vanilla extract
- 1 bananas, peeled and sliced
- 1 kiwi, peeled and sliced
- 1 cup sliced fresh strawberries

Direction

- Sift salt, cinnamon, light brown sugar and flour together in a bowl. Slice in the butter until the mixture forms coarse crumbs. Scatter ice water on, toss with a fork to moisten evenly. Pat to shape a round, wrap in plastic. Chill for half an hour.
- Warm the milk in the top half of a double boiler until it starts to bubble. Whip 1

tablespoon of hot milk, sugar and egg whites in a bowl. Beat the egg white mixture into the leftover hot milk. Heat and mix about 10 mins but do not boil, until the mixture is just thick enough to coat the back of a metal spoon. Take away from the heat, mix in the vanilla. Cool until it reaches room temperature.

- Heat oven to 375°F (190°C). Grease an 8-inch tart pan with a removable bottom gently.
- Roll out to shape the tart dough to a quarter inch thick on a floured surface. Push the chilled dough into the prepared tart pan. Cut off the edges, poke the bottom with a fork. Bake in the heated oven for 15 to 18 mins until golden brown. Take out and transfer to a wire rack, cool completely.
- Scoop the filling mixture into the shell. Bake in the heated oven for 18 to 20 mins. Cool to room temperature on a wire rack. Chill for 8 hours. Put sliced strawberry, kiwi and banana on top of the filling just before serving.

Nutrition Information

- Calories: 115 calories;
- Total Fat: 3.1
- Sodium: 72
- Total Carbohydrate: 18.7
- Cholesterol: 8
- Protein: 3.6

---

300.   Big Guy Strawberry Pie

Serving: 8 | Prep: 30mins | Cook: 30mins |Ready in:

Ingredients

- 1 cup water
- 3/4 cup white sugar
- 1/4 teaspoon salt
- 2 tablespoons cornstarch
- 1/4 teaspoon red food coloring (optional)
- 1 cup all-purpose flour
- 1/2 cup butter

- 3 tablespoons confectioners' sugar
- 1 teaspoon vanilla extract
- 1 quart fresh strawberries, hulled

Direction

- Mix together the food coloring (if using), cornstarch, salt, white sugar and water in a saucepan, then boil. Let it cook for around 5 minutes or until it becomes thick, then put aside to cool. Set an oven to preheat to 175°C (350°F).
- Mix together the vanilla, confectioner's sugar and flour in a big bowl. Slice in butter until the mixture looks like small crumbs. Press it into a 9-inch pie pan. Use a fork to prick all over and let it bake for 8-10 minutes in the preheated oven or until it turns light brown.
- Put the berries in the shell when the crust is cool and pour the thickened mixture on top. Let it chill in the fridge.

Nutrition Information

- Calories: 277 calories;
- Total Carbohydrate: 41.5
- Cholesterol: 31
- Protein: 2.3
- Total Fat: 11.9
- Sodium: 157

---

301. Crumb Topped Strawberry Rhubarb Pie

Serving: 8 | Prep: 30mins | Cook: 50mins | Ready in:

Ingredients

- 1 cup all-purpose flour
- 1/8 teaspoon salt
- 1/3 cup chilled butter
- 2 tablespoons cold water, or more as needed
- 1 1/4 cups white sugar
- 1/3 cup all-purpose flour

- 1/2 teaspoon ground cinnamon
- 1/4 teaspoon ground nutmeg
- 2 cups rhubarb, sliced 1/2-inch thick
- 2 cups sliced fresh strawberries
- 1/3 cup chopped pecans
- 1 cup all-purpose flour
- 2/3 cup white sugar
- 1/3 cup chilled butter

Direction

- Set oven to preheat at 200°C (400°F). In a bowl, whisk salt and 1 cup of flour.
- Use a pastry cutter to cut 1/3 cup of butter into the flour mixture until it looks like coarse crumbs. Moisten with 1 tablespoon water at a time, just until the mixture stays together. Make the dough into a ball, and on a floured work surface, roll it out into a 12-inch circle. The crust will become thin. Softly fold the dough into quarters, and arrange it into a 9-inch pie dish; unfold the middle crust and the dough in the pie dish. Cut the crust and leave behind 1/2 inch of overhang, and crimp or flute the edge of the crust. Let the crust chill in the refrigerator while you are preparing filling.
- Combine nutmeg, cinnamon, 1/3 cup of flour, and 1 1/4 cups of sugar in a bowl until thoroughly mixed. Mix in the rhubarb and strawberries, and transfer into the crust-lined pie dish. Sprinkle pecans on top. Mix 1 cup of flour with 2/3 cup of sugar in a bowl, and use a pastry cutter to cut 1/3 cup of butter into the mixture until it looks like coarse crumbs; over the pie filling, top with sprinkles of the crumb topping evenly. Use strips of aluminum foil to cover the pie's edge.
- In the preheated oven, bake until the crumb topping is golden brown and the filling around the edges bubbles, for 50 to 60 minutes. For the last 10 minutes of baking, take off foil to brown the pie edge.

Nutrition Information

- Calories: 506 calories;

- Total Fat: 19.2
- Sodium: 148
- Total Carbohydrate: 81.1
- Cholesterol: 41
- Protein: 4.9

302. Deep Dish Strawberry Pie

Serving: 8 | Prep: 20mins | Cook: 25mins | Ready in:

Ingredients

- 1 pastry for a 9-inch deep dish pie crust
- 1/2 cup semi-sweet chocolate chips
- 2 quarts fresh strawberries, hulled, divided
- 1 cup white sugar
- 2 tablespoons lemon juice
- 3/4 cup ginger ale
- 3 1/2 tablespoons cornstarch

Direction

- Set an oven to preheat at 230°C (450°F). Press pie shell into a 1/2-inch deep dish pie plate. Use a fork to prick the pastry's bottom and sides.
- In the preheated oven, bake until lightly brown for 10 to 12 minutes. Let it cool down thoroughly on a wire rack.
- In a saucepan over medium-low heat, melt chocolate chips and stir continuously for 1 to 3 minutes. Paint melted chocolate in the cooled pie crust's inside and bottom. Freeze the chocolate-painted crust for 30 minutes to harden the chocolate.
- In the center of the chocolate crust, place the best looking strawberry, cut-side down. Place around the center strawberry as many attractive strawberries as possible, to make circles around the center.
- In a bowl, mash the reserved strawberries; pour into a saucepan. Add lemon juice and sugar; boil and stir regularly.
- In a bowl, whisk together cornstarch and ginger ale until smooth; mix into boiling

strawberry mixture gradually. Lower the heat to medium-low and simmer, stir continuously for 12 to 14 minutes, until thickened. Take off heat and let it cool down for about 5 minutes.
- Scoop strawberry sauce on top of the strawberries in the pie shell. Refrigerate until set for at least 8 hours.

Nutrition Information

- Calories: 332 calories;
- Sodium: 123
- Total Carbohydrate: 59.2
- Cholesterol: 0
- Protein: 2.9
- Total Fat: 11.1

303. Delightful Strawberry Dessert

Serving: 8 | Prep: 40mins | Cook: | Ready in:

Ingredients

- 3 egg whites
- 1 cup white sugar
- 3/4 teaspoon cream of tartar
- 1/2 cup saltine crackers, crushed
- 1/2 cup flaked coconut
- 1/2 cup chopped pecans
- 2 cups whipping cream
- 1/2 teaspoon unflavored gelatin
- 1/2 cup white sugar
- 4 cups sliced fresh strawberries

Direction

- Start preheating the oven to 375°F (190°C).
- Beat the egg whites in a large bowl until it forms the soft peaks. Put in the cream of tartar and one cup of sugar gradually; continue to beat until the whites form the stiff peaks. Fold in pecans, coconut and cracker crumbs gently.

Spread mixture up the sides and onto bottom of a 9-in. pie pan.

- Bake for 20-22 mins in the prepared oven, until lightly browned. Let cool completely.
- Beat the remaining sugar, gelatin and cream in a large bowl until it forms the stiff peaks. Then fold in the strawberries; transfer over the egg white layer. Place in the refrigerator, covered, for 120 mins.

Nutrition Information

- Calories: 440 calories;
- Sodium: 102
- Total Carbohydrate: 52.3
- Cholesterol: 66
- Protein: 4.5
- Total Fat: 25.4

304. Deni's Strawberry Cheese Pie

Serving: 8 | Prep: 15mins | Cook: |Ready in:

Ingredients

- 1 (9 inch) pie crust, baked
- 1 (8 ounce) package cream cheese, softened
- 1 (14 ounce) can sweetened condensed milk
- 1/2 cup lemon juice
- 1 teaspoon vanilla extract
- 2 cups fresh strawberries

Direction

- Whisk the cream cheese in a medium mixing bowl until fluffy. Put in the condensed milk and stir until smooth. Mix in the vanilla extract and lemon juice. Stir until everything is well-combined.
- Into the baked pastry shell, add the cream cheese mixture. Garnish with strawberries (whole or sliced depending on what you

prefer). Refrigerate for at least 2 hours before serving.

Nutrition Information

- Calories: 355 calories;
- Total Carbohydrate: 39.8
- Cholesterol: 47
- Protein: 7
- Total Fat: 19.3
- Sodium: 248

305. Easy Strawberry Pie

Serving: 8 | Prep: 20mins | Cook: 10mins |Ready in:

Ingredients

- 1 1/4 cups crushed buttery round crackers
- 1/4 cup butter, melted
- 1 (8 ounce) package cream cheese
- 2 tablespoons milk
- 2 tablespoons white sugar
- 1 cup strawberries, halved
- 1/2 cup heavy whipping cream
- 1 tablespoon heavy whipping cream
- 1 (3.5 ounce) package instant French vanilla pudding mix
- 1 1/2 cups milk

Direction

- Heat oven to 375°F (190°C).
- In a bowl, stir melted butter with cracker crumbs and push mixture into a 9-inch pie pan to make a shell.
- In the preheated oven, bake crust until slightly brown, about 8 minutes; let it cool.
- In a bowl, blend white sugar with 2 tablespoons milk and cream cheese with an electric mixer, until smooth and creamy. Put cream cheese mixture evenly into pie shell. Put strawberry halves on top of cream cheese mixture.

- In a bowl, whip all the cream with an electric mixer about 3 minutes until it becomes fluffy and forms stiff peaks. In a separate bowl, whip 1 1/2 cups milk with French vanilla pudding mix for 2 minutes until it begins to thicken. Let it rest 3 more minutes to firm up. Slowly fold whipped cream into pudding mix and put pudding mixture evenly on top of strawberries. Let the pie refrigerate for 2 hours before serving.

Nutrition Information

- Calories: 342 calories;
- Protein: 4.8
- Total Fat: 25.4
- Sodium: 408
- Total Carbohydrate: 24.9
- Cholesterol: 73

306.   Easy As Pie Strawberry Pie

Serving: 8 | Prep: | Cook: |Ready in:

Ingredients

- 1 (9 inch) pie crust, baked
- 1 (10 ounce) package frozen strawberries
- 1 (8 ounce) jar ready-to-use strawberry glaze
- 1 (8 ounce) container frozen whipped topping, thawed

Direction

- Mix glaze and strawberries together in a medium bowl. Pour into pie shell. Put whipped topping on top.

Nutrition Information

- Calories: 220 calories;
- Sodium: 138
- Total Carbohydrate: 25.9

- Cholesterol: 0
- Protein: 1.2
- Total Fat: 12.3

307.   Favorite Strawberry Rhubarb Pie

Serving: 8 | Prep: 15mins | Cook: 40mins |Ready in:

Ingredients

- 3 cups sliced strawberries
- 3 cups sliced rhubarb
- 1 1/2 cups white sugar
- 1/4 cup instant tapioca
- 1 squeeze fresh lemon juice
- 1 recipe pastry for a 9 inch double crust pie
- 2 tablespoons butter, cut into small pieces

Direction

- Set oven to preheat at 200°C (400°F). Put a pie dish on top of a baking sheet.
- Mix together the lemon juice, tapioca, sugar, rhubarb, and strawberries in a bowl, and let sit for 15 minutes, stir from time to time. Press pie crust into a 9-inch pie dish; add the filling into the bottom crust. Scatter butter pieces on top of the filling, and put the top crust on the pie. Push the edges together and seal using a fork to crimp. Use a sharp knife to slice a few slits into the top crust.
- In the preheated oven, bake until the crust becomes golden brown and the filling bubbles up, from 40 to 55 minutes.

Nutrition Information

- Calories: 442 calories;
- Protein: 3.7
- Total Fat: 18.1
- Sodium: 257
- Total Carbohydrate: 68.5
- Cholesterol: 8

308. Fluffy Strawberry Pie

Serving: 8 | Prep: 20mins | Cook: | Ready in:

Ingredients

- 1 (3 ounce) package strawberry-flavored Jell-O® mix
- 1/4 cup white sugar
- 1/2 cup boiling water
- 1 (8 ounce) container frozen whipped topping, thawed
- 2 1/2 cups sliced fresh strawberries
- 1 (9 inch) prepared graham cracker crust
- 4 fresh strawberries, halved (optional)

Direction

- In a large bowl stir boiling water, sugar, and strawberry-flavored gelatin mix together, mixing until sugar and gelatin have dissolved.
- Chill gelatin mixture about 10 minutes until it begins to turn syrupy and thicken.
- Into the gelatin mixture, slowly fold frozen whipped topping until well-combined.
- Into the whipped topping mixture fold 2 1/2 cups of sliced strawberries.
- Into the graham cracker crust scoop filling and decorate the filling edge with 8 halves of strawberry.
- Chill before serving, for at least 2 hours.

Nutrition Information

- Calories: 318 calories;
- Total Carbohydrate: 45.9
- Cholesterol: 0
- Protein: 3
- Total Fat: 14.7
- Sodium: 222

309. Fresh Strawberry Almond Pie

Serving: 8 | Prep: | Cook: | Ready in:

Ingredients

- 1 1/2 cups crushed pecan shortbread cookies
- 1/4 cup blanched slivered almonds
- 1/3 cup butter, melted
- 6 cups fresh strawberries, hulled
- 1 cup white sugar
- 3 tablespoons cornstarch
- 1/3 cup water
- 1/4 teaspoon salt
- 1/2 teaspoon almond extract

Direction

- Set oven to preheat at 175°C (350°F).
- Mix all crust ingredients together in small bowl. Press it onto a 9-inch pie plate's bottom and up sides. Bake for 8 minutes. Let cool entirely.
- Mash enough strawberries to make 1 cup of liquid. In a 2-quart saucepan, combine sugar and cornstarch. Mix in water and mashed berries. Cook on medium heat and stir continuously until thickened and comes to a full boil (about 8 to 15 minutes). Continue boiling for 1 minute; take off heat.
- Mix in almond extract and salt; let cool for 10 minutes. Fill the reserved fresh strawberries into the baked crust; over the fresh berries, pour cooked mixture. Chill in the fridge for at least 3 hours. Top with walnuts and whipped cream if you wish.

Nutrition Information

- Calories: 333 calories;
- Total Fat: 14.5
- Sodium: 219
- Total Carbohydrate: 50
- Cholesterol: 24
- Protein: 2.8

310. Fresh Strawberry Cheesecake Pie

Serving: 8 | Prep: 15mins | Cook: 15mins |Ready in:

Ingredients

- 1 (9 inch) unbaked deep dish pie crust
- 1 (8 ounce) package cream cheese, softened
- 2 eggs
- 1/2 cup white sugar
- 2 tablespoons lemon juice
- 1/2 cup white sugar
- 2 tablespoons cornstarch
- 3/4 cup water
- 1 tablespoon lemon juice
- 2 tablespoons strawberry-flavored Jell-O® mix
- 1 quart fresh strawberries, hulled and sliced

Direction

- Set oven to preheat at 200°C (400°F).
- Bake pie crust for about 10 minutes until light brown.
- Take the crust out of the oven and lower oven temperature down to 175°C (350°F).
- In a bowl, beat together 2 tablespoons lemon juice, 1/2 cup sugar, eggs, and cream cheese until smooth and well combined.
- Transfer the filling into the crust.
- Bake for about 30 minutes until filling sets.
- Take it out of the oven and let it cool down entirely.
- In a saucepan, use a whisk to combine together strawberry gelatin, 1 tablespoon lemon juice, water, cornstarch, and 1/2 cup sugar until smooth; put on medium heat and heat to a simmer. Cook, stirring continuously, until the gelatin fully dissolves and the glaze thickens, about 5 to 10 minutes. Take off heat and let cool slightly.
- Place the strawberry slices on top of the cheese filling.
- Layer warm glaze on top of the sliced strawberries. Refrigerate to cool completely before serving.

Nutrition Information

- Calories: 369 calories;
- Protein: 5.4
- Total Fat: 18.7
- Sodium: 256
- Total Carbohydrate: 46.7
- Cholesterol: 77

311. Fresh Strawberry Pie I

Serving: 16 | Prep: 15mins | Cook: 15mins |Ready in:

Ingredients

- 2 (8 inch) pie shells, baked
- 2 1/2 quarts fresh strawberries
- 1 cup white sugar
- 2 tablespoons cornstarch
- 1 cup boiling water
- 1 (3 ounce) package strawberry flavored Jell-O®

Direction

- Combine corn starch and sugar in a saucepan; remember to mix the cornstarch thoroughly. Pour boiling water in, then cook on medium heat until thickened. Take off heat. Put in gelatin mix, and mix till smooth. Let the mixture cool down to room temperature.
- In the baked pastry crusts, layer the strawberries; place their points facing upwards. Pour the cooled gelatin over the strawberries.
- Refrigerate until firm. Top with whipped cream, if you want.

Nutrition Information

- Calories: 167 calories;
- Protein: 1.7
- Total Fat: 4.4
- Sodium: 104
- Total Carbohydrate: 31.6
- Cholesterol: 0

312. Fresh Strawberry Pie II

Serving: 8 | Prep: 40mins | Cook: 20mins | Ready in:

Ingredients

- 4 cups fresh strawberries, divided
- 1/2 cup white sugar
- 2 tablespoons cornstarch
- 1 pinch salt
- 1/2 cup water
- 1/4 cup water
- 3/4 cup white sugar
- 3 egg whites
- 1/2 teaspoon cream of tartar
- 1/8 teaspoon salt
- 1 teaspoon almond extract
- 1 (9 inch) prepared graham cracker crust

Direction

- Wash and hull strawberries; cut each into 4 equal pieces. In a saucepan, add 1/2 of the strawberries. Whisk a pinch of salt, cornstarch and 1/2 cup of sugar together. Mix sugar mixture and strawberries together; pour in 1/2 cup of water. Boil the mixture over medium heat with frequent stirs. Cook for 1 minute while constantly stirring. Take it away from the heat; set aside.
- In a saucepan, mix together 3/4 cup of sugar and 1/4 cup of water. Heat over medium-high heat for the sugar to dissolve; stir till the mixture begins to boil if necessary but do not stir when it is boiling. Boil without a cover until a soft ball forms when a small amount of mixture is placed in cold water or the mixture reaches the soft ball stage of 240°F (115°C).

- At the same time, in the bowl of a stand mixture, mix together 1/8 teaspoon of salt, cream of tartar and egg whites. Beat on medium speed until it forms medium-stiff peaks.
- When the sugar syrup is 240°, take it away from the heat. Keep the mixer running on high speeds; pour the hot syrup in a steady stream between the side of the mixing bowl and the beater. Beat until it is cool. Mix in almond extract.
- Combine the remaining fresh strawberries with the cooled cooked strawberries; transfer onto pie shell. Place meringue onto strawberries. Chill for at least 1 hour before ready to serve.

Nutrition Information

- Calories: 291 calories;
- Total Fat: 6.8
- Sodium: 209
- Total Carbohydrate: 56.3
- Cholesterol: 0
- Protein: 3

313. Fresh Strawberry Pie III

Serving: 8 | Prep: 20mins | Cook: | Ready in:

Ingredients

- 1 (9 inch) pie crust, baked
- 1 cup white sugar
- 3 tablespoons strawberry flavored Jell-O® mix
- 2 tablespoons cornstarch
- 1/4 teaspoon salt
- 1 cup boiling water
- 2 pints strawberries, cleaned and stemmed
- 2 cups whipping cream (optional)

Direction

- In a medium saucepan, combine salt, cornstarch, gelatin, and sugar. Mix in boiling water. Boil mixture over high heat for 3 minutes, stirring continuously. Let cool thoroughly.
- In pastry shell, spread whole strawberries. Pour gelatin mixture on top of the berries. Refrigerate before serving. Serve with whipped cream on top.

Nutrition Information

- Calories: 428 calories;
- Sodium: 208
- Total Carbohydrate: 45.3
- Cholesterol: 82
- Protein: 2.7
- Total Fat: 27.4

---

314.   Fresh Strawberry Pie With Orange Liqueur Glaze

Serving: 8 | Prep: 15mins | Cook: 30mins | Ready in:

Ingredients

- 1 (9 inch) refrigerated pie crust
- 1 cup fresh strawberries, hulled
- 3/4 cup water
- 3/4 cup white sugar
- 3 tablespoons cornstarch
- 3 tablespoons orange liqueur (such as Grand Marnier®)
- 3 cups fresh strawberries, hulled

Direction

- Set oven to preheat at 200°C (400°F).
- In the preheated oven, bake the pie crust until golden-brown and puffed, for 20 to 25 minutes. Place on a wire rack and let cool thoroughly.
- In a blender, puree 1 cup of strawberries until smooth. Add strawberry puree into a

saucepan. Mix in the cornstarch, sugar, and water. Heat up to a boil on medium heat until thickened, stir frequently. Take off heat and mix in the orange liqueur. Put aside.
- Place the leftover 3 cups of strawberries in a decorative pattern in the prepared pie crust. Add the glaze over the berries. Put in refrigerator until glaze is set, for about 4 hours.

Nutrition Information

- Calories: 241 calories;
- Total Fat: 7.7
- Sodium: 119
- Total Carbohydrate: 40
- Cholesterol: 0
- Protein: 1.9

---

315.   Fresh Strawberry Tart

Serving: 4 | Prep: 20mins | Cook: 20mins | Ready in:

Ingredients

- 1 (8 ounce) ball sweet pastry dough
- Sweet Cheese Mixture:
- 1 (8 ounce) package cream cheese, room temperature
- 2 tablespoons creme fraiche
- 2 tablespoons white sugar
- 1 large egg yolk
- 1/4 teaspoon salt
- 1/4 teaspoon vanilla extract
- 1/2 teaspoon grated lemon zest
- Strawberries:
- 1 pound fresh ripe strawberries, hulled, halved
- Glaze:
- 1/4 cup apricot jam
- 2 teaspoons water

Direction

- Set oven to preheat at 375°F. Line parchment paper on a baking sheet.
- On a lightly floured work surface, place the pastry dough. Roll out the dough into a round disk about 12 inches in diameter and 1/8-inch thick. Place onto the prepared baking sheet.
- Lightly brush water on the outside 2 inches around the edges of circle. Curl up tightly a bit of the dough's edge to create a rounder shape with a slightly thickened edge. If some edges are thicker than the rest, pinch off the excess and add to thinner edges to create even edges to the circle. Roll each edge again once more to make the edges that are thick enough to crimp. Flour fingers and crimp crust.
- "Dock" the bottom surface using a fork, the dough won't bubble up as it bakes when covered with tiny holes.
- In preheated oven, bake for 20 to 25 minutes until golden brown. Allow to cool for about 10 minutes. Keep the oven heated.
- In mixing bowl, add lemon zest, vanilla, salt, sugar, egg yolk, creme fraiche, and cream cheese. Thoroughly combine. Carefully and evenly pour a thin layer of mixture into pastry shell (some of the cheese mixture may not be used).
- Put the filled tart into the oven. Bake until crust is browned and cheese layer is set, for about 20 minutes. Allow tart to cool down completely to room temperature before placing berries.
- Place berries cut side down in a pattern, pointy end out beginning around the edges with the larger berries. As your work your way toward the middle, you can lean strawberries up a bit. Cut some halves of the berry in half again to fill any gaps on the cheese layer.
- Add 2 teaspoons water and apricot jam to saucepan. Heat on low heat until thin enough to brush. Allow to cool slightly before generously brushing over crust and all berries. Place tart on serving plate.

Nutrition Information

- Calories: 641 calories;
- Total Fat: 37.3
- Sodium: 595
- Total Carbohydrate: 67.6
- Cholesterol: 123
- Protein: 8.7

---

316.   Fruit Chiffon Pie

Serving: 8 | Prep: 30mins | Cook: 10mins | Ready in:

Ingredients

- For the Fresh Strawberry Filling:
- 1 (.25 ounce) package unflavored gelatin
- 1/2 cup cold water
- 2/3 cup white sugar
- 1 cup mashed strawberries
- For the Swiss Meringue:
- 3 egg whites
- 1/4 teaspoon cream of tartar
- 1/3 cup white sugar
- 1/2 cup heavy whipping cream
- 1 (9 inch) pie crust, baked

Direction

- Sprinkle the gelatin on top of the cold water and put aside to let it soften for 5 minutes.
- In a saucepan, mix 2/3 cup sugar, the mashed fruit and the rehydrated gelatin. Cook to a complete rolling boil while stirring continuously. Immediately take the pan off the heat and dip the bottom of the pan in cold water; let cool just until when dropped from a spoon, the mixture slightly mounds up.
- In a heat-proof mixing bowl, mix together egg whites, cream of tartar, and 1/3 cup sugar. Whisk it slightly to break the egg whites. Put the bowl on top of a pot of simmering water on the stove. Heat the mixture, whisk continuously until it is hot to the touch and reaches 63°C (145°F) on an instant-read thermometer. Remove the bowl from the heat right away and use an electric mixer to beat

until the meringue forms glossy, medium-stiff peaks.

- Fold the fruit mixture into the meringue with a spatula or whisk. Meanwhile, in a cold bowl, whip the cream until it has medium-stiff peaks.
- The filling should be at room temperature, not warmer, when adding the whipped cream. Add one third of the whipped cream into the filling mixture, mix gently until combined. Fold in the remaining whipped cream and pile the filling into the cooled baked pie shell. Chill several hours until set.

Nutrition Information

- Calories: 247 calories;
- Total Fat: 10.8
- Sodium: 131
- Total Carbohydrate: 35.6
- Cholesterol: 20
- Protein: 3.3

---

317. Lemon Poppy Seed Tartlet With A Strawberry Rose

Serving: 24 | Prep: 40mins | Cook: 12mins | Ready in:

Ingredients

- Cookie Base:
- 1 cup unsalted butter, at room temperature
- 3/4 cup white sugar
- 1 egg
- 2 tablespoons lemon juice
- 2 teaspoons lemon zest
- 1 teaspoon vanilla extract
- 2 1/2 cups all-purpose flour
- 2 tablespoons poppy seeds
- 1 teaspoon sea salt
- Filling:
- 1 (8 ounce) package cream cheese, at room temperature
- 1/4 cup sour cream
- 2 1/2 tablespoons white sugar
- 24 strawberries
- 1 small bunch fresh mint

Direction

- Preheat an oven to 175°C/350°F; line parchment paper on 2 baking sheets.
- Use electric mixer to beat 3/4 cup sugar and butter in big bowl till creamy. Beat vanilla extract, lemon zest, lemon juice and egg in; mix salt, poppy seeds and flour in till no floury streaks remain and dough comes together.
- Pinch 1 1/2 tsp-sized dough pieces off; roll into balls. Put balls on lined baking sheets; to create a small indent, press down on every ball using your thumb.
- In preheated oven, bake for 7 minutes till firm. Take out of oven; reinforce each indent with the back of a spoon. Bake for 5 minutes longer till cookie edges are barely golden.
- Put cookies on wire rack; fully cool.
- Mix 2 1/2 tbsp. sugar, sour cream and cream cheese till well blended in a bowl; use 1/2 tsp. cream cheese mixture to fill each cooled cookie.
- Use a sharp paring knife to create 4 deep cuts along bottom third of every strawberry. Carefully fan cuts out to open. Repeat the process, cutting in between the cuts from the row under, till you hit the top.
- Put a strawberry rose on every cookie; around each strawberry, tuck 1-2 mint leaves.

Nutrition Information

- Calories: 196 calories;
- Cholesterol: 39
- Protein: 2.8
- Total Fat: 12.1
- Sodium: 107
- Total Carbohydrate: 19.6

318. Lisa's Tomatillo And Strawberry Pie

Serving: 8 | Prep: 20mins | Cook: 50mins |Ready in:

Ingredients

- 1 pastry for 9-inch double crust pie
- 3 cups sliced ripe tomatillos
- 3 cups sliced strawberries
- 1/4 cup instant tapioca
- 1 1/2 cups white sugar
- 1 teaspoon lemon juice, or more to taste
- 3 tablespoons butter, sliced

Direction

- Preheat oven to 200°C/400°F. Prepare a 9-inch pie dish, press 1 pie crust into it.
- In a bowl, stir together lemon juice, sugar, tapioca, strawberries, and tomatillos. Let it sit for 15 minutes, or until sugar is dissolved, stirring occasionally. Spoon the strawberry-tomatillo mixture into the pie crust. Scatter slices of butter over the filling.
- Cover the pie using the second pie crust; seal by pinching the edges together. Cut slits on the top of the pie crust to allow ventilation. Transfer the pie to a baking sheet.
- Bake in the preheated oven for 50 minutes, or until the filling is bubbling and the top crust is golden brown.

Nutrition Information

- Calories: 470 calories;
- Protein: 4
- Total Fat: 20.2
- Sodium: 266
- Total Carbohydrate: 70.9
- Cholesterol: 11

319. Mile High Strawberry Pie

Serving: 15 | Prep: 20mins | Cook: 10mins |Ready in:

Ingredients

- Crust:
- 1 cup all-purpose flour
- 3/4 cup chopped pecans
- 1/3 cup margarine, melted
- 1/3 cup brown sugar
- Pie:
- 2 cups sliced strawberries
- 1 cup white sugar
- 2 egg whites
- 1 tablespoon lemon juice
- 1 (12 ounce) container frozen whipped topping (such as Cool Whip®), thawed

Direction

- Set oven to 350°F (175°C) to preheat.
- In a bowl, mix brown sugar, margarine, pecans and flour until crumbly; add to a baking tray.
- Bake in the prepared oven, mixing frequently, for 10 to 15 minutes until lightly browned. Add most of the crumbs to a 9x13-inch baking pan.
- In a bowl, whip lemon juice, egg whites, white sugar and strawberries for about 15 minutes with an electric mixer on high speed until smooth. Fold whipped topping into strawberry filling; add on top of crumbs. Scatter leftover crumbs on top of strawberry filling. Wrap dish with plastic wrap and put in the freezer for 8 hours to overnight until set. Slice into squares.

Nutrition Information

- Calories: 255 calories;
- Sodium: 61
- Total Carbohydrate: 32.3
- Cholesterol: 0
- Protein: 2.3
- Total Fat: 13.7

320. Mini Strawberry Tarts

Serving: 35 | Prep: 30mins | Cook: 18mins | Ready in:

Ingredients

- 2 (8 ounce) packages cream cheese, softened
- 2 cups butter
- 4 1/2 cups all-purpose flour
- 3 (3 ounce) packages strawberry flavored Jell-O® mix
- 1 cup white sugar
- 3 drops red food coloring
- 3 1/2 cups boiling water
- 1/4 cup cornstarch
- 1/4 cup water
- 3 pounds fresh strawberries, sliced
- 1 1/2 cups whipped cream, or to taste (optional)

Direction

- Preheat oven to 175 degrees C/350 degrees F. Grease mini muffin pans lightly.
- In a big bowl, put butter and cream cheese. Beat until fluffy and smooth with an electric mixer. Beat in flour gradually, one cup at a time, until everything has been incorporated. Roll the dough to 70 small balls. Press every ball into a mini muffin pan cup to make pastry crusts.
- Bake crusts for 15-18 minutes in preheated oven until golden brown. Take out of the oven. Let cool.
- In boiling water, mix food coloring, sugar and gelatin. Put on high heat; boil. Mix water and cornstarch together to create a paste. Mix cornstarch mixture in boiling gelatin until melted. Take off from heat. Completely cool for around 30 minutes.
- Evenly spoon cooled gelatin mixture in the tart shells. Push down a strawberry halfway into every tart. If you want, put a small amount of whipped topping/whipped cream on every tart prior to serving.

Nutrition Information

- Calories: 280 calories;
- Sodium: 135
- Total Carbohydrate: 28.9
- Cholesterol: 49
- Protein: 3.7
- Total Fat: 17.2

321. Mona's Fresh Strawberry Pie

Serving: 8 | Prep: 10mins | Cook: 20mins | Ready in:

Ingredients

- 1 (9 inch) prepared pie crust
- 2/3 cup water
- 1/3 cup pureed strawberries
- 1 cup white sugar
- 1 (3 ounce) package strawberry flavored Jell-O®
- 2 tablespoons cornstarch
- 1/4 teaspoon salt
- 2 pints strawberries, cleaned and stemmed

Direction

- Heat oven to 400°F (205°C). Line 2 layers of aluminum foil and a layer of dried beans or pie weights on pastry.
- Bake in the heated oven for about 10 minutes until the rim of crust is golden. Take out the foil and weights carefully and put in the oven again and bake for about 5 minutes more until the crust has firmed. Let crust cool.
- In a saucepan, heat pureed strawberries and water to a boil. Mix in salt, cornstarch, gelatin and sugar for 2 to 3 mins until dissolved, mixing continuously. Put strawberries evenly in crust and put gelatin mixture on berries.

Chill in the fridge overnight or until gelatin has set.

Nutrition Information

- Calories: 288 calories;
- Total Fat: 7.8
- Sodium: 234
- Total Carbohydrate: 53.7
- Cholesterol: 0
- Protein: 3

322. Most Spectacular Strawberry Pie

Serving: 8 | Prep: 20mins | Cook: 35mins | Ready in:

Ingredients

- 1 recipe pastry for a 9 inch double crust pie
- 1/4 cup white sugar
- 1/2 cup brown sugar
- 1/2 cup all-purpose flour
- 1 tablespoon cornstarch
- 1 teaspoon ground cinnamon
- 1/2 teaspoon ground nutmeg
- 1 tablespoon vanilla extract
- 1/2 teaspoon almond extract
- 4 cups fresh strawberries, halved
- 2 tablespoons butter

Direction

- Set oven to 425°F (220°C) to preheat. Line a 9-inch pie pan with one crust, making sure the edges extend beyond the pan a little.
- Combine vanilla and almond extract, nutmeg, cinnamon, cornstarch, flour, brown and white sugars in a large bowl. Put in strawberries; stir carefully until evenly coated. Transfer mixture to the crust, mounding it a little in the center.
- Slice the other crust into 1/2-inch strips; weave to create a lattice over the filling. Roll up additional dough on the underside crust to

seal down the lattice strips; press dough to make a fluted edges using your fingers. Place dots of butter in open squares. To make a golden crust, brush milk lightly over the lattice, then scatter top with sugar.
- Bake for 35 to 40 minutes in the preheated oven until golden brown.

Nutrition Information

- Calories: 393 calories;
- Protein: 4.2
- Total Fat: 18.2
- Sodium: 259
- Total Carbohydrate: 53.5
- Cholesterol: 8

323. No Bake Sugar Free Strawberry Cheesecake

Serving: 6 | Prep: 20mins | Cook: | Ready in:

Ingredients

- 3/4 cup graham cracker crumbs
- 3 tablespoons butter, melted
- 1/4 teaspoon ground cinnamon
- 1/4 teaspoon ground nutmeg
- 1 (8 ounce) package cream cheese, softened
- 1 1/2 cups milk
- 1 (1 ounce) package cheesecake flavor sugar-free instant pudding mix
- 2 pints fresh strawberries, sliced

Direction

- In a bowl put nutmeg, cinnamon, melted butter, graham cracker crumbs together and mix.
- Press the mixture into an 8-inch pie dish. Keep the dish in the fridge when you make the filling.
- Put cream cheese in a mixing bowl then use an electric mixer on medium speed to beat till

cream cheese gets soft. Slow the speed down to low then beat in milk slowly, a little by a little at a time (the mixture will be watery). Scrape cream cheese from the sides of the bowl by a rubber spatula if required.

- Beat in pudding mix till the filling becomes smooth and thick.
- Transfer 1/2 the cream cheese filling into the bottom of the graham cracker crust.
- Use 1/2 the strawberries to spread on the filling.
- Keep repeating cheesecake layer then strawberry layer.
- Keep pie in the fridge for at least an hour to let it chill till set and cold.

Nutrition Information

- Calories: 312 calories;
- Total Fat: 21.4
- Sodium: 448
- Total Carbohydrate: 25.2
- Cholesterol: 61
- Protein: 6.4

324.   No Crust Strawberry Pie

Serving: 8 | Prep: | Cook: |Ready in:

Ingredients

- 24 ounces fresh strawberries
- 1 (2.1 ounce) package sugar-free cook and serve vanilla pudding mix
- 1 (.6 ounce) package sugar-free strawberry flavored Jell-O®
- 2 cups water

Direction

- Rinse then hull strawberries. Spread evenly in a 10 inch pie pan.
- Mix water, gelatin mix, and pudding mix in a medium saucepan. Stir the mixture well and

bring to a full boil. Transfer mixture on strawberries and keep in the fridge for 4-6 hours. Use light frozen whipped topping to top before serving according to your liking.

Nutrition Information

- Calories: 57 calories;
- Total Fat: 0.3
- Sodium: 158
- Total Carbohydrate: 14.2
- Cholesterol: 0
- Protein: 1

325.   Old Fashioned Strawberry Pie

Serving: 8 | Prep: | Cook: |Ready in:

Ingredients

- 2 (9 inch) unbaked pie crusts
- 1 1/4 cups white sugar
- 1/3 cup all-purpose flour
- 1/2 teaspoon ground cinnamon
- 4 cups fresh strawberries
- 2 tablespoons butter

Direction

- Heat oven to 425°F (220°C). Put one crust in a 9-inch pie dish.
- Stir together cinnamon, flour, and sugar. Stir dry mix gently to the berries. Put filling into pan lined with pastry, and fleck fruit with margarine or butter. Top with the top crust and score the top. Pinch and flute the edges to seal.
- Bake until the crust is browned slightly, or for 35 to 45 minutes.

Nutrition Information

- Calories: 412 calories;

- Total Fat: 17.3
- Sodium: 301
- Total Carbohydrate: 62.7
- Cholesterol: 8
- Protein: 3

326. Quick And Easy Strawberry Shake Pie

Serving: 16 | Prep: 15mins | Cook: | Ready in:

Ingredients

- 1 (8 ounce) package cream cheese, softened
- 1/2 (14 ounce) can sweetened condensed milk
- 3/4 cup mashed strawberries
- 2 (8 ounce) containers frozen whipped topping, thawed, divided
- 2 (9 inch) prepared graham cracker crusts
- sliced fresh strawberries (optional)

Direction

- In a bowl, use an electric mixer to beat sweetened condensed milk and cream cheese until thoroughly mixed.
- Mix into the cream cheese mixture 1 container whipped topping and strawberries.
- Spread the filling into the 2 pie crusts. Top them with the rest of the whipped topping can.
- Decorate with strawberry slices if you want. Refrigerate for at least 2 hours.

Nutrition Information

- Calories: 329 calories;
- Total Fat: 20.5
- Sodium: 235
- Total Carbohydrate: 33.9
- Cholesterol: 20
- Protein: 3.7

327. Raw Vegan Strawberry Pie

Serving: 10 | Prep: 20mins | Cook: | Ready in:

Ingredients

- 1 cup almonds
- 1 cup shredded coconut
- 1 cup pitted dates
- 2 tablespoons coconut oil
- 1 pinch salt
- 2 cups strawberries
- 2 cups shredded coconut
- 2 tablespoons coconut oil
- 1 pinch salt
- 3 strawberries, sliced

Direction

- In a blender, put 2 tablespoons coconut oil, almonds, salt, 1 cup of coconut, and dates. Then puree until the ingredients form a dough.
- Transfer the dough into a pie pan then press to create the crust.
- In a blender, put 2 cups strawberries, salt, 2 tablespoons of coconut oil, and 2 cups of coconut. Then puree to form a cream.
- Spread the cream onto the crust. Add sliced strawberries on top. Chill for about 2 hours until the cream becomes thick.

Nutrition Information

- Calories: 348 calories;
- Total Fat: 27
- Sodium: 29
- Total Carbohydrate: 27
- Cholesterol: 0
- Protein: 5.2

328. Rock Creek Lake Fresh Strawberry Pie

Serving: 8 | Prep: 20mins | Cook: 20mins | Ready in:

Ingredients

- 1 pastry for a 9-inch pie crust
- 1 (8 ounce) package cream cheese, at room temperature
- 1/2 cup white sugar
- 1 cup fresh strawberries, hulled and halved
- 3/4 cup white sugar
- 3/4 cup strawberry juice
- 1/4 cup cornstarch
- 1/4 cup lemon juice
- 5 cups fresh strawberries, hulled and halved

Direction

- Set oven to preheat at 190°C (375°F). Into a 9-inch pie pan, press pie crust pastry; use a fork to prick holes 1 inch apart from each other.
- In the preheated oven, bake until pie crust is golden, for 15 to 20 minutes. Allow to completely cool on a rack.
- In a bowl, beat together 1/2 cup sugar and cream cheese until smooth; evenly spread over cooled pie crust' bottom.
- In a blender, blend together cornstarch, strawberry juice, 3/4 cup sugar, and 1 cup strawberries until smooth. Pour into a 3-quart pan on medium-high heat. Cook and stir until the mixture thickens and boils, for about 4 minutes. Take off heat and mix in the lemon juice.
- Into the hot strawberry glaze, mix in the leftover 5 cups strawberries; coat the strawberries by mixing. Allow to cool until lukewarm, for about 25 minutes. Add onto the cream cheese layer in pie crust. Refrigerate to set and until firm enough to cut, for no less than 3 hours and up to 1 day.

Nutrition Information

- Calories: 393 calories;

- Protein: 4.4
- Total Fat: 17.7
- Sodium: 202
- Total Carbohydrate: 56.9
- Cholesterol: 31

329. Scrumptious Strawberry Pie Bars

Serving: 9 | Prep: 25mins | Cook: 7mins | Ready in:

Ingredients

- Crust:
- cooking spray
- 9 graham crackers, crushed
- 1/3 cup butter, melted
- 1/3 cup white sugar
- 2 teaspoons shortening, softened
- 1/2 teaspoon ground cinnamon
- Filling:
- 1 1/2 cups heavy whipping cream
- 6 tablespoons confectioners' sugar
- 1 tablespoon vanilla extract
- 1 pound fresh strawberries, sliced
- 2 tablespoons strawberry syrup, or to taste

Direction

- Put beaters from an electric mixer and a large metal bowl into the freezer.
- Set the oven to preheat at 190°C (375°F). Use cooking spray to grease an 8-inch square pan.
- Combine cinnamon shortening, white sugar, butter, and crushed graham crackers in a bowl until well blended. Press into the greased pan to create the crust.
- In the preheated oven, bake crust until set for about 7 minutes. Allow to cool for about 5 minutes. Chill in the refrigerator for 10 minutes. Then put in the freezer and chill until cool when touched.
- In the chilled bowl, use an electric mixer to beat heavy cream on high speed until it forms soft peaks. Beat in 1 tablespoon confectioners'

sugar at a time. Add vanilla extract in; continue beating until it forms stiff peaks.

- Place 1 layer of strawberries on the cooled crust. Add 1 layer of whipped cream. Continue with another layer of strawberries and whipped cream. Place the rest of the strawberries on top. Top with a drizzle of strawberry sauce.
- Let set in refrigerator for about 1 hour. Slice it into 9 pieces before serving.

Nutrition Information

- Calories: 315 calories;
- Protein: 1.7
- Total Fat: 23.4
- Sodium: 110
- Total Carbohydrate: 25.8
- Cholesterol: 72

330.   Strawberry Banana Pie

Serving: 8 | Prep: 15mins | Cook: 20mins | Ready in:

Ingredients

- 1 unbaked pie crust
- 1/2 cup cold butter, cut into small pieces
- 1/4 cup packed brown sugar
- 1 cup all-purpose flour
- 1 tablespoon ground cinnamon
- 1 tablespoon ground nutmeg
- 2 tablespoons chopped walnuts (optional)
- 1/4 cup apple juice
- 3 ripe bananas, sliced
- 1/4 cup honey
- 1 cup chopped fresh strawberries
- 1/2 cup white sugar

Direction

- Preheat the oven to 190°C/375°F. Into a 9-in. pie pan, press prepped pie crust in. Put aside.

- In a food processor bowl, pulse nuts, nutmeg, cinnamon, flour, brown sugar and butter till it has an oatmeal-like texture. Refrigerate crumble topping till you use it.
- In a medium saucepan, put apple juice on medium low heat. Add honey and sliced bananas. Mix till honey dissolves. Stir white sugar and chopped strawberries in. Simmer for 20 minutes, uncovered. Put warm fruit mixture into prepped pie crust. Across pie's top, evenly distribute cold crumble topping.
- Bake in preheated oven for 20 minutes till set and golden brown. On a wire rack, cool pie 30 minutes prior to serving.

Nutrition Information

- Calories: 448 calories;
- Sodium: 202
- Total Carbohydrate: 64.2
- Cholesterol: 31
- Protein: 4.2
- Total Fat: 21

331.   Strawberry Brown Sugar Sour Cream Pie

Serving: 8 | Prep: 30mins | Cook: 1hours | Ready in:

Ingredients

- 1 egg, lightly beaten
- 3/4 cup brown sugar
- 3/4 cup white sugar
- 3/4 cup sour cream
- 1/4 cup whole wheat flour
- 3 cups sliced strawberries
- 1 unbaked 9 inch pie crust
- 1/3 cup brown sugar
- 1/3 cup whole wheat flour
- 3 tablespoons melted butter

Direction

- Heat an oven to 450°F (230°C).
- In a bowl, mix a quarter cup of wheat flour, sour cream, white sugar, 3/4 cup brown sugar and egg together. Put the sliced strawberries in the pie shell, scoop the sour cream mixture on top of the berries.
- Mix together a third cup of flour and a third cup of brown sugar in a separate bowl. Put in the melted butter and mix until the mixture looks like course meal. Scatter this mixture on top of berries and sour cream mixture in the crust.
- Put pie on lowest rack in heated oven. Bake for 15 minutes, then turn oven temperature down to 350°F (175°C). Bake for 45 minutes more. Take out of the oven, and cool entirely, overnight is best.

Nutrition Information

- Calories: 416 calories;
- Total Fat: 17.3
- Sodium: 175
- Total Carbohydrate: 63.4
- Cholesterol: 44
- Protein: 4.5

332.   Strawberry Butter Cracker Pie

Serving: 6 | Prep: 15mins | Cook: 30mins | Ready in:

Ingredients

- 3 egg whites
- 1 cup white sugar
- 1/2 teaspoon baking powder
- 1/4 teaspoon salt
- 1 teaspoon vanilla extract
- 14 buttery round crackers, crushed
- 2/3 cup chopped pecans
- 1 (8 ounce) container frozen whipped topping, thawed
- 2 cups fresh strawberries, sliced

Direction

- Preheat oven to 350°F (175°C). Grease a 9 inch pie pan.
- Whip egg whites in a large metal or glass mixing bowl until foamy. Gradually add vanilla, salt, baking powder and sugar, keep whisking until the whites form stiff peaks.
- Into meringue mixture, slowly fold pecans and crackers. Put into pie pan.
- Bake for 30 minutes in preheated oven. Cover and chill overnight.
- Just before served, cover pie with whipped topping completely, then set strawberry slices on top.

Nutrition Information

- Calories: 387 calories;
- Protein: 3.8
- Total Fat: 17.4
- Sodium: 230
- Total Carbohydrate: 52.7
- Cholesterol: 0

333.   Strawberry Cheese Pie

Serving: 8 | Prep: | Cook: | Ready in:

Ingredients

- 1 1/3 cups all-purpose flour
- 1/2 teaspoon salt
- 4 tablespoons shortening
- 2 tablespoons butter
- 3 tablespoons cold water
- 1 (8 ounce) package cream cheese, softened
- 3/4 cup confectioners' sugar
- 1 teaspoon vanilla extract
- 1 cup heavy whipping cream, whipped
- 1/2 teaspoon almond extract
- 1/4 cup chopped almonds
- 4 cups fresh strawberries, halved
- 1/4 cup currant jelly

Direction

- In medium bowl, mix together salt and flour. Cut in butter and shortening until all the flour has pea-sized crumbs. Sprinkle in one tablespoon water at a time. Lightly toss using a fork until dough creates a ball. Refrigerate dough for 15 to 30 minutes.
- Between two sheets of wax paper, roll dough out into a circle 11 inch in size. Take off the top wax paper sheet and put into a 9 inch pie pan. Thoroughly prick sides and bottom of pie shell to prevent it from shrinking.
- Bake at 220°C (425°F) for 10 to 15 minutes or until light brown. Let it cool down to room temperature.
- Mix together confectioner's sugar and cream cheese in medium bowl. Use an electric mixer to beat at medium speed until smooth. Beat in almond extracts and vanilla. Fold in almonds and whipped cream by hand until well combined. Add into the cooled crust. Put in refrigerator until firm.
- Use strawberries to fully garnish pie or just around the edge. In microwave oven, heat jelly just until soft and carefully brush over strawberries until glazed. Place in refrigerator until serving.

Nutrition Information

- Calories: 421 calories;
- Sodium: 256
- Total Carbohydrate: 41.7
- Cholesterol: 59
- Protein: 5.7
- Total Fat: 26.5

334.	Strawberry Cream Pie To Die For

Serving: 8 | Prep: 20mins | Cook: | Ready in:

Ingredients

- 1 quart strawberries, sliced
- 1 (13.5 ounce) package strawberry glaze
- 1 (4 ounce) package cream cheese, softened
- 1/2 cup confectioners' sugar
- 1/4 teaspoon ground cinnamon
- 1 teaspoon vanilla extract
- 1 cup heavy whipping cream
- 1 (9 inch) baked pie crust

Direction

- In a bowl, mix glaze and strawberries together and refrigerate to chill. Mix together vanilla extract, cinnamon, confectioners' sugar, and cream cheese in a bowl.
- Use an electric mixer to beat cream in a separate bowl just until it starts to thicken; put in cream cheese mixture and continue to beat until it thickens. Into baked pie crust, pour the cream mixture; layer strawberry mixture on top. Refrigerate before serving for no less than 1 hour.

Nutrition Information

- Calories: 353 calories;
- Sodium: 203
- Total Carbohydrate: 37
- Cholesterol: 56
- Protein: 2.9
- Total Fat: 21.3

335.	Strawberry Creme Brulee Pie

Serving: 8 | Prep: 30mins | Cook: 35mins | Ready in:

Ingredients

- 12 large strawberries, hulled and halved
- 1/3 cup brown sugar
- 1 cup all-purpose flour
- 1 tablespoon white sugar
- 1/4 teaspoon salt

- 1/2 cup butter, softened
- 2 tablespoons milk
- 1 pint heavy whipping cream
- 6 egg yolks
- 1/4 teaspoon salt
- 1/4 cup white sugar

Direction

- Toss brown sugar and strawberries in bowl; stand for 30 minutes while completing other steps.
- Preheat an oven to 175°C/350°F.
- Whisk 1/4 tsp. salt, 1 tbsp. white sugar and flour till combined thoroughly in bowl. Cut butter into flour mixture till it looks like coarse crumbs; drizzle milk in. Mix till dough just holds together. Turn out dough on floured surface; roll out to 10-in. circle then fit dough to 9-in. pie dish. Prick dough a few times on sides and bottom; fill with pie weights/dry beans.
- In preheated oven, bake for 25 minutes till golden brown. Remove crust; cool.
- Barely simmer cream in saucepan on low heat. Thoroughly whisk egg yolks in bowl with 1/4 tsp. salt; add 1 tbsp. hot cream to beaten yolks, constantly whisking. Add and whisk 2/3 cup of hot cream into the yolks. Whisk yolk mixture into leftover hot cream in saucepan, adding in thin stream. Whisk for 5 minutes till cream mixture is smooth and thick; don't boil custard will curdle. Take custard off heat; stand for 30 minutes till it reaches room temperature.
- From strawberries, drain juice; layer on bottom of baked pie shell. Spread cream custard on berries; refrigerate for 4 hours till set.
- Put oven rack 6-in. away from heat source; preheat oven broiler.
- Evenly sprinkle 1/4 cup white sugar over pie; broil for 5 minutes till sugar browns. Let pie stand for 5 minutes to cool sugar topping; serve.

Nutrition Information

- Calories: 479 calories;
- Total Fat: 37.1
- Sodium: 260
- Total Carbohydrate: 33.1
- Cholesterol: 266
- Protein: 5.2

336.   Strawberry Daiquiri Pie

Serving: 16 | Prep: | Cook: |Ready in:

Ingredients

- 1 (10 ounce) can frozen strawberry daiquiri mixer
- 1 cup sweetened condensed milk
- 1 (8 ounce) container frozen whipped topping, thawed
- 1 (10 ounce) package frozen strawberries, thawed
- 2 (9 inch) prepared graham cracker crusts

Direction

- Combine the whipped topping, sweetened condensed milk and daiquiri mix in a large bowl. Stir until creamy and smooth.
- Put in the thawed strawberries; blend into the mixture.
- Fill the pie crusts. Freeze until set or refrigerate for about 4 hours.

Nutrition Information

- Calories: 305 calories;
- Cholesterol: 7
- Protein: 3
- Total Fat: 12.7
- Sodium: 199
- Total Carbohydrate: 47.3

337.   Strawberry Delight Dessert Pie

Serving: 12 | Prep: 30mins | Cook: | Ready in:

Ingredients

- 1 1/2 cups graham cracker crumbs
- 1/4 cup white sugar
- 1/3 cup butter, melted
- 1 (8 ounce) package cream cheese
- 1/4 cup white sugar
- 2 tablespoons milk
- 3 1/2 cups frozen whipped topping, thawed
- 2 pints fresh strawberries, sliced
- 2 (3.4 ounce) packages instant vanilla pudding mix
- 3 1/2 cups milk

Direction

- Combine thoroughly the melted butter, 1/4 cup sugar, and graham cracker crumbs in a medium bowl. Layer this mixture into the bottom of a 9x13-inch pan. Let rest in the freezer while making the filling.
- Mix together the cream cheese, 2 tablespoons of milk and 1/4 cup sugar in a large bowl until smooth. Fold half of the whipped topping in. Spread the mixture on top of the crust. Evenly layer the strawberries over filling. Make instant pudding following package instructions, but only use 3 1/2 cups milk. Layer the prepared pudding on top of the strawberries. Refrigerate for 4 hours or overnight.
- Spread reserved whipped topping over the pudding before serving.

Nutrition Information

- Calories: 371 calories;
- Cholesterol: 40
- Protein: 5.3
- Total Fat: 19.9
- Sodium: 420
- Total Carbohydrate: 44.7

338.   Strawberry Delight Pie

Serving: 8 | Prep: 10mins | Cook: | Ready in:

Ingredients

- 1 (8 ounce) package reduced-fat cream cheese, softened
- 1/3 cup confectioners' sugar
- 1 teaspoon lemon juice
- 1 (8 ounce) container reduced-fat whipped topping, thawed
- 1 (8 inch) graham cracker crust
- 1 pint fresh strawberries, sliced
- 1/2 cup strawberry glaze

Direction

- In a bowl, whip lemon juice, confectioners' sugar, and cream cheese together with an electric mixer on low speed. Put whipped topping and whip until well incorporated. Scoop filling into graham cracker crust.
- In a bowl mix strawberries and glaze together until evenly coated; put berries on pie filling. Chill pie for at least 1 hour until cooled.

Nutrition Information

- Calories: 271 calories;
- Total Carbohydrate: 38.1
- Cholesterol: 16
- Protein: 4.2
- Total Fat: 10.4
- Sodium: 236

339.   Strawberry Dream Pie

Serving: 8 | Prep: 15mins | Cook: | Ready in:

Ingredients

- 1 (8 ounce) package cream cheese, softened
- 1/3 cup strawberry preserves
- 1 1/2 cups frozen whipped topping, thawed
- 1 (9 inch) prepared graham cracker crust
- 1 cup fresh strawberries
- 2 teaspoons white sugar
- 2 teaspoons grenadine syrup

Direction

- Combine strawberry preserves and cream cheese in a bowl. Fold in the whipped topping. Transfer the mixture into the prepared pie crust then set aside.
- Put grenadine syrup, sugar, and strawberries in a food processor or blender then turn the machine on to blend till slightly chunky. Spread on the cream cheese mixture. Put in the fridge for at least 2 hours to allow the mixture to chill before serving time.

Nutrition Information

- Calories: 340 calories;
- Total Fat: 20.8
- Sodium: 258
- Total Carbohydrate: 36.3
- Cholesterol: 31
- Protein: 3.7

340.   Strawberry Frangipane Tart

Serving: 10 | Prep: 30mins | Cook: 40mins | Ready in:

Ingredients

- Crust:
- 1 2/3 cups all-purpose flour, plus more for rolling out dough
- 1/2 cup almond flour
- 7 tablespoons white sugar
- 1/2 teaspoon salt
- 1/2 cup cold butter

- 1 egg, beaten
- Frangipane:
- 1/2 cup superfine sugar
- 7 tablespoons butter
- 1 cup almond flour
- 3 1/2 tablespoons all-purpose flour
- 1 egg yolk
- Jam:
- 1 3/4 cups strawberries
- 1/3 cup white sugar, or more to taste
- Topping:
- 2 cups strawberries, or as needed

Direction

- In a bowl, combine 1/2 teaspoon salt, 7 tablespoons white sugar, 1/2 cup almond flour, and 1 2/3 cups all-purpose flour. Use your fingers to mix in 1/2 cup cold butter until the mixture becomes coarse crumbs. Make a well; pour in beaten egg. Mix until it forms a dough; knead till just incorporated. Wrap the dough using plastic wrap; let sit in freezer for 15 to 20 minutes.
- Beat together 7 tablespoons butter and 1/2 cup superfine sugar in a bowl with an electric mixer until the mixture becomes creamy. Mix in 3 1/2 tablespoons all-purpose flour and 1 cup almond flour. Put in egg yolk; mix until frangipane is incorporated.
- In a pot over medium heat, put 1/3 cup white sugar and 3 cups strawberries. Cook and stir until the mixture begins to simmer. Turn the heat down to low; mash the strawberries. Cook until jam thickens, another 10 to 15 minutes. Strain the jam through a fine sieve; save pulp. Let cool.
- Set oven to preheat at 200 o C (400 o F).
- Flour a rolling pin and a work surface; roll dough out into a 1/8-inch thick circle and transfer to a tart pan. Use a double layer of aluminum foil to line crust and layer dried beans or pie weights on top.
- In the preheated oven, bake for 10 minutes.
- Remove foil and weights carefully; spread frangipane in layer 1/3 the thickness of the crust.

- Put back into the oven; bake for 15 to 20 minutes until the tart turns golden brown. Allow tart to cool for 5 minutes.
- Spread the saved pulp on top of tart; push in strawberries to cover surface. Evenly layer jam on top of tart. Cool until set, about 30 minutes.

Nutrition Information

- Calories: 437 calories;
- Total Fat: 21.7
- Sodium: 249
- Total Carbohydrate: 52.9
- Cholesterol: 85
- Protein: 10.6

341.   Strawberry Frozen Pie

Serving: 16 | Prep: 10mins | Cook: | Ready in:

Ingredients

- 1 (14 ounce) can sweetened condensed milk (such as Eagle Brand®)
- 2 (8 ounce) packages cream cheese, softened
- 2 (8 ounce) containers frozen whipped topping (such as Cool Whip®), thawed
- 2 pints fresh strawberries, hulled and sliced, or to taste
- 2 (9 inch) graham cracker crusts

Direction

- In a bowl, whisk cream cheese and sweetened condensed milk together until smooth; put in whipped topping and mix until smooth. Fold strawberries into whipped topping; split between the 2 pie shells.
- Keep in the freezer 2 to 3 hours until solid.

Nutrition Information

- Calories: 427 calories;
- Total Fat: 26.6

- Sodium: 292
- Total Carbohydrate: 43.4
- Cholesterol: 39
- Protein: 6

342.   Strawberry Glazed Pie

Serving: 8 | Prep: | Cook: | Ready in:

Ingredients

- 6 cups sliced fresh strawberries
- 2/3 cup white sugar
- 1 cup water
- 4 tablespoons strawberry flavored Jell-O®
- 4 tablespoons cornstarch
- 1 (9 inch) prepared graham cracker crust

Direction

- In a medium large saucepan, stir together the cornstarch, gelatin, water and sugar. Heat up to a boil for one minute. Take off from heat.
- Fold in the sliced strawberries, toss until evenly coated. Put into the graham cracker crust.
- Refrigerate until firm. Top with whipped cream and serve.

Nutrition Information

- Calories: 279 calories;
- Total Fat: 7.8
- Sodium: 185
- Total Carbohydrate: 52.2
- Cholesterol: 0
- Protein: 2.4

343.   Strawberry Kiwi Tartlets

Serving: 12 | Prep: 25mins | Cook: 30mins | Ready in:

Ingredients

- 1 egg
- 2 teaspoons water
- 12 frozen puff pastry shells, thawed
- 1/3 cup strawberry preserves
- 2 pints fresh strawberries, sliced
- 4 kiwis, peeled and seeded
- 2 tablespoons honey
- 1/2 cup heavy cream
- 2 teaspoons confectioners' sugar

Direction

- In a clean bowl, whisk together the water and egg. Brush the egg mixture to the puff pastry shells and bake. With regards to baking, follow the directions in the package of the shells.
- Using a saucepan, melt the preserves over low heat. When it's already melted, add strawberry slices after removing it from the heat.
- Blend in honey and kiwis in a food processor. Blend until it looks smooth. Mix together the sugar and cream in a large bowl until it forms stiff peaks.
- Prior to serving, add strawberries in each of the puff pastry shell and drizzle it with the kiwi sauce. Place whipped cream on top of it then serve.

Nutrition Information

- Calories: 301 calories;
- Total Carbohydrate: 34
- Cholesterol: 29
- Protein: 5.4
- Total Fat: 17.4
- Sodium: 241

344.   Strawberry Pie I

Serving: 8 | Prep: | Cook: |Ready in:

Ingredients

- 1 (9 inch) pie crust, baked
- 24 marshmallows
- 1 tablespoon milk
- 1 (10 ounce) package frozen strawberries, thawed and pureed
- 1 cup heavy whipping cream

Direction

- Mix milk with marshmallows in a saucepan over low heat until marshmallows are dissolved.
- Mix strawberries into the melted marshmallows. Beat cream in a medium bowl until soft peak. Into the marshmallow mixture, fold whipped cream.
- Scoop mixture into pie crust, chill for 4 to 6 hours. Serve cold.

Nutrition Information

- Calories: 281 calories;
- Cholesterol: 41
- Protein: 1.9
- Total Fat: 16.3
- Sodium: 132
- Total Carbohydrate: 33.7

345.   Strawberry Pie II

Serving: 8 | Prep: | Cook: |Ready in:

Ingredients

- 1 (9 inch) pie crust, baked
- 1 quart fresh strawberries
- 1 cup white sugar
- 3 tablespoons cornstarch
- 3/4 cup water
- 1/2 cup heavy whipping cream

Direction

- In the baked pie crust, place half of the strawberries. In a medium saucepan, smash the rest of the berries with sugar. Place the saucepan on medium heat and bring to a boil and stir regularly.
- Whisk together water and cornstarch in a small bowl. Stir this mixture slowly into the boiling strawberry saucepan. Lower heat and simmer until the mixture thickens for about 10 minutes, stirring continuously. Pour the mixture on top of the berries in the crust. Refrigerate for a few hours before serving. Whip cream in a small bowl until soft peaks form. Place a spoonful of whipped cream on top of each slice.

Nutrition Information

- Calories: 265 calories;
- Sodium: 109
- Total Carbohydrate: 41.9
- Cholesterol: 20
- Protein: 1.5
- Total Fat: 10.9

---

346.   Strawberry Pie III

Serving: 18 | Prep: | Cook: | Ready in:

Ingredients

- 2 cups crushed zwieback toast
- 3 tablespoons white sugar
- 3/4 cup butter, melted
- 1 (8 ounce) package cream cheese, softened
- 1 cup confectioners' sugar
- 1 (8 ounce) container frozen whipped topping, thawed
- 2 cups miniature marshmallows
- 2 cups water
- 2 (3 ounce) packages strawberry flavored Jell-O®
- 2 cups strawberries, partially frozen

Direction

- Set oven to preheat at 175°C (350°F).
- Combine together white sugar and zwieback crumbs in a medium bowl. Mix in margarine or butter. Combine well and pat the mixture into a 9x13 inch baking dish. In preheated oven, bake for 12 to 15 minutes, until light brown. Put aside and let cool.
- Whip cream cheese in a large mixing bowl until fluffy. Put in confectioners' sugar and beat till it becomes smooth. Fold in marshmallows and whipped topping. Evenly spread mixture atop cooled crust.
- In a medium saucepan, boil water. Take off heat and put in gelatin. Mix until gelatin dissolves, then mix in partly frozen strawberries. Add mixture on top of cream cheese layer. Refrigerate until really firm.

Nutrition Information

- Calories: 266 calories;
- Sodium: 149
- Total Carbohydrate: 30.5
- Cholesterol: 35
- Protein: 2.7
- Total Fat: 15.7

---

347.   Strawberry Pie IV

Serving: 8 | Prep: 30mins | Cook: | Ready in:

Ingredients

- 1 (8 ounce) container frozen whipped topping, thawed
- 1 (14 ounce) can sweetened condensed milk
- 2 cups diced fresh strawberries
- 1/4 cup lemon juice
- 2 drops red food coloring
- 1 (9 inch) prepared graham cracker crust

Direction

- Mix together condensed milk and whipped topping in a large bowl. Fold strawberries in and keep on stirring while adding food coloring and lemon juice. Into a graham cracker crust, pour the mixture; cover and let chill in the fridge for 2 to 3 hours.

Nutrition Information

- Calories: 391 calories;
- Sodium: 220
- Total Carbohydrate: 54.1
- Cholesterol: 17
- Protein: 5.6
- Total Fat: 18

| 348. | Strawberry Pie V |

Serving: 8 | Prep: 10mins | Cook: 10mins | Ready in:

Ingredients

- 2 1/2 cups water
- 2 cups white sugar
- 5 tablespoons cornstarch
- 1 (3 ounce) package strawberry flavored Jell-O® mix
- 2 quarts strawberries, hulled
- 2 (9 inch) pie shells, baked

Direction

- Mix cornstarch, sugar and water in a saucepan. Cook over medium high heat, mixing continuously until it boils and thickens. Take off from heat and mix in the strawberry gelatin. Let it cool slightly.
- Put strawberries in the pie shells, make the tips of the strawberries point up. Cover the berries with gelatin mixture.

Nutrition Information

- Calories: 537 calories;

- Sodium: 289
- Total Carbohydrate: 96.8
- Cholesterol: 0
- Protein: 4.9
- Total Fat: 16

| 349. | Strawberry Pie VI |

Serving: 8 | Prep: 30mins | Cook: | Ready in:

Ingredients

- 1 (3 ounce) package strawberry flavored Jell-O®
- 2/3 cup boiling water
- 3 cubes ice
- 1 (8 ounce) container frozen whipped topping, thawed
- 1 cup strawberries, hulled and sliced
- 1 (9 inch) prepared graham cracker crust

Direction

- Mix boiling water and gelatin in a medium bowl. Stir for 3 minutes or till all gelatin is dissolved. Put ice in and stir till gelatin becomes thick and cool. Fold in strawberries and whipped topping. Allow the mixture to chill till the mixture mounds then transfer mixture into crust. Keep in the fridge for at least 2 hours before serving time.

Nutrition Information

- Calories: 281 calories;
- Total Fat: 14.6
- Sodium: 221
- Total Carbohydrate: 36.6
- Cholesterol: 0
- Protein: 2.7

350. Strawberry Pina Colada Pie

Serving: 10 | Prep: 20mins | Cook: | Ready in:

Ingredients

- 1 (8 ounce) package PHILADELPHIA Cream Cheese, softened
- 1/4 cup milk
- 1 pkg. (4 serving size) JELL-O Vanilla Flavor Instant Pudding & Pie Filling
- 1 (8 ounce) can DOLE Crushed Pineapple in Juice, undrained
- 1 (8 ounce) tub COOL WHIP Whipped Topping, thawed, divided
- 1 (6 ounce) HONEY MAID Graham Pie Crust
- 1/4 cup BAKER'S ANGEL FLAKE Coconut, toasted
- 1 1/4 cups sliced fresh strawberries

Direction

- In large bowl, whisk milk and cream cheese with an electric mixer until well combined. Put dry pudding mix and pineapple; stir well. Slowly mix in 2 cups of the whipped topping; scoop into crust.
- Chill 3 hours or until set.
- Just before serving, garnish with remaining whipped topping, strawberries and coconut. Store leftovers in the fridge.

Nutrition Information

- Calories: 278 calories;
- Sodium: 339
- Total Carbohydrate: 32.5
- Cholesterol: 26
- Protein: 2.6
- Total Fat: 15.3

351. Strawberry Pretzel Pie

Serving: 16 | Prep: 20mins | Cook: 10mins | Ready in:

Ingredients

- 2 cups coarsely crushed pretzels
- 3/4 cup margarine, melted
- 1 tablespoon white sugar
- 1 (8 ounce) package cream cheese, softened
- 1 cup white sugar
- 1 (8 ounce) container frozen whipped topping, thawed
- 2 (3 ounce) packages strawberry flavored Jell-O®
- 2 cups boiling water
- 2 (10 ounce) packages frozen sweetened strawberries (do not thaw)

Direction

- Heat oven to 400°F (200°C).
- Stir 1 Tbsp. sugar, melted margarine and crushed pretzels together in a medium bowl. Push mixture firmly down the bottom of a 9x13 inch baking dish. Bake for 8 to 10 minutes in a preheated oven until lightly browned. Let cool completely.
- Whip together 1 cup sugar and softened cream cheese in a medium bowl until fluffy and smooth. Fold in whipped cream and put mixture evenly on prepared crust.
- In a medium heat-proof bowl, put gelatin and boiling water. Gradually whisk to dissolve gelatin entirely. Put in frozen strawberries and keep mixing just until thickened. Chill until the mixture is semi-firm but still pourable. Put gelatin mixture on top of cream cheese layer. Chill for 2 hours or more before slicing.

Nutrition Information

- Calories: 332 calories;
- Cholesterol: 15
- Protein: 3.4
- Total Fat: 17.3
- Sodium: 368

- Total Carbohydrate: 43.6

352. Strawberry Pudding Pie

Serving: 8 | Prep: 15mins | Cook: |Ready in:

Ingredients

- 1 (9 inch) prepared graham cracker crust
- 1 (3.4 ounce) package instant vanilla pudding mix
- 20 strawberries, hulled
- 1 (18 ounce) jar strawberry glaze
- 1 (16 ounce) package frozen whipped topping, thawed

Direction

- Make the pudding following the directions on the box. Put the pudding evenly in the bottom of the pie shell. Put the strawberries big side down on to the pudding.
- Put the strawberry glaze on top of the strawberries, to cover completely. Top with whipped topping.

Nutrition Information

- Calories: 445 calories;
- Protein: 2
- Total Fat: 20.9
- Sodium: 398
- Total Carbohydrate: 62.3
- Cholesterol: 0

353. Strawberry Tart With Truvia® Natural Sweetener

Serving: 8 | Prep: | Cook: |Ready in:

Ingredients

- Crust:
- 1 1/4 cups flour
- 4 teaspoons Truvia® natural sweetener spoonable*
- 1/4 teaspoon salt
- 6 tablespoons unsalted butter
- 2 tablespoons cold shortening
- 1/4 cup ice water
- Pastry Cream:
- 1 1/3 cups 1% low-fat milk
- 2 tablespoons Truvia® natural sweetener spoonable, plus
- 1/2 teaspoon Truvia® natural sweetener spoonable**
- 2 tablespoons cornstarch
- 2 tablespoons flour
- 4 large egg yolks
- 3/4 teaspoon vanilla
- 1/8 teaspoon salt
- Fruit Topping:
- 1 pint fresh strawberries
- 1/2 teaspoon Truvia® natural sweetener spoonable***

Direction

- Set oven to preheat at 375 o F.
- For the crust: Mix together the salt, Truvia(R) natural sweetener and flour in a small bowl and refrigerate until chilled. Mix the shortening and butter into the refrigerated flour mixture using your fingers or a pastry blender until the butter becomes as small as peas. Put in the ice water and combine until the dough forms. Shape dough into a flat disk, then cover and refrigerate for 30 minutes.
- On a floured surface or between sheets of parchment paper, roll the dough out to the thickness of 0.5 cm. Place into tart pan(s) that has removable bottom, be careful not to stretch the dough as it will shrink while baking. To cut off excess pastry, roll the rolling pin over the tart pan. Prick the shells' bottom to keep it from puffing while baking. Use aluminum foil or parchment paper to line the shells and fill them with rice, dried beans or pie weights. Bake until crust is light brown, about 25-30

minutes. Take away the weights and let crust thoroughly cool down before filling.

- For the pastry cream: beat together egg yolks, cornstarch, flour and Truvia(R) natural sweetener in a medium bowl on high speed until pale yellow and thick, about 2 minutes. In the meantime, in a medium saucepan, heat milk over medium heat and set to a simmer.
- Slowly pour the heated milk into the egg mixture while mixing on low speed. Pour the mixture back into the sauce pan and cook, whisking continuously to keep it from scorching. Continue heating over medium heat until it starts bubbling, then keep on whisking and cooking to completely cook the eggs, about 30 seconds.
- In a clean bowl, put cooked pastry cream and mix in vanilla. Use parchment paper or plastic wrap to cover the pastry cream's surface to keep a skin from forming. Refrigerate until cooled.
- For the tart assembly: Layer the pastry cream evenly in the tart shell's bottom. Garnish strawberry slices in a decorative pattern atop the cream. Sprinkle with 1/2 teaspoon of Truvia(R) natural sweetener. Serve immediately.

---

354.   Strawberry Tarts

Serving: 6 | Prep: | Cook: |Ready in:

Ingredients

- 12 (4 inch) prepared tart shells, baked
- 2/3 cup white sugar
- 2 1/2 tablespoons cornstarch
- 1 pinch salt
- 1 cup apple juice
- 3 cups fresh strawberries

Direction

- Glaze" Blend salt, cornstarch and sugar. Mix into apple juice. Cook, constantly stirring, on

medium heat until thick and smooth. Cool for 10 minutes.

- Spread a bit of glaze on the shell's bottoms. Put washed and hulled fresh berries on glaze, slicing if needed to fit in the tarts. Carefully spoon leftover glaze on berries, cover them well. Chill for 2-4 hours. Top with whipped cream (optional).

Nutrition Information

- Calories: 643 calories;
- Total Carbohydrate: 96.7
- Cholesterol: 0
- Protein: 7.7
- Total Fat: 25.3
- Sodium: 288

---

355.   Strawberry Yogurt Pie I

Serving: 8 | Prep: | Cook: |Ready in:

Ingredients

- 2 (8 ounce) containers strawberry flavored yogurt
- 1 (12 ounce) container frozen whipped topping, thawed
- 1 cup strawberries, finely chopped
- 1 (9 inch) prepared graham cracker crust

Direction

- Stir yogurt with 3 and 1/2 cups of the dessert topping until combined. If necessary, sweeten the strawberries. Stir in strawberries and scoop into crust.
- If possible, chill in the freezer for at least 3 hours or overnight until it's firm.
- Take out from freezer and spread remaining dessert topping on top. Freeze to store.

Nutrition Information

- Calories: 317 calories;
- Total Carbohydrate: 36.1
- Cholesterol: 1
- Protein: 3.9
- Total Fat: 18.1
- Sodium: 221

356. Strawberry Yogurt Pie II

Serving: 8 | Prep: 10mins | Cook: |Ready in:

Ingredients

- 1 (9 inch) pie shell, baked
- 1 (16 ounce) package frozen strawberries, defrosted
- 2 (8 ounce) containers strawberry flavored yogurt
- 1 (8 ounce) container frozen whipped topping, thawed
- 1 (.25 ounce) package unflavored gelatin

Direction

- Put yogurt and strawberries in food processor or blender. Blend to cut strawberries into small chunks.
- Mix together gelatin and whipped topping in a large bowl. Stir the strawberry mixture in. Pour this into baked pie crust and refrigerate overnight.

Nutrition Information

- Calories: 246 calories;
- Sodium: 151
- Total Carbohydrate: 31.5
- Cholesterol: 1
- Protein: 4.1
- Total Fat: 12.3

357. Strawberry Mango Pie

Serving: 8 | Prep: 30mins | Cook: 20mins |Ready in:

Ingredients

- 2 mangos - peeled, seeded, and cubed
- 1/4 cup apple juice
- 15 fresh strawberries, hulled and halved
- 1/2 cup white sugar
- 3 tablespoons honey
- 1/2 cup cold butter
- 1/4 cup packed brown sugar
- 1 cup all-purpose flour
- 1 tablespoon ground nutmeg
- 1 tablespoon ground cinnamon
- 1 (9 inch) refrigerated pie crust

Direction

- Set oven to preheat at 190°C (375°F). Refrigerate a mixing bowl to chill.
- In a saucepan, put in the apple juice and mangoes; simmer over medium-low heat. After 10 minutes, stir into the mangoes the honey and 1/4 cup white sugar. Put in the strawberries. Reduce the heat to low and continue simmering until the fruit becomes soft.
- Into the cold mixing bowl, add the butter and cut into small pieces. Mix butter with the cinnamon, nutmeg, flour, brown sugar, and the remaining1/4 cup white sugar. Use two forks or your fingers to mix the butter into the dry ingredients until it turns coarse and crumbly. Rest in the refrigerator until needed.
- Into the prepared pie crust, pour the mango mixture. Spread the crumb mixture evenly over the top of the fruit.
- In the preheated oven, bake until the top is golden brown, about 20 minutes. Take out of the oven and let it cool down for at least 30 minutes before serving.

Nutrition Information

- Calories: 423 calories;

- Total Carbohydrate: 60.6
- Cholesterol: 31
- Protein: 3.7
- Total Fat: 19.8
- Sodium: 203

358.   Summery Strawberry Pie

Serving: 8 | Prep: 20mins | Cook: 5mins | Ready in:

Ingredients

- 1 (9 inch) prepared graham cracker pie crust
- 1 (8 ounce) package Neufchatel cheese, softened
- 2 tablespoons white sugar
- 2 teaspoons pure vanilla extract
- 2 tablespoons milk
- 1 pint fresh strawberries, hulled
- 1 cup strawberry glaze

Direction

- Heat oven to 350°F (175°C).
- Bake pie crust in the heated oven for about 5 minutes until lightly browned, let cool completely before assembling.
- In a bowl, whisk together milk, vanilla extract, sugar, and Neufchatel cheese together until slightly thinned; put onto the pie crust evenly with a spatula.
- Put berries over the cheese filling in the pie crust with the points upward, pressing down gently to sink in the cheese filling. Cover the cheese filling as much as possible with berries.
- Put strawberries glaze evenly on the pie.
- Chill at least an hour prior to serving.

Nutrition Information

- Calories: 289 calories;
- Total Fat: 14.2
- Sodium: 312
- Total Carbohydrate: 35.6

- Cholesterol: 22
- Protein: 4.5

359.   Sweet Lady Dane Strawberry Pie

Serving: 8 | Prep: 30mins | Cook: 30mins | Ready in:

Ingredients

- 3 cups sliced fresh strawberries
- 1 cup white sugar
- 3 tablespoons cornstarch
- 3/4 cup cold water
- 1 cup half-and-half
- 1 egg
- 1 egg yolk
- 3/4 cup white sugar
- 1/3 cup all-purpose flour
- 3 tablespoons butter
- 2 teaspoons vanilla extract
- 2 cups fresh strawberries, halved
- 1 (9 inch) prepared graham cracker crust

Direction

- In a saucepan, mash together 1 cup sugar and 3 cups sliced strawberries over medium heat. Heat the strawberry mixture up to a boil, stir regularly.
- In a small bowl, mix water and cornstarch and pour into the mashed strawberries; lower heat to medium-low.
- Simmer the strawberry mixture, stir continuously, until thickened, for about 10 minutes. Put aside.
- In a saucepan, heat half-and-half up to a boil; take off heat.
- Use an electric mixer to beat egg yolk and egg together in a bowl until frothy; mix in 3/4 cup of sugar slowly, then beat until the egg mixture is pale yellow, thick, and when the beater is lifted out of the bowl, it can create a ribbon, for about 3 minutes.
- Mix in the flour until the mixture is smooth.

- Stream hot half-and-half into the egg mixture steadily and gradually, beat continuously.
- Pour mixture back to the saucepan on medium heat. Cook and stir continuously using a wooden spoon, till the custard begins to boil and thickens. Lower the heat to medium-low; keep on cooking, stir continuously until flour is cooked, for 2 to 3 more minutes.
- Take the custard off heat, and mix in vanilla extract and butter.
- In an even layer, spread the custard atop the graham cracker crust's bottom. Pour the cooked strawberry mixture on top of the custard. Garnish with fresh strawberries on top.
- Refrigerate for no less than 3 hours before serving.

Nutrition Information

- Calories: 477 calories;
- Total Fat: 16.8
- Sodium: 226
- Total Carbohydrate: 79.5
- Cholesterol: 71
- Protein: 4.6

---

360. The Old Boy's Strawberry Pie

Serving: 8 | Prep: 15mins | Cook: 1hours | Ready in:

Ingredients

- 1 recipe pastry for a 9 inch single crust pie
- 3/4 cup white sugar
- 3/4 cup all-purpose flour
- 6 tablespoons butter
- 1 pinch ground nutmeg
- 4 cups fresh strawberries, hulled
- 1/2 cup white sugar
- 1/2 cup all-purpose flour
- 1 tablespoon cornstarch

Direction

- Heat the oven to 200°C or 400°F. Put one drip pan on bottom shelf to capture pie juices.
- Prep topping: combine nutmeg, butter, 3/4 cup of flour and 3/4 cup of sugar in medium bowl till fluffy.
- In one deep bowl, put the cleaned strawberries. Combine half cup of flour, cornstarch and half cup of sugar in another bowl. Slowly glaze the berries in this mixture; ensure to not mash the berries.
- Put the berries to prepped pie crust piling them in the center; piling is important as berries sinks while baking. Put crumb topping over berries to cover and top crumbs with approximately 15 the size of a pea butter blobs. Use foil to encase pie crust edges to avoid excessive browning.
- Let pie bake for 20 minutes in prepped oven, then lower the heat to 190°C or 375°F and bake for 40 minutes longer. On the final 10 minutes of baking time, scatter a small amount of additional sugar on crumb topping then complete the baking.

Nutrition Information

- Calories: 410 calories;
- Total Fat: 16.6
- Sodium: 179
- Total Carbohydrate: 62.9
- Cholesterol: 23
- Protein: 4

---

361. Two Tier Strawberry Pie

Serving: 8 | Prep: 20mins | Cook: 10mins | Ready in:

Ingredients

- 1 (3 ounce) package cream cheese
- 1/2 cup confectioners' sugar
- 1/2 teaspoon vanilla extract

- 1/2 teaspoon almond extract
- 1 cup heavy cream
- 1 (9 inch) baked pie shell
- 1/3 cup white sugar
- 2 tablespoons cornstarch
- 1/3 cup water
- 1/3 cup grenadine syrup
- 1 tablespoon lemon juice
- 2 cups fresh strawberries, hulled

Direction

- Stir confectioners' sugar and cream cheese in a medium bowl until creamy and smooth. Mix in almond extract and vanilla. Beat cream in a separate bowl until it forms peaks. Fold it in the cream cheese mixture. Put evenly on the bottom of baked pie shell. Refrigerate.
- Stir cornstarch and sugar together in a saucepan. Mix in water until smooth. Put in lemon juice and grenadine. Heat up to a boil on medium heat. Cook for 5 minutes, mixing frequently or until thickened. Let cool then refrigerate.
- Mix together cooled cornstarch mixture and strawberries just before serving until coated. Put over cream cheese layer evenly.

Nutrition Information

- Calories: 378 calories;
- Sodium: 169
- Total Carbohydrate: 41.6
- Cholesterol: 52
- Protein: 3.1
- Total Fat: 22.6

362.   White Chocolate Strawberry Mousse Pie

Serving: 16 | Prep: 15mins | Cook: 10mins | Ready in:

Ingredients

- 2 cups crushed shortbread cookie crumbs
- 3 tablespoons butter, melted
- 2/3 cup heavy whipping cream
- 12 ounces white chocolate, chopped
- 1 1/2 cups heavy whipping cream
- 1 teaspoon vanilla extract
- 2/3 pound strawberries
- 1/3 pound chopped strawberries

Direction

- Preheat an oven to 175°C/350°F>
- Mix butter and cookie crumbs in bowl; press crumb mixture in bottom of 8-in. springform pan.
- In preheated oven, bake for 10 minutes till set and browned; completely cool.
- Heat 2/3 cup cream in small saucepan on medium heat for 3-4 minutes till just barely bubbling. Put white chocolate in bowl; put hot cream on chocolate. Whisk till mixture is smooth and white chocolate melts. Cool down to room temperature.
- Use electric mixer to beat 1 1/2 cups cream in chilled metal/glass bowl till soft peaks form then add vanilla extract; beat till stiff peaks form.
- In food processor/blender, puree 2/3-lb. strawberries.
- Fold 1/2 whipped cream into cooled white chocolate mixture then fold white chocolate mixture into leftover whipped cream. Add strawberry puree; fold just till combined. Put strawberry mixture over crumb crust in springform pan. Put chopped strawberries over; refrigerate for minimum of 4 hours till chilled.

Nutrition Information

- Calories: 396 calories;
- Total Fat: 27.7
- Sodium: 176
- Total Carbohydrate: 33.8
- Cholesterol: 60
- Protein: 3.8

Chapter 11: Awesome Fruit Pie Recipes

***

---

363.   Apple Pie III

Serving: 8 | Prep: 30mins | Cook: 1hours | Ready in:

Ingredients

- 3 transparent apples - peeled, cored and sliced
- 3 Granny Smith apples - peeled, cored and sliced
- 1/3 cup white sugar
- 1/4 cup all-purpose flour
- 1/4 teaspoon ground cinnamon
- 2 cups all-purpose flour
- 1 teaspoon salt
- 2/3 cup shortening
- 3 tablespoons butter
- 1/4 cup cold water
- 1 tablespoon half-and-half
- 1 teaspoon white sugar

Direction

- In a big bowl, add sliced apples. Combine cinnamon, 1/3 cup of sugar and 1/4 cup of flour together in a small bowl then dredge the mixture on top of apples. Cover and let rest in the fridge overnight.
- Start making the pie with the pastry. Combine salt and 2 cups of flour in a big bowl. Slice in 2 tablespoons of butter and shortening until the mixture turns into rough crumbs like cornmeal. Shape a well in the center of the mixture, pour in cold water. Whisk together to shape a ball. Let sit for 20 minutes.
- Roll the dough out and use it to line a pie pan. Distribute the apple mixture onto the pan lined with pastry, spread 1 tablespoon of butter on top. Lay top crust over, seal the edges. Slit some vents in the top of the crust for the steam to escape while baking. Use a pastry brush to brush half-and-half on top of the crust. Dredge 1 teaspoon of sugar on top.
- Preheat the oven to 205°C (400°F) then bake the pie for 10 minutes. Lower the heat to 175°C (350°F). Keep baking until the crust turns golden brown, 30 to 40 minutes.

Nutrition Information

- Calories: 408 calories;
- Total Fat: 22.1
- Sodium: 324
- Total Carbohydrate: 50.1
- Cholesterol: 12
- Protein: 4

---

364.   Chemical Apple Pie (No Apple Apple Pie)

Serving: 8 | Prep: | Cook: | Ready in:

Ingredients

- 1 recipe pastry for a 9 inch double crust pie
- 2 cups water
- 1 1/2 cups white sugar
- 1 1/2 teaspoons cream of tartar
- 25 buttery round crackers
- 1/2 teaspoon ground cinnamon
- 2 tablespoons butter

Direction

- Start preheating the oven to 450°F (225°C).
- Roll out the pastry. Put aside. Boil water in large saucepan.

- Mix cream of tartar and sugar together in small bowl. Put mixture into the boiling water. Stir. Put in crackers, 1 at once. Boil about 3 mins without stirring.
- Add cracker mixture to the pastry-lined pie pan. Sprinkle cinnamon over crackers; then dot with margarine or butter. Add top pastry to cover. Seal the edges then cut steam vents in the top.
- Bake for half an hour in prepared oven, until the crust turns golden brown. Partway through baking, you may need to cover the top pastry to avoid overbrowning.

Nutrition Information

- Calories: 456 calories;
- Total Fat: 20.9
- Sodium: 355
- Total Carbohydrate: 64.9
- Cholesterol: 8
- Protein: 3.5

---

365.   Nectarine Pie

Serving: 8 | Prep: | Cook: | Ready in:

Ingredients

- 2/3 cup white sugar
- 4 tablespoons all-purpose flour
- 1/2 teaspoon ground cinnamon
- 1 cup heavy whipping cream
- 1/4 teaspoon almond extract
- 5 nectarines
- 1 (9 inch) unbaked pie shell

Direction

- Set the oven for preheating to 400°F (205°C). Add water in a big pot and bring to a boil over high heat.
- Combine cinnamon, sugar, flour, almond extract and heavy cream. Put aside.

- On the pot of boiling water, drop the nectarines in for 30 to 45 seconds. Transfer the nectarines right away under the running cold water and peel it off. Halve the nectarines and remove its' pits. Arrange the nectarines halves in the crust of the pie, cut side down. Add the cream mixture all over the nectarines.
- Place inside the preheated oven and bake for about 35 to 40 minutes at 400 degrees F (205 degrees C). Best served warm or cold.

Nutrition Information

- Calories: 333 calories;
- Sodium: 128
- Total Carbohydrate: 39.8
- Cholesterol: 41
- Protein: 3.3
- Total Fat: 18.8

Index

Conclusion

Thank you again for downloading this book!

I hope you enjoyed reading about my book!

If you enjoyed this book, please take the time to share your thoughts and post a review on Amazon. It'd be greatly appreciated!

Write me an honest review about the book – I truly value your opinion and thoughts and I will incorporate them into my next book, which is already underway.

Thank you!

If you have any questions, **feel free to contact at:** *publishing@crumblerecipes.com*

Sarah Williams

crumblerecipes.com

Printed in Great Britain
by Amazon

35729465R00117